The Persistence of Memory

My Father's Ukrainian Shtetl
A Holocaust Reckoning

Arthur Kurzweil

Ben Yehuda Press
Teaneck, New Jersey

THE PERSISTENCE OF MEMORY

©2022 Arthur Kurzweil All rights reserved.

No part of this book may be used or reproduced in any manner whatsoever without written permission except in the case of brief quotations embodied in critical articles and reviews.

Published by Ben Yehuda Press
122 Ayers Court #1B
Teaneck, NJ 07666
http://www.BenYehudaPress.com

To subscribe to our monthly book club and support independent Jewish publishing, visit https://www.patreon.com/BenYehudaPress

Ben Yehuda Press books may be purchased at a discount by synagogues, book clubs, and other institutions buying in bulk. For information, please email markets@BenYehudaPress.com

Set in Arno Pro by Raphaël Freeman MISTD, Renana Typesetting

ISBN 13 978-1-953829-36-8

22 23 24 / 10 9 8 7 6 5 4 3 2 1 20221127

Dedication

For our children
and
For our grandchildren

Even as man is obliged to instruct his child, so is he obliged to teach his children's children, for it is said: "But make them known to thy sons and thy sons' sons" and, not alone to his son and his son's son, but each and every scholar in Israel is commanded to instruct all who desire to be his disciples, even though they be not his sons, for it is said: "And thou shalt teach them diligently unto thy children", which is traditionally interpreted to include one's disciples; for disciples, too, are called children.

– Maimonides, *Mishneh Torah*, "Torah Study"

Acknowledgements

Gratitude and heartfelt thanks to:

Miriam (Mimi) Pauker, Ed Rothfarb, Elie Wiesel z"l, Ken Kurzweil, Adam Sher, Catharine Murray, Dr. Lucjan Dobroszycki z"l, Yurij Petryk z"l, Halia Lutsyshyn, Olexandra Mrachyska, Lev Mykyta, Andiy Kernytsky, Pavlo Bishko, Anna Baranowa, Dr. Joanna Tokarska-Bakir, and Lubomir Jacynicz z"l.

My children, Moshe Kurzweil, Miriam Kurzweil Plumer, and Malya Kurzweil Levin.

Special thanks to Laura Logan, my talented, eagle-eyed editor, and Larry Yudelson, my publisher.

Most importantly, this book would never have been written without the encouragement of my wife, Bobby Dor Kurzweil. The title of this book, The Persistence of Memory, was also suggested to me by Bobby. It is borrowed from the most well-known surrealist painting, sometimes referred to as "Melting Clocks," by the artist Salvador Dali.

…the destiny of a person is connected not only with those things he himself creates and does, but also with what happens to the soul in its previous incarnations. The encounters and events of life, its joys and sorrows, are influenced by one's previous existence. One's existence is a continuity, the sustaining of a certain fundamental essence; and certain elements may rise to the surface which do not seem to belong to the present, which a person has to complete or fix or correct – a portion of the world it is his task to put right in order for him to raise his soul to its proper level.

– Rabbi Adin Steinsaltz, "The Soul of
Man," in The Thirteen Petalled Rose

*   *   *

If you see what needs to be repaired and how to repair it, then you have found a piece of the world that God has left for you to complete. But if you only see what is wrong and ugly in the world, then it is you yourself that needs repair.

– Rabbi Menachem Mendel Schneerson, The Lubavitcher Rebbe

*   *   *

And it is this (the Torah) that has stood by our ancestors and for us. For not only one (enemy) has risen up against us to destroy us, but in every generation, they rise up to destroy us. But the Holy One, Blessed be He, delivers us from their hands.

– The Passover Haggadah

*   *   *

The gates of prayer were locked, the gates of tears were not locked.

– Talmud, Bava Metzia 59a

Contents

Part III: Dobromyl: Making Contact

Part IV: Dobromyl At Last

Part V: "If You See What Needs to Be Repaired"

Part VI: Searching for My Murdered Family

Preface

ABUSCH

> …Names affect one's life…the names given to people are "the works of the Lord upon the earth."

> – Talmud: *Berakhos* 7b (Steinsaltz edition)

My name is Abusch.

I was given the name Arthur when I was born. But I was also given a Hebrew name, Avraham Abusch, on the occasion of my bris (ritual circumcision). I never liked the name Arthur; I don't feel it is really my name. And I always loved the name Avraham Abusch.[1] I feel the name is a part of me.

Ever since I learned that I was named after my paternal great-grandfather, I have been far more than casually interested in my name. More to the point, I became extremely interested in the man after whom I was named. In a way, it became an obsession.

Avraham Abusch was a metal worker. He made pots and pans, gutters for roofs, and other metal products in Dobromyl, Poland (now Ukraine). He was born in 1867 and he died in 1950. According to his birth record, he was born in the nearby city of Przemysl, Poland. According to his death certificate, he died in his synagogue in Brooklyn, New York on Passover.

---

1. Rabbi Adin Steinsaltz, my teacher, told me that my great-grandfather's original name was not Avraham Abusch. Abusch is a diminutive for Abba (father). So while my official Hebrew name is Avraham Abba, I follow my great-grandfather's example and privately call myself Abusch.

His family and friends called him Abusch. He had a full beard as a young man, and he was known by all of his grandchildren as the one who let them play with his gold pocket watch. I inherited that watch from my aunt Ruth who was given it by Avraham Abusch himself.

My father recuperated from typhus and diphtheria when he was 4 years old, sitting on his grandfather's lap and looking out the window. Avraham Abusch would sing to my father. The songs gave him strength. That's what my father told me.

Abusch sailed on the ss *Mauretania* from Southampton, England to the Port of New York on September 17, 1927.

For over sixty years of my life, I have searched for Abusch and dreamed about Dobromyl, the *shtetl* where my father was born and where he spent the first eight years of his life. I have searched for my great-grandfather and I have searched for Dobromyl and I have searched for myself. Sometimes I believe I am the reincarnation of Abusch. I was born a little over a year after he died. Many people who knew him have told me that I remind them of him.

In some way, all of my years of genealogical research and all of my travels have been for one reason: to find Abusch. He is within me. Throughout my life, it has always been that way.

*   *   *

It is said that when parents give their child a name, thinking that they know exactly why they are doing so, the truth is that they don't know why they are choosing it. And if they make a mistake and give a wrong name, the child will afterward change it because the name is not his correct one.

– Rabbi Adin Steinsaltz, *The Sustaining Utterance*

Avraham Abusch Kurzweil, the author's great grandfather

Introduction:
What is the Most Important
Principle in Judaism?

Hillel and Rabbi Akiva, two of the greatest Jewish sages, each expressed their opinion.

Hillel says, "What is hateful to you, do not do to your fellow: this is the whole Torah; the rest is commentary; go and learn." (Talmud, *Shabbat* 31a)

Rabbi Akiva teaches: "And you shall love your neighbor as yourself" (Lev. 19:18). "This is the fundamental principle of Torah" (Sifra 2:16:11).

Both teachings were on my mind when I began my relationship with Dobromyl and its citizens.

It could easily have been otherwise.

I could have adopted the rage and outrage of so many Jews who have said things to me like, "The Ukrainians were worse than the Nazis."

I could have gone to Dobromyl, looked around, and left. It would have fulfilled my dream of actually seeing my father's place of birth and the hometown of my grandparents and great-grandparents.

I could have traveled to Dobromyl with a huge chip on my shoulder. And I could have easily justified my bitterness. After all, every relative of mine who lived in Dobromyl during the Holocaust (with a few exceptions) was – one way or another – murdered.

I could have had the attitude that I wanted nothing to do with the local Ukrainian people.

I could have tried to find out what, if anything, they teach the children of Dobromyl about the Holocaust. There was hardly a trace of any Jewish life for decades after the Holocaust. I could have tried to remind them or teach them about the murders, the tortures, the inhumanity.

I could have thought about the fact that non-Jewish neighbors in Dobromyl often betrayed their Jewish neighbors.

I could have been angry that the school in Dobromyl was named after Stepan Bandera, the infamous anti-Semite.

I could have been repelled by the Christian icons in town, and the beautiful churches. I could have thought about the great synagogue of Dobromyl in flames with Jews inside.

I could have thought about the probable teachings in the local churches that the Jews killed Jesus.

But the words of Hillel and Rabbi Akiva echoed in my brain. My family lived in Dobromyl and vicinity for generations. Many of the non-Jews who are now there, are, after all, the children and grandchildren and great-grandchildren of our former neighbors.

Neighbors. How do I love my neighbors as myself? And how do I prevent myself from treating people in ways I would not like to be treated?

The first step was simply to say hello.

A Note to the Reader

Remembering To Forget

According to the Book of Exodus, the descendants of Amalek, the Amalekites, attacked the Children of Israel on their journey to the land of Israel. Amalek and the Amalekites have come to represent the enemies of the Jewish people; they are the archetypal Jewish symbol of evil.

The Torah states: *"You must obliterate the memory of Amalek from under the heaven; you must not forget."* – Deuteronomy 25:19

What a strange paradox. We must *not forget to obliterate the memory of Amalek.*

Which is it? Do I obliterate the memory, or do I remember it?*

A word of caution to readers of this book: Proceed at your own risk.

I will plant some horrifying, inhumane images in your mind.

They might never leave your memory; you may regret it.

Read it so as not to forget.

But try to forget some of it – for your own sake.

Mine was a journey of remembering and forgetting, and this book records that journey.

*There is a practice among *sofers*, Jewish scribes: when a scribe wants to test his quill, he writes *Amalek* and crosses it out to fulfill the commandment of blotting out the memory of Amalek.

Please note: I am writing these words on April 24, 2022, exactly two months since Russia invaded Ukraine. Time will tell the outcome of this horrendous war. *May God help the Ukrainians to maintain their independence, freedom, and their national identity.*

Part I

Obsessions

If a man loves his fellow, the Divine Presence rests with them.

– Rabbi Mendel of Kosov

Meeting with Elie Wiesel

In 1975, when I was 24 years old, I devised a plan to meet Elie Wiesel. I needed to talk to someone urgently. No, I felt I needed to speak with Elie Wiesel urgently. I felt I needed help, or guidance, or therapy. I felt he'd understand me.

Although he had not yet received the Nobel Peace Prize, his fame had already spread throughout the world with his books like *Night, A Beggar in Jerusalem, The Jews of Silence* and *Souls on Fire*. His reputation grew as an eloquent spokesperson on behalf of Holocaust survivors. He was the most highly sought-after speaker on the Jewish lecture circuit, speaking about *Chasidic* and Talmudic and biblical personalities and ideas, and he was a Distinguished Professor of Jewish Studies at the legendary City College in New York City.

One evening my plan to meet Professor Wiesel hatched. I confess I'm tickled by my own luck and ingenuity. Please know that this is the story of an unknown 24-year-old, out of school and out of work, mixed up young man, and how he managed not only to meet Elie Wiesel, arguably the most well-known personality in the Jewish world at the time, but to meet privately, once a week with Elie Wiesel for the better part of a year, between October of 1975 and June of 1976.

I knew I needed some Jewish psychological counseling, I needed it badly, and I figured Elie Wiesel could help me. I was desperate, and I needed the best.

A local New York Jewish newspaper announced that Elie Wiesel was scheduled to speak at a large synagogue on Long island, on the occasion of the publication of his newest book *Messengers of God: Biblical Portraits and Legends*.

The synagogue's sanctuary was standing room only that night. The guest speaker was over a half hour late (the infamous Long Island Expressway took the blame) but Elie Wiesel proceeded to deliver a spellbinding lecture to a large, packed auditorium. He spoke about the biblical Joseph, calling him the first psychoanalyst, weaving passages from the Midrash to explore the nature of dreams, and making references to then Secretary of State Henry Kissinger, comparing him to Joseph as the Jew inside the government.

The audience was captivated; the speaker was breathtaking.

After the lecture, the audience was directed to a table in the synagogue lobby where new copies of *Messengers of God* were piled high – for sale and for a signature from the author.

The hardcover edition of the book was $8.95, rather low in comparison to today's book prices, but it was still financially out of my reach as an unemployed guy wearing an old jean jacket, messy hair, and with my master's degree, figuratively speaking, in my back pocket.

But here's where my plan comes in.

A previous book by Elie Wiesel, a collection of essays called *One Generation After*, includes an essay titled, "To a Young Jew of Today." It was a sort of "open letter" to young Jews, but when I read it I felt Elie Wiesel was writing to me directly, almost personally. I brought my paperback edition of *One Generation After* to the lecture with the hope I could get close enough to Elie Wiesel to make some personal contact with him.

As soon as the lecture was over, the almost hypnotized audience went to the synagogue's lobby. When I arrived at the lobby it was already filled with a swarm of book buyers, and an ever-increasing crowd of autograph seekers gathered around the author.

I tried to get close but the table was two to three semi-circles deep with people who were asking for personal inscriptions in their books.

The idea then came to me spontaneously. It was the answer to my question that evening: How can I connect with Elie Wiesel in a meaningful, or at least memorable way? I knew I needed him.

I needed to talk with someone who could understand my obsession. What was the obsession? It was, it is, my father's town of Dobromyl, a small *shtetl* in – depending upon the year – Austria, Poland, the Soviet Union, or Ukraine.

If anyone would understand, it would be Elie Wiesel. He too came from a little town in Eastern Europe. He too dreamt – and wrote – of his boyhood in Sighet as I dreamt of my father's boyhood – in Dobromyl.

I experienced the pull toward Dobromyl as a strange psychological phenomenon, perhaps otherworldly, from another time and place – calling to me. While it is reasonable for a young man to be interested in his father's boyhood town, the extent of my interest often felt out of reasonable proportion. It was as though I had little or no control over a persistent tug in the direction of some mythic place, my father's town of Dobromyl.

I opened my paperback copy of *One Generation After* to the page where the essay "To a Young Jew of Today" began. With one hand – my thumb on the inside and my four fingers on the other side – I held the book wide open, to the title page in the middle of the book, to the open letter, "To a Young Jew of Today." I then stuck my arm, book in hand, between and past the people in front of me. From Elie Wiesel's vantage point, an arm with one of his books in its hand had just emerged from a crowd of admirers and autographic hounds, and with the words "To a Young Jew of Today" facing him.

Suddenly the autographs for his new book stopped and the author looked past the people standing in front of him – and in my direction. In a soft voice Elie Wiesel said to me, "May I ask you …?" The people in front of me, who had been blocking me from him, parted like the Red Sea. " … what is your name?"

I said with enthusiasm, "Arthur Kurzweil." So, after the words, "To a Young Jew of Today" its author wrote, "– Arthur" and signed his name. The page became, "To A Young Jew of Today – Arthur. (signed) Elie Wiesel."

It worked. I made contact. He asked me my name.

I wasn't just one more nameless face in the crowd, not just one more attendee to Elie Wiesel's countless lectures. In fact, that open letter was written to "a young Jew of today," and by singling out that page I was able to say to Elie Wiesel, "Your letter was delivered."

He knew that this is what I was saying, and I knew that he knew. He also knew that I knew. We had a moment of connection.

A little over a week later I sat down at my typewriter and wrote a letter from me – "A young Jew of today – Arthur" to Elie Wiesel. I sent it registered mail, return receipt requested.

In my letter I reminded him of our brief encounter at the Long Island synagogue. I was the guy with the opened book.

I then went on to write that his "Letter to a Young Jew of Today" got me thinking of an idea: I proposed that he and I co-author a book-length conversation. He would be "Elie Wiesel" and I would be "a Young Jew of Today." We would talk about all kinds of things and I would record the conversations and edit them into a book we would call "Elie Wiesel Speaks with a Young Jew of Today." This was my proposal.

I went to the post office and mailed him the registered letter. To my surprise I received a letter in response within a week. It was two typed sentences on a small piece of Elie Wiesel's stationery: "I like your idea. Please call me." Below was his handwritten private phone number.

I immediately called. It was a Friday, late morning. The conversation was brief. We set a time, date and place to meet. It would be the following Thursday at his office at City College at 8:00 A.M. As soon as I hung up the phone I began reading or mostly re-reading everything I could find written by him. As I read, I took notes and wrote out lists of questions to ask. By the time the next Thursday came around, I had seven pages, handwritten on a long yellow pad of paper, filled with notes and questions to bring with me.

The following Thursday morning was a rainy, windy one. I finally arrived at the building, dried off a little and knocked on Elie Wiesel's office door. I was greeted warmly and I set up my tape recorder and microphone on the edge of his desk.

The tape was rolling and I asked him a question about his new book. He replied, "Yes."

I asked him a second question about his latest book. He said, "No."

I asked him a third question about a point he had made about Joseph in his lecture and Elie Wiesel replied, "Perhaps."

It wasn't going too well.

I was beginning our book-length dialogue. I was trying to be a "Young Jew of Today," but all I was receiving were one-word answers.

Elie Wiesel obviously knew I was squirming in my seat, and out of compassion he said, "Please turn off the tape recorder."

He then said to me, "You wrote to me with an offer of a conversation. But this is not a conversation. This is a journalist's interview. It is easy to find a journalist for an interview. But you offered me a conversation."

Before I had time to feel any worse than I already did, Wiesel mercifully said, "Let's try again. Let's start again next week at the same time. We should have a topic. Let's decide on a topic." I eagerly agreed. Then he added, "Beginnings. Yes, let's talk about beginnings," he confidently suggested.

I agreed with enthusiasm. "Beginnings," I declared.

We stood up, shook hands, and I left the office.

But then, alone outside of the building, I thought, in a near panic, *Beginnings? Sure. But beginnings of what?*

During the next week, I didn't really think about what he might have meant. I had no idea what he meant. But it was in the back of my mind constantly. Ultimately, I decided I would simply begin our "conversation" by asking Elie Wiesel what he means by beginnings. Since my whole approach would be different (i.e., not an interview), I felt if I asked such a question I would be able to inspire a response.

But it didn't happen that way.

Instead, as we sat down at his desk, Elie Wiesel started the conversation. He looked at me with his now famous, ancient, painful, piercing, compassionate eyes and asked me, "Arthur, what is your oldest memory as a Jew?"

Within a nanosecond I knew the answer. I said, "I am a little boy sitting on my grandfather's lap in a tiny, long and narrow shul in Brooklyn on *Rosh Hashanah*. It was the type of place where everyone knew everyone.

"My grandfather was the shul's president and sat in a seat of honor next to the Holy Ark on a raised platform. The *bimah* was in the center of the shul and the people on the *bimah* faced the ark – and therefore they faced us.

"Each *Rosh Hashanah* I would spend some time sitting on his lap – especially during the blowing of the *shofar*, my favorite moment. We had a perfect view of the rabbi blowing the *shofar*.

"As I grew, I had the whole scene vividly in my mind – except for one thing: the face of the rabbi. I could never recall what his face looked like. I could remember so many other things so clearly – the women's section behind a curtain, the old men rocking back and forth while they were praying. But I could not recall the rabbi's face.

"Then, while thinking about my grandfather and his shul and his *tallis* (prayer shawl), I strained to catch a whiff of a memory of the rabbi's face while blowing the *shofar*. And it suddenly came to me. He was crying. The rabbi was crying. In fact, tears were streaming down his face.

"My grandfather's long *tallis* enwrapped both of us. I can still feel the wool cloth all around, rubbing my cheek, and I smelled my grandfather's aroma, a warm, cozy scent. In the synagogue, the rabbi is blowing the *shofar* and he is crying. Tears are flowing from his eyes and down his cheeks." This, I told Elie Wiesel, is my earliest memory as a Jew.

Wiesel looked at me as though he was in shock. "This is *your* earliest memory? This is *my* earliest memory," he declared. "I am sitting on my grandfather's lap on *Rosh Hashanah* in my town of Sighet and the rabbi is blowing the *shofar* and he is crying. This is my earliest memory as a Jew."

He then leaned back on his chair and said, "Do you know why you remember the *shofar*? *Shofar* means memory. It is a call to remember. They blow the *shofar* to make you remember; to remind you.

"Did he have his *tallis* over his head?" Wiesel asked.

I answered yes and he responded, "It is a powerful image. I remember my grandfather. I remember his crying also. But only in prayer, never in life. Only in prayer. We would go to our rebbe on *Rosh Hashanah* – and he'd cry. The happiest people cried. On *Rosh Hashanah*, you cry."

Elie Wiesel shifted in his chair and then said to me, "Maybe our generation is sad because people don't know how to cry. O r they cry for the wrong things. They remember the wrong things."

I was thrilled to know that our earliest memories matched, but more importantly I discovered the key to the doorway through which I would find my way to having one long conversation with Elie Wiesel once a week for almost nine months.

The key was this: If I shared myself with Elie Wiesel, he would share himself with me; if I told him a story, he would tell me a story; if I would ask a theological question, he would push the question to its extremes to test it; if I would make a statement, he would also push me to clarify, to test the ideas in each statement I made. He was gentle but demanding.

Elie Wiesel looked directly into my eyes and said, "Beginnings. Your beginnings, my beginnings. In my case it's almost a keyword. I believe in memory so much. I think memory is what makes man human. If you have no memory, you are not a man. You are not Jewish certainly. Only if we can remember – back to Abraham, back to Adam – can we go on. But, you see, memory is misunderstood. Some people think memories are nice memories, sad memories. They are not only that. They are much more than that. It's almost a kind of universal resources of mankind. If you go deep down and deep enough, you will come up with things that you haven't witnessed or heard or read, and yet you will remember them. That is what I call beginnings."

"My father was born in a town on the Polish/Russian border. It is called Dobromyl," I said. "Sometimes I wish I lived there, in a small Jewish town like Dobromyl. I've imagined it all my life. My father is a great storyteller and he told me stories of his boyhood in Dobromyl."

"I don't know this town. Where was it near?" Wiesel asked.

"Not far from Przemysl," I suggested.

"In my town, we received a lot of our religious books from Przemysl," he said with some excitement in his voice and eyes. I later learned that Przemysl, which was where my great grandparents were married, was also a center for Jewish book publishing.

Our conversation was suddenly interrupted by a phone call. Elie Wiesel said he was expecting a call from someone in Paris. I sat there during the phone call – which was in French. I was frankly relieved. I had had enough for one day. It's very hot to get close to a soul who is on fire.

When Elie Wiesel got off the phone, we agreed to meet at the same time the following week. During that week, I had vivid dreams of being in Dobromyl – even though I had never been there.

The next week when I arrived, shortly before 8:00 A.M. at the building on the City College campus where the Jewish Studies department was located, the building was closed, its doors locked. It was early in the morning, so there was only a little evidence of the college being open. I waited for 15 minutes and finally Elie Wiesel appeared with keys to the building and to his office.

"I apologize for being late," he said to be as he held the door open for me twice, the outer door and the inner door. My spirits were lifted merely by Elie Wiesel holding each of the doors for me. It felt good when a man like Elie Wiesel holds the door for a *chutzpadik* young man of 24 years.

We finally settled down to the same places we were the week before: he was seated at his desk and I was next to him and facing him. He was turned toward me. Our knees almost touched.

He saw that I had brought a book. He said to me, "I see a book. I love books. When I travel, sometimes I have more books in my suitcase than clothing. Did you bring a book to show me? What book did you bring?"

The Book that Changed My Life

One day, several months before I began to meet with Elie Wiesel, I discovered a book that changed the trajectory of my life. It was shelved inside the world-famous New York Public Library, at 42nd Street and Fifth Avenue in Manhattan.

As a child and as a teenager, I looked for any reference I could find for the town of Dobromyl. Our home encyclopedia made no reference to it, nor did the rather large atlas we owned. I did find one huge atlas in the public library of my suburban New York town in which Dobromyl was indicated by the tiniest dot on the map.

I had heard that the NYPL housed a fantastic map collection. In fact, one of the departments of the library is called the Map Division. They have an extraordinary collection of atlases, historical maps and documents, and at the time the library staff was delightful and helpful. I had a conversation with one of the librarians, telling her about my interest in the town of Dobromyl.

First, we went to the best English language gazetteer – a geographical dictionary – in the library. We looked up the name of the town. It was there, along with its latitude and longitude, and the names of the countries in which it was located at different times in its history. The librarian then went to the back room and after several minutes she returned with a large map the size of a big poster. The map was part of a highly detailed series of maps declassified from U.S. military intelligence. The maps were so detailed that there were dots where houses were located. I had suddenly gone from an atlas with

Dobromyl as a dot to a detailed map of Dobromyl as well as of the villages surrounding it.

The librarian then said, "Have you checked the Jewish Division?"

I didn't know there was a Jewish Division.

"Check there. It's right down the stairway outside our doors. They might have something."

In the Jewish Division, on that particular day, there were a few *Chasidim*, a few modestly dressed young college-aged women, and a modern looking man. There were long tables with chairs, and a front desk with a librarian seated there. A card catalog against one wall held thousands of cards, alphabetically by author, title, and subject. Next to the card catalog was a table with small book request forms. The forms were necessary in order to see a book.

I went to the file drawer for "Dob-Doz" in the alphabet and was quite shocked to find a card indicating the library had a book about Dobromyl.

A book about Dobromyl? It seemed impossible. How could there be a book in the New York Public Library about a town I could not even find on most maps and encyclopedias?

As quickly as I could, I filled out the book request form with the name of the book (*Memorial Book Dobromil*), the number under which the book is catalogued, and my name. I brought it to the librarian and was asked to wait for the book at one of the tables. Someone would find me once the book was retrieved from storage.

The handful of people in the room were scattered throughout the Jewish Division with its long tables. I looked around at each of them, wondering what they were searching for – in what I have come to learn is one of the great collections of Judaica in the world. I wished I had the courage to go over to them and ask; instead I waited patiently, wondering what a book on Dobromyl could be.

After about 10 minutes someone brought the book over to me. And there it was: a book that was about to become a marker and turning point in my life.

The book, *Memorial Book Dobromil*, is a hardcover book of about 550 pages. There were three sections. One was Hebrew, one was

Yiddish, and one was English. I began flipping through the pages and suddenly saw a large group photograph of about fifty men. One of the men was the person after whom I was named – my great-grandfather, Avraham Abusch. His large white beard and handsome face was prominent in the photo.

The Dobromyl *Yad Charutzim* ("Hand of the Diligent"), a craftsman association. The author's great-grandfather, Avraham Abusch, is in the second row, seated, fifth from left.

For the next few minutes, I stared at the photo, looking at all fifty men at what I later learned was taken at a gathering of members of *Yad Charutzim*, the Jewish skilled artisans organization. My great-grandfather, I was told by a great-uncle of mine, was its president.

I flipped through the pages of the book. My hands were shaking. I suddenly saw a photograph of my grandmother, Malya, and then another photograph of my great-grandfather, Avraham Abusch.

I later learned that this book was one of several hundred books of this type published after the Holocaust. They were generally published by *landsmannschaften*, which were organizations of people from specific towns in Europe. So, for example, there was a Dobromyl Society, consisting of people who immigrated to the United States from Dobromyl. They established free loan societies for their membership, and they usually maintained a cemetery for their membership as well. They also often published a book memorializing their former towns. These books are referred to as memorial or *yiskor* books.

The Dobromyl memorial book contained essays about the history of the town, prominent personalities in the town, social customs of the town's population, and finally the fate of the town during the Holocaust.

I sat in the Jewish Division for a few hours that day, reading and rereading the essays written in English and looking closely at each of the many photographs scattered throughout the volume. I learned about Jewish life in Dobromyl, the celebration of holy days, the Jewish schools, the Jewish tradesmen, some of the more well-known personalities in town, and how the Jewish population was destroyed in the early 1940s.

Dobromyl was a *shtetl* – a small Jewish town.

There were glaziers and tinsmiths and leather smiths and butchers and tailors and drivers and cap makers and matchmakers and shoe-makers and sign painters. There were milk sellers and bakers and peddlers and letter carriers, painters and tanners, clothes sellers and wood sellers, butchers and tobacco sellers, liquor sellers and wheel smiths and confectioners.

There were about 5,000 people living in Dobromyl before the Holocaust; half of them were Jewish. The population of the inner town was Jewish and outside the center of town lived Poles and Germans and Ruthenians.

There were rabbis and yeshivas, Zionists and Socialists, and social clubs and trade organizations. Occasionally a bookseller came through town. There were taverns and meeting halls, Zionist organizations and free loan societies. There was a Jewish cemetery that was centuries old. There were general stores, a public bathhouse, several small synagogues and many Hebrew and Torah tutors.

I was lost in thought. Had it not been for the destruction of European Jewry, where would I be? What would I be doing?

Would I be a tinsmith like my great-grandfather Abusch, or a glazier like another of my great-grandfathers? Would I be a tanner, like one of my great-great-grandfathers, or a seller of tobacco like another of my great-great-grandfathers?

Would I be living in Dobromyl, where my father was born, or in Chyrow where my grandmother's family lived? Or would I be in Kroscienko where another branch of my family lived? Or maybe I'd be in the branch of my family living in Przemysl or Jaroslaw.

Had the man across from me not been engrossed in the Talmudic text in front of him, he would have seen me shake. As a person to whom the New York Public Library was the center of the world, I was overcome by the just-discovered fact that my great-grandfather had his picture in a book in that very place. A picture of my great-grandfather. I could say it over and over and it would still sound unbelievable to me.

I could sit still no longer. I ran to the librarian at the desk in the front of the room to share my discovery. To the best of my recollection, she took the matter quite casually. What was at the time the most exciting thing that had ever happened to me was taken in stride by the woman at the desk before me. I didn't understand why she couldn't appreciate the importance of my discovery. Part of me still doesn't. Because that discovery opened up the door to a search that has taken me many years and which, at the time, offered no end in sight. The discovery of that photograph said one thing to me – one thing that changed my life: *You have a past*, it said, *a past and a history, and you can discover it if you want.*

The reason I recognized the photograph of my great-grandfather, Abusch, is because I had taken a great interest in him for years. I was told that I was named after my great-grandfather, so I had always asked questions about him, collected pictures of him, and he became my imaginary friend. Actually, he became my imaginary conscience. For the longest time, I have envisioned him in heaven, watching me. This didn't upset me, nor did it frighten me, but I have to admit that there have been many times when I would base my choices on what I thought my great-grandfather in heaven would think. Even during the periods of my life when I rejected the notions of God, heaven and anything supernatural, I still remained in the state of mind which had me think of how my great-grandfather would feel if I did what I knew to be wrong. In those times, I did not believe that he was watching and judging; rather that being named after him, I had a responsibility to maintain his good name.

In the library, I took the book on Dobromyl to the photocopy services and had a few pages duplicated. One was the picture of my great-grandfather. Another was the title page of the book. And a third was a street map of the *shtetl*, Dobromyl, complete with little squares representing houses, and captions of many of the houses in Yiddish which I would have to get translated. I took the photocopies and went to visit my parents.

My father was amazed at the discovery I had made and was most excited by the map of the *shtetl*. Glancing at the map for no more than a few seconds he unhesitatingly pointed to a spot on the map and said, "We lived here."

The spot he pointed to had a number, and we looked at the number guide to the map where my father read the Yiddish caption. It said, "The Glazier Ennis." We looked at each other and smiled. Ennis (which I later learned was really "Inies") was my grandmother's maiden name and her family were glaziers. So, not only did the book have a picture of my great-grandfather on my grandfather's side of the family, but it also had a map with the house of my grandmother's family.

How many times I had been in that house in my dreams! How many times I imagined eating at the table, playing outside, walking through the fields with my grandmother, helping her carry milk cans back to the house. That house came to represent an entire world that I somehow longed for but felt I'd never find. It was a world which I knew was destroyed, a world which only my dreams could capture. I would never know if I was nearly correct in the way I imagined it. But now I had it on a map. Now I could place it at the exact point on earth where it still might be standing.

Where it still might be standing. This was another part of my daydreams. Often, I wondered what happened to the house where my father grew up. Who lived there now? Who sat in the doorway that

Ruchel Ennis, the author's maternal great-grandmother, in Dobromil.

I have wanted to sit in? It was years later that I spoke to a man who
went back to Dobromyl shortly after the war. The inner part of town,
which was once almost completely Jewish, was already occupied by
residents of Dobromyl or newcomers to the town, as though it had

always been theirs. They lived in our houses, ate at our tables, and slept in our beds.

As my father and I looked at the map, he remembered more stories about his childhood and the town. I was delighted. I was also impressed by my father's memory. He had left Dobromyl as a child of eight, and he had often been told by other family members that he could not remember much, probably because they themselves could not recall much, though they were older. But as my father looked at the map of the town where he spent the first eight years of his life, he proved them wrong time and again. He began to identify many places on the map with ease and finally turned to me and said, "See, I remember the place well."

I returned often to the New York Public Library Jewish Division to look at the Dobromyl book. I was like a little child who asked for the same picture book from the librarian and sat with it, reliving the same fairy tale. It was not much different for me. Each time I returned to the book, I became more familiar with the faces in the photographs and they became my neighbors. The only section of the book that I avoided with each visit was "The Destruction of Dobromyl." I could not read it nor look at those pictures. Not yet. I was not ready. I was still building the town. There was no way I would let it be destroyed so quickly.

One day I decided to actually use the photocopy of the title page I had made the first day I discovered the book. It included the names of a few men who had apparently put the book together. The title page of the Dobromyl book indicated that the Dobromyler Society was located in New York, so I deduced that the men on the book committee were also New Yorkers. I decided to call them.

I searched through the several New York City area phone books for the names and finally came across one that matched. They were all uncommon names which made my search easier. The man whose phone number I found was a Philip Frucht, who lived in the Bronx. I dialed his number and a man answered.

"Is this Philip Frucht?' I asked.

"Yes."

"Are you the man who helped to put the book on Dobromyl together?"

"Yes. Who are you?"

"My name is Arthur Kurzweil," I answered. "You might have known my family. There was a picture of my great-grandfather in the book."

"What did you say your name was?" he asked.

"Kurzweil."

"I'm sorry," he said. "I knew most of the people in Dobromyl, but this family I must not have known."

"But you must have known them. There was a picture in the book," I pleaded.

Again, I repeated my name, but it did not help. It was then that an idea struck me. Though I knew my grandfather to be named Julius, his name in Yiddish – and therefore in Dobromyl – was Yudl. I also knew that though my grandfather was a roofer in Brooklyn he was a tinsmith in Dobromyl. So, I asked Mr. Frucht, "Did you know Yudl the tinsmith?"

Frucht's voice perked up. "Who are you to Yudl?" he demanded.

"I'm his grandson" I said.

The next thing I knew, Mr. Frucht was shouting into the next room to his wife telling her that he was speaking to Yudl's grandson. He sounded as excited as I was.

"What did you say your name was?" he asked me again.

"Kurzweil," I said, pronouncing it the way I was always taught to say it. Kerz-*while*.

"You mean *Koortz-vile*," Frucht pronounced it. "No wonder I didn't recognize it."

Inside, I was a bit ashamed. Though it was the way I was taught since childhood, it was not the way my grandparents said our name, or my great-grandparents, or their parents, or any of the people in Dobromyl. I must have spoken my name incorrectly a hundred thousand times. I robbed it of its Jewishness and made it American.

I have come to believe that names are terribly important. I have already mentioned the significance of the knowledge that I had of being named for my great-grandfather, Abusch. Actually, the importance of that went further. Several times I have been told that I resembled Abusch, in personality as well as in looks – from old photographs of him. Psychologically, this had an impact, the same way it would if I was told that I was a bad boy. Children who are labeled bad often live up to the name. I, too, wanted to live up to the name of my great-grandfather. He was a kind man, I was told, so I wanted to be a kind man. He always had a good sense of humor, so I wanted to have a good sense of humor. He was religious yet modern and I wanted to be religious yet modern. He was a role model which I took very seriously because of our shared name. How I would love to know for whom he was named!

Surnames are equally important. I could never understand how a person could change their last name. Of course, I know the history of it: it was often a survival tactic in response to antisemitism. But for me, changing one's name is like cutting off an arm. It is part of you. How can you bear to lose it?

After Mr. Frucht gave me a lesson in pronouncing my own name, I asked him if he knew my family. He did, indeed, and quite well. I learned many things from the conversation which followed, including the fact that my grandfather Yudl had once been a president of the Dobromyler Society. Frucht proceeded to tell me many stories about Dobromyl and his relationship to my family and finally suggested other people who would be equally able to fill me in on further details. After completing my talk with Mr. Frucht, I was elated and mystified. Perhaps it was the quality of Frucht's stories. He spoke about Dobromyl as if it still existed as a *shtetl*. The affection he had for his town was inspiring, and it brought the town that much closer to me. But one of his comments made the biggest impact of all. After we spoke about Dobromyl, the conversation turned to me. "What do you do?" he asked. I told him that I was (at that time) a librarian, the head of a department, with a staff of people working with me. Mr. Frucht replied, "That's wonderful. It's always nice to hear about the success of a Dobromyler."

That was all he needed to say to make my day, or perhaps my year! Here was a man, born and raised in Dobromyl, calling me a Dobromyler, calling me a member of the *shtetl*. He didn't know that I have walked the streets of the *shtetl* in my dreams, that I imagined the town to be mine for years, or that I longed so often to go there. He didn't know that I have relived, so many times, the stories told to me by my father. Yet he called me a Dobromyler. My wish had been realized.

I felt like I was in a Chagall painting, floating through and high above the *shtetl*. And it was during this floating that the sky lit up and lit my way. I found myself thinking that if I could find a photograph of my great-grandfather, Avraham Abusch, in a book in New York's 42nd Street library, there must be more information to find. What other books were waiting to be discovered? What other sources of information could help me find my way back to Dobromyl?

Often, I have wondered how many people would think all of this crazy. I still wonder. There is a touch of madness to all of this dreaming and feelings. Why in the year 1970 would a young man in his twenties, born and raised in New York suburbs, be elated at being called a member of a *shtetl*? What is the point? What does it mean? Who really cares?

I have no answer for it, except to say that the more I learn about the *shtetlach* of my ancestors, the more at home I feel. It was in these places that my ancestors struggled to survive, and something within me drives my body and soul to visit the streets of my family's past. I visit them in photographs, in stories, in names, and in dreams. And Mr. Frucht merely said out loud what I had been unable to say myself. I am a Dobromyler; I was born in New York but come out of a *shtetl*. In fact, as I reach farther and farther back in my past, I have come out of Egypt as an Israelite. This is what the Passover *Haggadah* says, and it is true. My experience with Dobromyl teaches me this.

I am a child of America, but I am a Dobromyler.

At the end of my conversation with Mr. Frucht, he said, "The Dobromyler Society still meets once a year. And next month is our annual meeting in New York City. Why don't you come to the meeting?" He gave me the date, time and place, and I told him I would make every effort to attend.

When that date arrived, I travelled to Manhattan and went to the hotel where a room was rented for the meeting. My usual habit is to get to appointments early, and this was no exception. But when I arrived at the room, I was not the first person to arrive. Four elderly gentlemen were sitting near the door. One man said to me, "You're in the wrong room." I understood why he said this. After all, what did a young guy in his 20s want with the Dobromyler Society? I said to them, "Is this the Dobromyler Society?" and they said, "Yes, who are you?" Well, by that time I knew who I was – I was Yudl the tinsmith's grandson. Their serious faces turned into smiles and they greeted me warmly. Almost immediately after this, other members of the society began to arrive. The men began to introduce me to a few of the others, but rather quickly the annual meeting began.

Before I went to the meeting, I asked my father what they do at meetings of the Dobromyler Society, and he said, "They fight!"

Well, the annual meeting began and the president of the group began by saying, "I'd like to begin by introducing a guest." He was about to introduce me when a man in the third row (there were about 30 people in attendance) stood up and shouted, "That's new business!" *And they began to fight.* After the dispute ended, a 93-year-old man walked over to me and whispered, "I played the fiddle at your grandparents' wedding." And with that statement, I suddenly knew why I had come to the meeting. This elderly gentleman helped to bring me back, in my imagination, to Dobromyl. Suddenly I was attending my grandparents' wedding.

*   *   *

On May 20, 1976, Elie Wiesel ended the once-a-week meetings he and I had been having for nine months.

Looking back, what a fantastic opportunity I had.

Each week, on Thursday mornings at 8:00, during both the Fall and Spring Semesters at City College in New York, in 1975/76, Elie

Wiesel – who would go on to receive the Nobel Peace Prize, invited me into his office for a private conversation. He was a professor at the University, and I was a young man of 24, totally obsessed with genealogy in general and my father's birthplace, Dobromyl, a small town in Ukraine, in particular.

Inscribing his newest book at that time, *Messengers of God*, Elie Wiesel wrote to me, "To Arthur – with gratitude for our sharing sources and obsessions."

From his writing, Elie Wiesel seemed to be obsessed with his town of Sighet, his boyhood town in Transylvania. And I was obsessed with Dobromyl – not my boyhood town, but my father's.

I had been reading books and essays by Elie Wiesel when I was in my early 20s. The Vietnam War was raging and college campuses seemed unsafe after the National Guard shot and killed four people at Kent State University, racial unrest was at a peak, and I had my head in the clouds. Beneath those clouds was the little town of Dobromyl, where my grandfather worked with his father as the town tinsmith. He made gutters, pots and pans, and other things.

Four images have dominated my imagination about Dobromyl since childhood: Grandma's dairy business, the snow, Great-Grandfather's lap, and the river.

Grandma's dairy business

My grandfather came to America in 1925. Three-and-a-half years later he had saved enough money to send for his wife (my grandmother) and his three children. During those years my grandmother had a dairy business. It was simple. My grandmother would walk to the farms on the outside of town, and she would carry two empty jugs with handles, one in each hand. She would buy milk from the farmers and carry the filled jugs back to town, where she would sell it to her customers. The filled milk jugs were too heavy to carry with one in each hand, so she carried one a short way with both hands and then returned for the second one. She did that over and over until she was back home, ready to sell the milk she had purchased.

Malya Kurzweil, the author's paternal grandmother,
with her three children, Ruth (with ball), Raphael (with
violin), and Saul, the author's father, (with books)

Passport photo of the author's grandfather, Yehuda Yaakov Kurzweil

Snow

All of my life, during snowstorms, my father would recall a winter of his childhood in Dobromyl when the snow was so deep that when his mother opened the door the snow had piled up and they could not get out without digging their way out of the doorway.

My great-grandfather's lap

My father contracted diphtheria and typhus at the same time. He told me many times that for much of the recuperation period, he sat on his grandfather's lap, looking out the window. His grandfather (Abusch) would sing to him and tease him. I've always imagined this lap to be the coziest place in the world.

The river

My father would often recall the location of the river that ran through Dobromyl. It was very close to his house: "Out the door and a short walk to the right," my father would say. My father recalled that on hot summer days people would swim in the river. When I finally got to Dobromyl, I walked from his childhood house to the river. It was just where he said it was.

Countless nights throughout my childhood and into my teens I would lie in bed and imagine Dobromyl, the river, the snow, the milk jugs, and the cozy lap of my great-grandfather.

Genealogical Research[1]

Finding the Dobromyl book and speaking to Philip Frucht launched my casual interest about family history into an obsession. I ultimately wrote a book about it entitled *From Generation to Generation: How To Trace Your Jewish Genealogy and Personal History*. Often, I wonder when it really began. For a while I thought it was with the discovery of the Dobromyl book, but something had to have brought me to the library. Then I thought of the stories that my father told me, but something made me ask him to tell them to me over and over again.

I recall an incident that occurred early in my childhood. I was in my family's synagogue on *Rosh Hashanah* and I recall sitting next to my father and listening to the rabbi's sermon, which I did not understand. I must have been eight years old or so. But at one point in the sermon, the rabbi said that at that time of year God opens the Book of Life, a book with everyone's name in it, and God decides who will live and who will die.

I remember wondering, as the rabbi made that statement, how God organized his book. Was it alphabetically, or by family? I imagined it to be by family, and to this day I visualize it in that way. In fact, I sometimes imagined that one day I would be God's librarian for those books. Obviously, my interest in family relationships had an early beginning.

---

1. Please note that many of the sources I discovered in the 1970s are now available on line at websites such as Jewishgen.org, Ancestry.com and others.

I began to contact people in my family on a random basis, taking trains and buses (and making phone calls to people too far to visit) to gather information about the family. Each conversation led me to more people, and in very little time I had more than a hundred names of cousins and ancestors. I was particularly interested in talking to the oldest members of the family, asking them to reach back in their memories to the earliest people and stories that they could recall.

The family tree grew with amazing speed, and I was admittedly surprised by the cooperation I had gotten. Everyone was interested in telling me what they knew. I even received letters from people who had heard of my interest and had decided not to wait for me to get around to them. I found that I had gathered names, dates, towns, and stories about a huge number of people. The family, which I never knew to be that large, became enormous. Of course, many of the names I had gathered were of people who were no longer living, but the living family was still quite large. One factor became very helpful to my research. There is a Kurzweil Family Circle, a cousin's club which has been in existence for more than 85 years. While the organization did not have any historical information to share, it did have a membership list as well as a cemetery plot. I visited the cemetery and sent questionnaires to the members of the Family Circle.

The questionnaires asked for information about each person's immediate family and their ancestors. I included return envelopes and in a short period of time my mailbox was overflowing with completed questionnaires. I spread them all out on the floor and began to build a sizable family tree stretching back several generations. I also received more names and addresses of people who were not members of the Kurzweil Family Circle and I wrote to them as well. Then I sent additional letters out to people asking for stories and I received more history about the family.

In the course of my research I discovered a branch of the family who have lived in Israel for a few generations, branches of the family in cities around the United States, and most surprising of all, I found the name of a cousin who was still living in Poland. At that time, he was just a strange name on a piece of paper, but he quickly became my cousin Joseph, with a wife Daniele and a daughter Anna. They lived in Warsaw, and Joseph was the only member of the Kurzweil family who survived the war and remained in Poland. He was a writer of, among other topics, Jewish history, which was surely a rare thing for anyone in Poland at that time. We wrote to each other regularly. He is now deceased, as is his wife. Anna still lives in Warsaw with her daughter.

In time, I had accumulated a lot of information and was becoming quite familiar with the history of the family. My questions to older relatives surprised them. I asked them about things that they themselves hadn't thought about for decades. A crucial point came when I felt as if I was living in a different place at a different time. My dreams at night took place far away in time and space. It was becoming unusual for me not to have a dream about some ancestor or other. I entered the world of my ancestors in my conscious and subconscious life. At times I felt it unhealthy. Newspapers interested me less than historical accounts of Eastern Europe which I borrowed from the library.

My picture collection grew as well, undoubtedly helping my dreams create vivid images of the *shtetl* and the past. Some people loaned me photographs, others gave them to me. I also discovered a large box of pictures that my parents had, filled with old photos of family members and street scenes. Eventually, I had just about exhausted every possible lead that I had on people who could contribute information about the family.

The process of meeting these people was wonderful. In effect, I was doing two things at once: building a family history and making new friends and acquaintances. Both were rewarding and priceless. It was fascinating to learn what paths my cousins' lives had taken. We all descended from the same people, but because of the different choices our ancestors made, we went, of course, in varied directions. The physical resemblance between people who had never seen each other before was uncanny. My cousin Joseph from Warsaw, for example, looks remarkably like my father.

When I completed the stage of research which dealt with people I had known or was referred to, I began searching through phone books. Since Kurzweil is an uncommon name, it was a rather easy task – at least compared with searching for a name such as Schwartz or Cohen. The New York Public Library had a collection of just about every available phone book in the world, so I spent hours with them, looking for Kurzweils to call or write. My efforts were met with remarkable success. I found people who were definitely related to me but who knew nothing about my family. Several generations back, their ancestors and mine went in different directions, and eventually we lost contact. Now, for the first time, my cousins were getting to know one another. It was relatively easy for me to figure out if someone was a cousin. I had accumulated enough names and places to be able to discover the links in a rather short time. My family tree was organized well enough for me to have easy access to the material within it.

One phone call to an unknown Kurzweil met with an unusual series of circumstances. I called a man whose name was Arthur Kurzweil, just like mine. I identified myself on the phone and told him what I was doing. He voiced disinterest and told me that he'd call me back if he became interested. I was upset by this, having experienced nothing like it in the months that I was pursuing my family history. But I decided, some weeks later, to call again and try my luck. I asked him politely what his grandparents' names were, and when he told me I immediately knew who he was. His grandparents came to America long before most Kurzweils and because of this, they grew apart from the rest of the family, most of whom came to the U.S. rather late, historically. So, it was obvious why we would not have known about him.

When he told me their names, I proceeded to tell him the names of some of his aunts and uncles.

"Your aunts and uncles must be Bessie, Morris, Pauline. . . ."

"Who told you this?" he asked.

"And your parents must be Harry and . . ." I continued.

"Are we related?" he asked.

We certainly were, and I explained exactly what the relationship was. He still wasn't convinced. The phone conversation ended shortly after that, and there was still doubt in his voice. Later on – months later – he told me that he thought I was representing a business that does family-tree research for a fee.

His disbelief troubled me, as did his unwillingness to cooperate, since he could have been the link between me and many other people in his "missing" branch of the family. I wanted to make the family tree as complete as possible, and he was a source for quite a bit of information. Rather than give up, I decided to tackle the problem with even more energy than usual. It brought me to examine public records.

Until this point, I had very little experience with the use of public records. Actually, the only time I ever used them for my family tree research was to get the death certificate of my great-grandfather, Abusch. Death certificates often provide the names of the deceased's parents, including the mother's maiden name. In this case, I was able to verify what I was already told by relatives as to my great-great-grandparents' first names, and I also learned the maiden name of Abusch's mother. This was important for two reasons. First, it added another major branch to my family tree. Second, it led me to the knowledge that my great-grandparents were first cousins.

I began to research this unknown branch of the family. I used census records which gave me information about household members in 1900. I sent for immigration records which provided still more information, and I went to the Surrogate's Court and looked up the wills of several people. It all added up to a lot of facts, though it was a difficult way of doing what could probably have been done in a conversation. But it was also a fortunate thing because in the process of looking for the items I was after, I discovered things about other branches of the family. In the end, I had a thick file of data on my entire family, provided by public documents in the United States. This included the names of towns in Europe where people originated, ages of immigration, names of steamships they sailed on to this country, and even copies of the passenger lists of the ships. I have in my possession the passenger list of the ship which took my father and his brother, sister, and mother to America in 1929. It is an important document to me, for obvious reasons.

Over the years, many people have asked me if I was related to Professor Baruch Kurzweil of Israel. When Professor Kurzweil died in 1972, I still had no idea if he and I were related, though I knew quite a bit about him because I was in the habit of looking for the name "Kurzweil" in just about every book I picked up. Since at the time, Baruch was perhaps the most famous Kurzweil in the world, his name had shown up often. Baruch Kurzweil was a leading literary critic in Israel. He was an Agnon expert and was also known for his critique of the work of Gershom Scholem. His criticism of Scholem made him quite a controversial figure (as did many other of his points of view) since Scholem was seen as almost untouchable when it came to Kabbalah, his field of research.

But though my knowledge of the work of Professor Kurzweil grew, I still did not have an answer to the question of whether we were related. No one in my family, immediate or more distant, knew the answer, though many of us had been asked the very same question. Then one day I received a reply to one of the many letters I had sent to Kurzweils around the world. I went through scores of telephone directories from the U.S. and other countries at the New York Public Library, and wrote to as many Kurzweils as I could find. While many people were in the habit of checking phone books for their last name out of curiosity whenever they traveled, I did the same – and then I wrote to the people I found! The letter I received on one particular day was from Israel. It was from an Amram Kurzweil, who began his letter with a warm message of support for what I was doing regardless (he said) of whether we were related or not. He then drew for me his family tree, listing descendants as well as ancestors. At the top of his tree was the following sentence: "My grandfather's father (whose name I do not know) came from the town of Przemysl." It was the same town that I knew to be my great-great-grandfather's! As I examined the family tree further, I discovered the name Baruch Kurzweil.

This discovery had two pieces of significance to it. First, it answered my question about Professor Kurzweil. Secondly, it taught me something about family history research. From all of my research on Baruch Kurzweil, I was led to believe that his family came from an altogether different part of Europe than my family. Items about Professor Kurzweil, from many different sources, including his biography and even some family background. Again, the region of his ancestry was given as a different part of Eastern Europe. Ordinarily, I would have drawn the conclusion that we were not related. The fact of the matter is that the accounts that I read never went back far enough. But Amram Kurzweil, who is Professor Kurzweil's uncle, knew an earlier town of origin than any of the encyclopedic sources I had found, and so I was able to discover that our families were originally from the same place. Of course, this still does not absolutely prove that we are related, but if two Kurzweils come from the same relatively small town in Eastern Europe, it is likely that we are.

Another letter from a Kurzweil in Israel brought interesting results: One day I received a detailed piece of correspondence from a man named Dov Kurzweil. While he was eager to exchange notes of the histories of our families, it was clear from his letter that we would not be able to establish any family links – at least not from what he knew. While Kurzweil is not a common name, it is not altogether rare in Europe, so it is quite possible that many Kurzweils are not related (though I must add that I am beginning to doubt that since I continue to discover more previously unknown cousins). I wrote Dov back, thanking him for his letter, adding that there appeared to be no relation.

Months later, a letter arrived from a man in California, also a Kurzweil. He responded to one of my many inquiries to Kurzweils around the country and world. Again, as I read his letter it became clear that he was not related. His letter, however, was quite enthusiastic, and he indicated that he would love to hear from me and share information regardless of whether we were cousins. He said this because I told him in my letter that I had collected a mass of material on Kurzweil families around the world. One comment in his letter was odd. Near the end he wrote, "My father was an atheist, but I always assumed that we were Protestant."

As I reread his letter, I had the feeling that some of the details he provided were familiar. Though it was obvious that his family and mine were unrelated – at least for the past several generations – I was sure that I recognized some of what he had written. Then I remembered: The information that he gave me and the information provided by Dov

Kurzweil in Israel matched. They were not related to me, but they were related to each other! I wrote him back, explaining this to him, and adding that it appeared that his family was originally Jewish. I waited for a reply from him, sure that I would get one based on the enthusiasm which he registered in his letter, but he never answered me.

In addition to my search and living relatives, I became rather knowledgeable about the public documents and other sources of genealogical information, which led me to write my book on genealogy. The Immigration and Naturalization Service (INS), for example, which is now a part of Homeland Security, responded to my requests and in one case sent me a copy of my great-grandfather's Declaration of Intention (to become a citizen). When most of our immigrant ancestors came to America, they usually filled out a form called a Declaration of Intention. Through this form, the immigrant was declaring their desire to become a U.S. citizen and renouncing any previous vow of allegiance to other countries or their leaders.

My great-grandfather's declaration provided me with his age (at the time he immigrated to the United States), his occupation (tinsmith), his parents' names (my great-great-grandparents), the names and birthdates of his six siblings (my great- aunts and uncles – three of whom were murdered during the Holocaust), his place of birth (the town in Poland where he was born), his place of residence (Dobromyl), and the name of his deceased wife and the year she died.

From one document I now had names, dates, and places! So many people have said to me over the years, "I don't know which town my ancestors came from and nobody in my family knows." Well, The INS knew because your immigrant ancestor told them – and they have kept all the files!

The National Archives in Washington, D.C. responded my request for copies of steamship passenger lists (the ships' manifests). I now have the passenger lists for all four of my grandparents and for my great-grandfather. These lists were compiled aboard the ship, often providing the original surname which was changed after arrival to the U.S. for one reason or another.

One of the big misconceptions about Jewish immigration to the

United States is that immigrants' names were often changed at Ellis Island, in New York, when the immigration officials were not able to understand an immigrant's surname. *This is untrue.* The ships' manifests already provided the surname for each passenger. The immigration officials were given the steamship manifests upon arrival. There was no mystery as to what a person's surname was.

The two most common reasons surnames were changed were (1) at the encouragement of relatives who had already arrived in America and who discovered that a shorter or more "American" sounding name would serve them better; or (2) at the encouragement of public school teachers, whose advice was often to "Americanize" surnames.

I remember when my father's passenger list arrived in the mail. I carefully cut the envelope open and took out the photocopy of the ship's manifest, a list of everyone on the ship – including my grandmother, my uncle, my aunt and my father. It provided me with each passenger's name, age, occupation, languages spoken, amount of money they were carrying, closest relative they were leaving, name and address of their final destination, and place of birth. For my grandmother and her three children the place of birth said DOBROMIL.

The YIVO Institute for Jewish Research was founded in Vilna before the Holocaust and reconstituted itself in New York. It maintains perhaps the finest archives and libraries of Eastern European Jewish material in the world. YIVO has a collection of "survivor books," that is, books listing names of Jewish Holocaust survivors. At the end of the war, the organized Jewish communities urged survivors to register as survivors, in an effort to reunite families when possible. In one of the survivor lists from Poland, I discovered the name of a cousin of my father named whose last name is Kurzweil.

It was also in YIVO where I found an encyclopedia of *Chasidic* rabbis titled *HaChasidut* by Y. Alfasi. It lists hundreds of *Chasidic* leaders from the founder of Chasidism, the Baal Shem Tov, to the 1970s. I located this book in the YIVO library and found a listing for my great-great-great-grandfather, Chaim Joseph Gottlieb, known as the Stropkover Rav. He was my mother's direct ancestor. More about him later.

The International Tracing Service (ITS), located in Arolsen, Germany, continues to do what it began doing even before the war ended: helping people find people. The International Tracing Service has tried to gather every Holocaust document containing names, including train transports to death camps, inmate lists, and "death books." My correspondence with the ITS resulted in information about several people in my family who were murdered during the Holocaust.

Yad Vashem, Israel's official memorial of the Holocaust, is a remarkable resource for people looking for information about family members who were affected by the Holocaust. Of particular interest is their Central Database of Shoah Victims' Names, which they describe on their website:

> Yad Vashem, together with its partners, has collected and recorded the names and biographical details of millions of victims of systematic anti-Jewish persecution during the Holocaust (Shoah) period. More than four million eight hundred thousand of the near six million Jews murdered by the Nazis and their accomplices are commemorated here. This database includes information regarding victims of the Shoah: those who were murdered, many whose fate has yet to be determined as well as some who survived.

The New York Public Library is a world-class library, with incomparable specialized collections. In addition to their Map Division and their Jewish Division, there is a Local History and Genealogy Division. It was there that I learned about city directories, the precursors to telephone directories. A telephone directory provides names, addresses and phone numbers while a city directory provides names, addresses and occupations. I was able to find the addresses where my family first lived when they came to America and their occupations as well. I also investigated the United States Federal Census going back to the late 1800s. Census records are available in many public libraries throughout the U.S.

In the 1970s, long before personal computers and cellphones and the internet, there were two kinds of printed telephone directories. The white pages were alphabetical listings of individuals. Almost every town had white pages issued by the phone company. The yellow pages were business telephone directories, organized alphabetically by category. In those days, the New York Public Library devoted an entire wall of a rather large room to their collection of every white pages telephone book in the United States. I spent almost three weeks checking for my last name, Kurzweil, in every book on that long, tall wall.

A library annex in the New York Public Library is located on 43rd Street between 10th and 11th Avenues. In this building the library houses, among many other things, all the old telephone directories. They didn't throw them away, year by year. They saved them. In addition, they have also collected and saved every available telephone book in the world.

One day I went into the Annex and I said to the librarian, "Is it true that the library saves old phone books?

The librarian said, "Yes. What would you like to see?"

So, I said, "What do you have?"

The librarian said, "Tell me what you want to see and I will tell you if we have it."

So, I said, "Tell me what you have and I can tell you what I want to see."

The librarian said, "It doesn't work that way here. Tell me what you want to see and I will tell you if we have it."

So, I said, "OK. I'd like to see the 1803 Polish phone books."

The librarian said, "There were no telephones in 1803!"

So, I said, "I realize that. So if you tell me when there were telephones in Poland, I can tell you what I want to see."

He was getting angry with me, so I said, "What I really want to see is every Polish telephone book you have ever received."

This actually satisfied him. He asked me to sit at a nearby table and to wait for the result of my request. About one half hour later two clerks wheeled in two book trucks piled high with telephone directories. I had before me every Polish telephone directory the New York Public Library had ever received. There were dozens of them in no particular order, and in one afternoon I searched through all of them. The first thing I did was to see how far back they went – what is the earliest Polish telephone book the New York Public Library ever received? I not only discovered that the earliest two books (one was "Warsaw" and the other was "Everything but Warsaw") were from 1936, but in those books, I found the names of people in my family who were murdered during the Holocaust. I was permitted to make photocopies of the pages of interest to me. One of the pages listed two people with the surname of Stelzer. My father had a cousin whose surname was Stelzer, from the town of Yaroslow. I photocopied the page and visited him in his home in Queens, N.Y. I said to him, "This is a page from the 'Everything but Warsaw' phone book. And here are two people with your last name in the listing for Yaroslow. Do you know who these people are? He said, "Of course I do: one is my father and one is my uncle. They were both murdered by the Nazis."

In Warsaw, Poland, The Jewish Historical Institute helps people looking for genealogical information on their families. One of the staff members told me that there was a family who visited the Institute in search of their Jewish roots. When the staff member asked if they knew which town the family came from, they insisted that it was "Anatevka."

The fact is there is no town of Anatevka. Anatevka is the name of the fictitious town in the musical *Fiddler on the Roof.*

Combing through the Polish phone directories gave me some insight into the members of my family who had lived in eastern Europe during the Holocaust. But it was the New York City white pages that led me to a gold mine of information to add to the details about my family's life in the "old country."

Interviewing relatives surpassed my expectations. For months, I was calling elderly relatives and making appointments to visit them. Now that I am over 70, I know the people I visited were not elderly. I was simply in my 20s at the time. Time gives you perspective.

I visited almost every Kurzweil in my grandparents' generation who lived in the New York area in the 1970s. Those I could not visit I called on the telephone and interviewed. I have recordings of hours of telephone conversations with some of my father's first, second and third cousins. I spent at least one hundred hours sitting at kitchen tables or in living rooms of my grandfather's siblings and cousins, trying to find out as much as I could about the family history. I knew pretty early in this whole genealogical process that I was not looking for names and dates to put on a family tree. I certainly was gathering family tree information, but it was just an excuse. I was really trying to grasp Dobromyl, or grasp *at* Dobromyl, which for me was some kind of idyllic little village in my Jewish imagination.

My grandfather's cousins were all immigrants. They knew Dobromyl and knew some of the other little villages and towns near Dobromyl. They had vivid recollections. This contributed to my imagination. Although I lived in New York City for most of the 70s, in my mind I was in Dobromyl, walking down the roads, passing the little houses, passing the shops, going to the marketplace, going to the synagogue. Greeting people in the street.

I once spoke to a woman who was a Kurzweil from Dobromyl and living in Queens, New York. While on the phone with her, I made an appointment to see her – and I had the feeling she wasn't quite sure who I was. I must have mentioned enough names to give her confidence to invite me to visit. I told her I wanted to interview her about her memories regarding Dobromyl and I also wanted to see any old family photos she might have. I was in her apartment for a while before she knew precisely who I was. When I said, "I am the grandson of your second cousin Yudl," she said, "Why didn't you tell me that when you called?" I did.

My good friend Richard Carlow, whom I have known for over 60 years, recently told me that part of his family came to America from…Dobromyl! When he told me, I couldn't believe it. But he mentioned to me one day that he was speaking with members of his family and when he asked what town they came from, they said Dobromyl. Richard and I have been the closest of friends for almost our whole lives. In addition, when I returned to my research (thanks to Jewishgen.com), I learned that people in his family and people in my family married one another back in Dobromyl. So, at least by marriage, Richard and I are related. I wonder how many weddings and funerals our families both attended!

The result of all of my research on the Kurzweil family was a book I privately published called *The Kurzweil Family History and Genealogy*. It contains all of the genealogical information I had gathered as well as the photographs I had collected or copied.

But after all of the research and all of the interviewing of relatives, it was not enough for me. I needed to go to Dobromyl. I needed to see and touch the place for myself.

The Stropkover Rebbe

After initially researching my father's family for several years, I decided, reluctantly, to try to trace my mother's side of my family. I wasn't too optimistic because my mother had a small family; there weren't as many people to speak with as there were in my father's family. In addition, while my father's family was a somewhat traditional Jewish family, my mother's family was more assimilated into American culture. And my mother, unlike my father, was born in New York City, so she didn't have any old country *shtetl* stories to tell me like my father did.

But out of respect for my mother and out of curiosity, I announced to my mother that I was ready to trace her family tree. I asked her who I could speak with – knowing full well that there were few, if any possibilities. My mother surprised me when she reminded me that her first cousin, Maurice, was born in Slovakia. "Why not talk to him?" she suggested.

I immediately called him and made an appointment for us to meet. He lived a half hour's drive from our home on Long Island, and a week later I was sitting with him at his dining room table, asking him what he knew about the family history. He was a gentle man with a Hungarian accent. I was disappointed when he said he knew very little. He told me that he was born in Slovakia, and that he had an uncle, the brother of my grandfather, named Pinchas, who was murdered in Auschwitz. But that was about it.

He then said, "Wait a moment! I do remember something interesting. When I was a boy in Slovakia and I didn't behave myself, my parents would always scold me in the same way. They would say, 'That's no way to act, particularly as an *eynikl* ["descendent" in Yiddish] of the Stropkover Rebbe.'"

"The Stropkover Rebbe?" I asked. "Who was he?"

"He was the *Chasidic* Rebbe from the town of Stropkov."

I understood what he meant. Just as the first Satmar Rebbe was from the town of Satu Mare, Romania, and the first Bobover Rebbe was from the town of Bobova in Galicia and the Lubavitcher Rebbe a Chasidic line from the town of Lubavitch, the Stropkover Rebbe was from the town of Stropkov, Slovakia!

"We come from a *Chasidic* rebbe?" I asked, quite excitedly. "What was his name?"

"I don't know his name. I never liked being scolded in that way so I must have blocked it out – until now!

Well, you might need to be a librarian to appreciate this, but I have come to the conclusion that there is a book on every topic in the world. The next day, in the library of the YIVO Institute for Jewish Research in New York City, I found a book on *Chasidic* rebbes indexed by town! In the book, entitled *HaChasidut*, I discovered the name Rabbi Chaim Yosef Gottlieb, the Stropkover Rebbe. My mother's family name was Gottlieb. Putting this discovery together with other research I have since done, I had found my ancestor, my great-great-great-grandfather.

Now that I had his name I was able to discover a book that he wrote, in the library of the Jewish Theological Seminary in New York City, which also contained a lengthy biography of him. The biography described him as a great scholar, a miracle worker – and an exorcist! And, to my great surprise, I found out that in Jerusalem, there is a yeshiva named after him called The Rabbi Chaim Yosef Gottlieb Yeshiva, located on Chaim Ozer Street near the Old City.

In 1983, when I was 32 years old, I traveled to Israel and went to the address. There it was before me, the yeshiva, a modest sized building, named for one of my ancestors, in the holy city of Jerusalem! The day I arrived there, an old man with a long white beard and a kind face – a

Blima Rath and Asher Yeshiya Gottlieb,
the author's maternal great-grandparents

chusid, dressed in a black suit and white shirt, as *Chasidim* do – sat on
a chair at the door outside of the yeshiva. I quietly approached him
and said, "Hello. Is this the Rabbi Chaim Yosef Gottlieb Yeshiva?" I

knew that it was, but it was my way of starting a conversation with the old man.

The man looked up at me standing before him and politely and gently said (in broken English and a thick accent), "Yes, it is. And who are you, may I ask?"

Proudly, I responded, "I am an *eynikl* of the Rebbe!"

The old man said, "I too am an *eynikl* of the Rebbe." So, there I was, standing before the yeshiva named for my ancestor and speaking with an old *chusid* who was a relative of mine.

"Who are you?" he asked. I knew from the way he asked his question that he was implying that he wanted to know just how I was related to him – and to the Rebbe.

"I am the Rebbe's great-great-great grandson. My grandfather was Zalman Leib Gottlieb."

He said, "Zalman Leib? Zalman Leib from Bistritz? He seemed quite excited to hear my grandfather's name.

"Yes! My grandfather was born in Bistritz!"

"Zalman Leib. Zalman Leib. Your *zadie* [grandfather in Yiddish] was Zalman Leib from Bistritz!"

He then asked, "Zalman Leib, the brother of Pinchas?"

"Yes! My grandfather had a brother named Pinchas. He was murdered in Auschwitz."

"I know," he said, rolling up his sleeve and showing me the numbers on his arm tattooed there by the Nazis. "I am a survivor of Auschwitz. I was there with Pinchas. We learned Torah together in Auschwitz."

My mind was exploding. I was actually speaking to a man who was in the death camp Auschwitz with my great-uncle, Pinchas Gottlieb.

"You learned Torah with Pinchas in Auschwitz?" I repeated, thinking it was impossible.

"Yes," he said. "We reviewed what we could from memory."

"My name is Arthur-Avraham Abusch Kurzweil. What is your name?" I asked.

"I am Akiva Gottlieb. Would you like me to tell you a story that your great uncle Pinchas told me when we were in Auschwitz"

"Of course!"

Pinchas Gottlieb, the author's great-uncle,
who was murdered in Auschwitz

And here is the story he told me . . .

One day, a rabbi had a vision of Elijah the Prophet. Elijah appeared before him, and the rabbi said, "Elijah, I know that God sends you into our world with certain tasks to perform. I wonder – could I follow you as you do God's work?"

Elijah responded firmly, "No you cannot."

The rabbi asked, "Why?" And Elijah said, "You will ask me too many questions, and I don't have time for your questions."

The rabbi pleaded with Elijah and promised that he would not ask any questions. Reluctantly, Elijah agreed, saying that if questions were asked, the rabbi would have to leave. Off they went together.

Later that day, they came to a small shack in which a young couple lived. They lived in poverty; all they owned was an old cow whose milk they sold to make a meager living. Elijah asked the couple if they could stay for the night and the couple, who were quite lovely, eagerly agreed in the spirit of the patriarch Abraham, who was well known for offering hospitality. The couple gathered some straw to make it a little more comfortable for their guests to sleep.

The next morning the rabbi awoke and found that Elijah was praying to God. He heard Elijah ask God to kill the couple's only cow. Outraged, the rabbi said, "Elijah, they were such lovely but impoverished people. All they had was their cow. Why would you pray to the Almighty to kill the cow!"

Elijah indignantly responded, "You see, you already have questions. I don't have time for your questions. The rabbi withdrew the question and begged Elijah to give him another chance.

Off they went. Later that day they arrived at a mansion of a wealthy but nasty, stingy man. Elijah asked the man if they could stay for the night. The rich man reluctantly agreed, and told them to sleep in his cold, unfurnished cellar.

In the middle of the night, the rabbi awoke to some noise and discovered that Elijah was reinforcing the walls and patching up any cracks that he saw. Deeply confused, the rabbi said, "Elijah, this man doesn't deserve the mansion he lives in. Why are you repairing his cellar?"

Elijah responded angrily, reminding the rabbi of their agreement not to ask questions. Once again, the rabbi pleaded to be forgiven and to be given one last chance to follow Elijah silently. Elijah agreed, and said, "Any more questions and you will have to leave me."

Once again, off they went and arrived at a wealthy neighborhood filled with people enjoying their wealth. Elijah and the rabbi went to the local synagogue, with pews made of gold and silver, but found the congregation to be quite unfriendly and cold. Nobody greeted the two strangers; nobody offered a kind word. Elijah look at this congregation and said, "I bless you that you all become leaders."

And Elijah and the rabbi left the synagogue and the community. The rabbi wondered why Elijah would give these inhospitable people such a blessing, but he said nothing.

They then came upon a neighborhood filled with people living in poverty. They were warm and friendly, but their living conditions were squalid. Elijah looked at them and blessed them saying, "I bless you that one of you should be a leader." Once again, he rabbi wondered why Elijah would give them such a blessing.

Upon leaving this neighborhood, the rabbi said to Elijah, "I can't take this any longer. Nothing that you are doing makes any sense. I know I have to leave but I beg you, Holy Elijah, can you please explain to me what you have been doing? I don't understand anything."

And Elijah said, "You will have to leave. I don't have time for your questions, but I will offer you an explanation of what you have seen."

Elijah continued. "Remember the poor couple. You overheard me praying to the Lord, 'Kill the cow.' My mission there was that it was the time for the wife to die. So, I pleaded with the Almighty, 'Don't take the wife; take the cow.'"

"Remember the wealthy mansion owner? He didn't deserve that mansion. But I knew there was a treasure buried within the cellar walls. I patched up those walls so he will never find the treasure."

"And remember the wealthy congregation with the synagogue containing gold and silver pews? You were shocked when I blessed them to all become leaders. Don't you know what happens when everyone thinks he or she is the leader? That wasn't a blessing; it was a curse."

"And finally," said Elijah the Prophet, "in that neighborhood of squalor, you were surprised that I blessed them that one of them should be a leader. Rabbi, you compared this blessing to my previous 'blessing' that they all become leaders. Rabbi, all that poor neighborhood really needed was one good leader to lead them out of their poverty."

The rabbi then left Elijah, but he did take with him one thing: the knowledge that we do not see everything that is happening. We only see a small part of what is occurring in God's world.

"This is the story," said the old rabbi at the Stropkover Yeshiva, "that your great uncle, Pinchas, told me in Auschwitz."

I was blown away by the story and by the immediate realization that it was told by my great uncle Pinchas in, of all places, Auschwitz. And it reminded me of a story I remembered learning from the Talmud. It is a story about the great Talmudic sage, Rabbi Akiva, who, while traveling, stopped in a town and asked people if they could provide him with a place to sleep for the night. No one made an offer. They all refused. So, Rabbi Akiva bedded down for the night in a field and the Talmud says he had with him an oil lamp, a rooster, and a donkey. In the evening, a wind blew out the light, a cat came and ate the rooster, and a lion came and ate the donkey. As each occurrence took place, R. Akiva responded, "All that the Holy One, blessed be He, has done, He has done for the good." Later that night, foreign troops attacked and looted the nearby town. Only R. Akiva, whose presence was not betrayed by his light, rooster, or donkey, was untouched. (*Berachos* 60b)

Both of these stories concur with the attitude of the Talmudic sage Nachum Ish Gam Zu, Rabbi Akiva's teacher for 22 years, who responded to every event in his life, "This too is for the good (*Gam zu l'tova*)," part of which became the nickname of Nachum Ish Gam Zu – Nachum the man of "This too").

It is important to note that according to Jewish tradition a person can only say "*Gam zu l'tova*" ("This too is for good") to oneself, about one's own experiences, and not to anyone else. If I encounter a person who is suffering, it is my duty to help to relieve the suffering – not to say that it is for the best, God forbid. But if I myself am suffering, I have the right to say this to myself. As it is explained, this is not a way of accepting harsh judgment but because what people experience as a descent is, in reality, an elevation.

In addition, the story told by my great-uncle about Elijah the Prophet and the Rabbi, and in of all places at Auschwitz, was not told by me, but by the victim himself. I assume that as a deeply pious and religious *chusid*, my great uncle Pinchas was telling the story to himself to be reminded of this theology.

It is also crucial to keep in mind that traditional Jewish theology includes the notion that our soul is immortal. We, as individuals, are not just a body, nor are we a body that has a soul. *We are a soul that has a body.* Our soul existed before our current body and it picks up the body to live for a certain number of years, and then the soul drops the body and goes on with its journey.

Jewish belief also includes the concept of *"Gilgul haNefesh,"* the reincarnation of the soul. Explanations and illustrations of this can be found in the authoritative text, the Zohar, as well as in many other books of Kabbalah and Chasidism. Despite what many Jews think, reincarnation is very much a part of our theological system, but it is unfortunately not learned or taught in most non-Orthodox strands of Judaism. Death is not the end of our existence. Death is something that happens to the body, but the eternal soul within each of us does not and cannot die.

As my teacher, the late Rabbi Adin Steinsaltz explains in his book *The Thirteen Petalled Rose*, in the chapter called "Repentance":

> The soul that has fulfilled its task, that has done what it has to do in terms of creating or repairing its own part of the world and realizing its own essence, can wait after death for the perfection of the world as a whole. But not all the souls are so privileged: many stray for one reason or another; sometimes a person does not do all the proper things, and sometimes he misuses forces and spoils his portion and the portion of others. In such cases the soul does not complete its task and may even itself be damaged by contact with the world. It has not managed to complete that portion of reality which only this particular soul can complete; and therefore, after the death of the body, the soul returns and is reincarnated in the body of another person and again must try and complete what it failed to correct or what it injured in rebbe past.

It is surely not the purpose of this book to explore Jewish theology in depth, nor to justify suffering. But after all of my travels, and with the knowledge of the suffering of the Jews and the Kurzweil family during the Holocaust, I want to share my Jewish studies on the subject of suffering with you. And I want to remind myself of two other of Rabbi Steinsaltz's teachings as a final word of comfort:

> The process of the soul's connection with the body – called the "descent of the soul into matter" – is, from a certain perspective, the soul's profound tragedy.
>
> But the soul undertakes this terrible risk as a part of the need to descend in order to make the desired ascent to hitherto unknown heights.
>
> It is a risk and a danger, because the soul's connection with the body and its contact with the material world where it is the only factor that is free – unbounded by the determinism of physical law and able to choose and move freely – make it possible for the soul to fall and, in falling, to destroy the world.
>
> Indeed, Creation itself, and the creation of man, is precisely such a risk, a descent for the sake of ascension.
>
> – *The Thirteen Petalled Rose*, "The Soul of Man"

* * *

> There is no way of comparing the pleasures of this world – for all their sweetness, intensity, and variety – with the pleasure of the next world.
>
> We have no common denominator.
>
> Just as we cannot compare a color, such as blue, with a number.
>
> We can have more blueness or less, a larger number or a smaller one; we cannot compare them.
>
> All we can say about the joys of the next world is that they are so superior to the joys of this world that it is worth going through the torments of Hell in order to attain them.
>
> – "Hidden Aspects of Shabbat" in *The Candle of God*

My Father

Two things made my father stand apart from the fathers of my childhood friends. One was the fact that he was born in Poland (while all of their fathers were born in the U.S.); the other was that he was a war hero, although he never referred to himself in that way, nor would he accept it as a description to be even remotely true.

When my oldest daughter, Malya, was in middle school, I actually hired her to interview my father about his experiences in World War II. The result was twelve hours of tape recordings. While my father was usually quite hesitant to talk about his war experiences, Malya was able to finally get almost the whole story of his war experiences out of him.

My father enlisted and ultimately joined the 82nd Airborne Division of the U.S. Army. A squad leader (a staff sergeant) with 10 men, he parachuted over enemy lines on the French beaches near Normandy shortly before the great invasion called D-Day. Of his 10 men, nine were killed while he and the other man were shot and left for dead. He was found and obviously survived, going on to be involved with some dangerous missions for which he received the Bronze Star for Bravery (also referred to as "heroic achievement").

My father was a master storyteller. From time to time some of my young friends, 10–12 years old, would come to my house – not to spend time with me, but with the hope that my father would get into the mood and tell war stories. On occasion, he did. A few of the boys would sit in a semi-circle around my father and listen with rapt

Saul Kurzweil, the author's father

attention as he told his stories. I would sit there patiently, admittedly proud, not only of the contents of the stories, but also of the fact that he never made himself the hero. He would say things like, "I must have been out of my mind" or "What was I thinking?" or "I was convinced from the day I became a soldier that I would never come home alive." He also made sure to tell the story of his commanding officer reprimanding him for standing up while hiding in enemy territory. The officer said, "Get down; do you want to get yourself killed?"

But between the lines, my friends and I knew that the harrowing stories were about him and his bravery. Once, when I called him a war hero he said, "War hero? I had no idea what I was doing. It was like I was in a fog. I just did what I was there to do."

My boyhood friends would, for a short time, treat me as special after these war story sessions. And the sessions, which often went on for over an hour, ended each time with my father saying, "O.K. Enough. That was a long time ago."

To us, World War II did feel like a long time ago, although for my father, at times, it was like yesterday. After all, it was only a relatively few years between the mid 1940s when my father "saw action" and the late 1950s when he told of his experiences. In addition, due to his war wounds, my father was partially disabled. He had limited mobility of his arm. I can vividly recall the faces of my friends when one of them would ask my father if he was wounded during the war. He would point to the places on his body and explain that he was shot in the chest, right through the dog tag he was wearing. The bullet came out of his body, under his armpit and then went through his arm and out the other side. After describing the trajectory of the bullet, he added that by hitting his metal dog tag, the bullet pulled some of the metal into his chest where it would stay for the rest of his life.

My father never spoke about Dobromyl to my friends; he seemed to save those stories just for me. Of course, when I was a boy, I asked him over and over to tell me the same stories. My friends were not interested in short tales of a small town in Poland (today *Dobromyl* is in Ukraine). It was the army stories that kept them coming back for more – or even for the same stories repeated over and over again.

Throughout my life it often struck me as ironic and sad that my father left Europe in the late 1920s only to have to return in the early 1940s. He arrived in the United States as a Jewish boy who spoke no English and came back from the war as a hero who fought against Hitler's armies during the Holocaust.

He arrived in New York as a boy of eight, with his mother and two siblings. His father had arrived in the United States four years earlier, and lived alone in Brooklyn, working as a roofer, working to save money to send for his wife and children. In fact, one of his children, my aunt Ruth, had not yet been born when my grandfather left Dobromyl. My grandmother was pregnant with her. How I would love to know what the conversations between my grandmother and grandfather were about as they discussed his plan to leave for America.

In addition to leaving his wife for those years, my grandfather also left three married siblings, each of whom had little children of their own. They lived in Dobromyl, in poverty, and were murdered during the Holocaust. I do not know the circumstances of their murders. I only know what the various possibilities were – and I will go into detail about the fate of Dobromyl's Jews later in this book. The one thing I know for certain is that they were never heard from again.

My father left Dobromyl in 1929. He was eight years old. He never went to school in Dobromyl. He was too busy battling diphtheria and typhus simultaneously.

One day, a few years ago, a metal detector friend of mine in Ukraine sent me two amulets in Hebrew that were identical. The writing on them was meant to ward off diphtheria:

> May it be Your will
> Before you, the Lord our God.
> That you protect this child,
> And prevent the evil eye from harming him
> And protect him from diphtheria…

I often play various versions of "What if?" in my mind. For example, what if my father had not survived the diphtheria? Would I have never existed, or doesn't it work that way? Perhaps I would have been born

Amulet to ward off diphtheria

to another mother and father, or maybe just to my mother with some other father.

Maybe souls line up and are placed into the body of the next baby about to be born. But it wouldn't be "me" then. It would be a different combination of DNA, making me – or my body at least – entirely different. If a person is a combination of a body and a soul, what would happen if my soul were in a different body, and in a different family? My soul would then have a completely different set of situations and challenges, but it would be the same soul. I often think that this is the situation in the context of reincarnation: a body dies, but the soul lives on and is placed in a different body. So, if the soul I have (or the soul I am) was once in a different body, its assignment would then be in my current body, with all of the circumstances I have experienced in the life I currently lead. I once heard it said that souls choose their parents, depending on the kind of tests that each soul wants to face. But I don't think so; it doesn't make sense to me (as if this whole line of thinking makes any sense at all).

My father was given the name "Saul" (Shaul in Hebrew) when he was born. His mother once told him that when he was ill with diphtheria his name was changed to Chaim Shaul in the synagogue in front of an open Torah scroll, following the Jewish custom of naming a baby on a day when the Torah is taken out during a prayer service. Chaim in Hebrew means life, so a name change to Chaim is a good omen.

Ever since my father told me of his name change, I have imagined my grandmother, in Dobromyl, carrying my father to the synagogue to change his name. Some say the custom of name-changing is to fool the angel of death. I used to imagine the angel of death looking for my father but not being able to locate him. But I've learned that this is based on an old wives' tale that has circulated for generations, perhaps for centuries.

But this is not the reason. It is taught in Kabbalistic literature that when a baby is named by his or her parents, the parents are not actually selecting the name. Rather, a Divine spirit inspires parents to give the baby its "proper" name – which is a name that reflects the essence of the baby's soul. And if parents give their children the "wrong" name, then one of that person's tasks during his or her life is to find their real name.

Therefore, when an ill person's name is changed, the hope is that the new name reflects a new essence, thereby changing the fate of the person.

By the way, my grandmother told my father (who told me) that due to his childhood illnesses, he would never live a healthy, normal life. She was wrong. My father was healthy and strong and lived to the age of 93.

Facts about Diphtheria:

- As the diphtheria bacterial infection continues to attack, a pseudo membrane forms in the throat. It looks like leather, so much so that its name, *diphtheria,* coined in 1826, comes from the Greek word *diphtheria,* for leather or hide (as the throat looks during the disease).
- Diphtheria has been referred to as "the strangling angel of children" because a child's throat can suggest the image of a classic angel with wings, and because death is usually caused by an inability to breathe.
- In Spain, the year 1613 is known as "El Año de los Grotillos," *The Year of Strangulations,* because of the diphtheria epidemic in that year.

- The victims of diphtheria are mostly children.
- In 1901 in St. Louis, 11 children were given what turned out to be contaminated diphtheria anti-toxin. Ten of the 11 children died. This occurrence was in large part the stimulus for the development of federal regulations of biologic products.
- There was a diphtheria epidemic in the U.S. from 1921–1925. Each year there were an estimated 100,000 – 200,000 diphtheria cases, mostly children, and 13,000 – 15,000 deaths in the United States.
- According to the Centers for Disease Control and Prevention (CDC), diphtheria peaked in 1921, the year of my father's birth, with 206,000 cases in the U.S.
- Before there was a vaccine, Presidents Abraham Lincoln, Grover Cleveland and James Garfield each had children who died from diphtheria.

Reincarnation

How can I explain or understand my obsession with genealogy in general and Dobromyl in particular? It has not been like a regular hobby; sometimes, it is all-consuming. I confess that there have been moments when I have gotten a flash of awareness that I've had some connection with Dobromyl in a past life.

When I first arrived in Dobromyl, it seemed oddly familiar to me. I truly felt that I had walked the streets before. I admit that I had been looking at photographs and imagining my being there for most of my life, so it could be that I only visited Dobromyl in my imagination. But something else might have been at work.

I know that it is difficult to acknowledge, but I know for a fact that the Jews of Dobromyl were not all saints. Sometimes, for example, a person who is extremely religious and demanding on oneself can walk down the street and totally ignore a person walking in the other direction. Multiply this by 2,500 (the approximate number of Jews in Dobromyl before the Holocaust) and we can truly seem like an unfriendly people. Strict adherence to the kosher laws of Judaism also, in a way, forced Jews to keep separate from others. I once read a book on the history of immigration to America in which the author described what it was like to be on those steamships. Jews often stayed in corners of public spaces in order to make sure that the children did not accept any food from the non-Jews who were there.

In another context, I remember, for example, walking to the synagogue in Brooklyn on Shabbos mornings. I would often pass an individual or family walking to a synagogue in the other direction. I would say, "Good Shabbos" to them and they would totally ignore me. It would piss me off, and I would wonder, *What is wrong with these people*?! (It was not until quite recently that I learned that this custom of not talking to anyone on the street is deliberate. It's based on the idea that such encounters can result in frivolous talking, perhaps even gossip. A religious community whose members are serious about their religion might easily adopt this custom.) There was one time I was so annoyed by being ignored that I said, "Merry Christmas" as the people passed. That sure got their attention!

I also know that during Stalin's time, Communists – including Jewish Communists – would harass and sometimes even kill people who resisted the new Communist regime. I wonder: could members of my family have been among the killers?

Or perhaps someone in my family in Dobromyl was not honest in his or her business dealings.

If my soul was actually in another body in a previous generation, and if somehow, I was involved in some activities damaging to Dobromyl, this could surely explain why I felt such an inner compulsion to do things that would help the Dobromyl of today to rebuild.

My mentor, Rabbi Adin Steinsaltz has written about this:

> "…our souls can feel all kinds of pain in the context of our life experiences. But the soul suffers additional pains that are not intrinsically linked to our life process and experiences. An individual soul can also suffer the pain of the past. This includes the past within a single lifetime, as well as past incarnations. When the past is known to us, it is possible to see a coherent sequence that unites the events of our lives. About our previous incarnations, however, we seldom remember anything. Yet this past is still attached to our individual souls…
>
> "We can, in fact, carry a lot of baggage from past lives. We are not entirely aware of this baggage, and it acts within us in a concealed way that we cannot comprehend. At times, this pain becomes exposed when we experience a similar event in the present life

and respond to it in a more extreme way than the current situation would warrant. This inherited suffering, which is generated in the unknown past, as well as in the immediate environment, can play a significant role in the direction we decide to take in life. We might, for example, end up following a path that is the continuation of a past we do not recall.

Because these past events and experiences are usually unknown to us, we lack the wherewithal to rectify them. We can say only that we are making an effort to correct what we can in whichever way we see fit, whether we know and understand the issues or whether they are concealed. In our nightly prayers, we ask for forgiveness for sins, faults, and wrongs we have committed and that others have committed against us, and we express the intent to rectify our actions in the current incarnation and in other ones. We are meant to know only that within our own soul, there are depths that may not be exposed to us during our lifetime, but despite this concealment, their influence is felt.

– Rabbi Adin Steinsaltz, *The Soul*

The destiny of a person is connected not only with those things he himself creates and does, but also with what happens to the soul in its previous incarnations. The encounters and events of life, its joys and sorrows, are influenced by one's previous existence. One's existence is a continuity, the sustaining of a certain fundamental essence; and certain elements may rise to the surface which do not seem to belong to the present, which a person has to complete or fix or correct – a portion of the world it is his task to put right in order for him to raise his soul to its proper level.

– Rabbi Adin Steinsaltz, "The Soul of Man" in *The Thirteen Petalled Rose*

Bobov and Lubavitch

Shtetl life, or, more accurately the romantic *shtetl* life of my imagination, brought me, for ten years, to the periphery of the Bobover *Chasidim*.

As a result of the fact that my now ex-wife and I got married and looked for a place to live in the New York City area where we would have room for children, we found ourselves moving to an apartment in the neighborhood in Brooklyn called Kensington, specifically Ocean Parkway and Cortelyou Road.

From time to time, a man named Tuvia (like Tevye, but with a Polish pronunciation), had been calling me on the telephone to ask me questions about genealogical research. We had conversations every few months for a few years, and he closed each genealogy conversation by saying he would like to invite me to "Bobov, to see the Ruv." At first, I had no idea what Bobov was, but I soon learned that it was the largest group of *Chasidim* in the ultra-Orthodox neighborhood of Boro Park in Brooklyn – which itself was the largest ultra-Orthodox neighborhood in America. And "the Ruv" was the leader of the group, more commonly known as a *Chasidic* rebbe. The Bobover *Chasidim* began in the town of Bobova in Poland, and the current rebbe at the time was Rabbi Shlomo Halberstam (who has since died; one of his sons is now the rebbe).

Though I had some curiosity, I kept putting off acceptance of Tuvia's invitations until one day, after we had moved to Kensington, Tuvia called once more. When I told him I had moved, he asked me where, and when I told him he excitedly said that "Bobov" was just a few blocks from the apartment. Tuvia invited me one more time and this time I accepted.

Tuvia decided that the best invitation would be for a Friday night, during a religious service called *Kabbalat Shabbat*, the "reception of the Sabbath." It was a time, on Friday evenings, when the *Chasidim* would gather and, in addition to performing the *Kabbalat Shabbat* ritual, in Bobov it included sharing dinner with the Ruv. Tuvia and I decided that the coming Friday would be perfect – why delay my introduction to Bobov any longer? I wore my black suit and walked to Tuvia's home, and then the two of us proceeded to "go to Bobov." Tuvia referred to Bobov as if it was the town of Bobova in Poland itself. Of course, it was where the great synagogue and world headquarters for Bobov *Chasidim* was located in Brooklyn.

When we arrived, there were hundreds of *Chasidim* of all ages gathering for the weekly event. The large room was furnished by a long dais in the middle of the room, surrounded by fifteen tiered bleachers flanking the dais on three sides. The bleachers were already filling up, and Tuvia guided me to a place on one of the bleachers where I would stand for the next three or four hours. I was squeezed in between Tuvia and a young man, dressed like almost everyone there except for me. While the *Chasidim* worn black robes, tied with a black tassel-like rope and with *streimels* (most made of mink fur) on their heads, I was in my black suit and, I'm happy to say, my black Stetson hat, which I had recently purchased. I knew that many Orthodox synagogues were filled with men wearing black suits and black Stetson hats, and I had planned to attend one of the orthodox synagogues in my new Brooklyn neighborhood, so I was prepared.

The men on the bleachers looked like a sea of black and white in their robes and shirts – and I was one of them. The bleachers were now filled to capacity. Suddenly the Bobover Ruv entered the hall. He was wearing a long elegant blue robe, the only bit of color in the otherwise black and white sea. The entire room was now filled with song and clapping as the Ruv made his way to the center seat at the dais. Other men joined him on the dais, some from the Ruv's family as well as, I was told, a few dignitaries – who were actually old men who had been with the Bobover Ruv from the very beginning of Bobov's history in the U.S. (when the Ruv and one of his sons arrived in America, having escaped the Holocaust. His wife and other children were all murdered by the Nazis.)

After the Ruv sat down, he began to sing "*Sholom Aleichem,*" the traditional prayer written to welcome the angels to the dinner. The place was silent, so despite his rather weak voice, his singing filled the place. What seemed like thousands of *Chasidim* stood still or rocked back and forth as the Ruv completed his singing.

While all this was happening, my head was exploding. The scene didn't seem like it was taking place in America. It was as though I was transported to 18th century Poland, where I am sure the very same scene took place. I was in an Eastern European *shtetl*, complete with *Chasidim*, a *Chasidic* rebbe, and the chanting of Jewish prayers. I wondered if I would ever be able to leave the place. The *Chasidic tisch* (table) is an important ritual in *Chasidic* life. One highlight is the distribution of the *shirayim*, the remains of the rebbe's meal, to the congregation. And I was one of the *Chasidim*!

The evening included singing, words of Torah in Yiddish from the rebbe, and dinner – for the rebbe – while everyone else watched and participated. How did we participate in the rebbe's Shabbat meal? When the rebbe was served a plate of fish, he would cut a piece for himself and then set the plate aside for others to share. The fish was supposed to feed everyone in the hall! It was a great honor to eat from the rebbe's plate. The piece of fish was passed around, hand to hand, as each of the *Chasidim* took a little piece off for themselves. By the time it got to the fellow next to me, there was a piece of fish less than the size of the nail on a pinkie finger. The young man next to me took a little bit, and then passed it to me. The piece of fish was now barely more than a tiny speck – and there were four more men standing on my row of the bleachers, waiting for their piece! With my sharpest fingernail, I cut a speck of a speck of fish off and gave the rest – almost microscopic in size, to Tuvia. I recited the blessing for eating fish and "ate" my piece. I could honestly say that I ate from the same piece of fish eaten by the rebbe. I was flying high!

The rest of the evening was filled with words of Torah in Yiddish from the rebbe. In between each teaching, the *Chasidim* would sing or chant. Finally, at around one o'clock in the morning, while many of the *Chasidim* went home, a few hundred – including me that night – stayed for the dancing and blessings from the rebbe. The smaller group reconvened in a smaller room and basically did a line dance, with each *Chasid* holding on to one shoulder of the person in front of him. The snake line, winding around the room, was accompanied by chanting. After about an hour of this dance and chanting, suddenly everyone charged in the direction of the Ruv, who was standing at one corner of the room.

People began pushing toward the Ruv for, what I later found out, was an opportunity to receive a blessing from him. The *Chasidim* were elbowing their way to the Ruv, pushing and shoving in an attempt to get close to the Ruv. As I was literally being tossed around by the frenzy of the others, my mood suddenly changed, and I just wanted to get out of there. I managed to escape and told myself that these *Chasidim* were acting like animals, and I wanted nothing to do with them. My dream of having found an American *shtetl* evaporated in the face of the rough-and-tumble behavior of those seeking a blessing from the Ruv. I left and walked home, convinced I would never return.

During the following week, I reflected on my Bobov experience, feeling warm and protected by the other *Chasidim* on the bleachers, and then feeling vulnerable and offended by the mad rush to get a blessing from the Ruv. And although I felt I would not go back, the next Friday night I found myself walking to Bobov again. I decided to give the whole thing one more chance.

It was basically the same as the week before. I took a place on the bleachers. I participated in the singing (especially when the singing was a simple *niggun* (a wordless melody, sung over and over again). I listened to the discourses of the Bobover Ruv (they were in Yiddish, so I didn't understand any of it). And I was somewhat successful in receiving a tiny piece of food originally on the Ruv's plate. I realize, as I look back on it, that I was not discouraged in the least by not being able to understand either the Hebrew prayers or the Ruv's Yiddish sermons. Just the fact that I was playing the role of a *chusid* satisfied me and actually spoke to me deeply. Had the Holocaust not occurred I had no doubt that I'd be in much the same situation, as a fervent follower of some *Chasidic* rebbe, gathering in one of the *Chasidic shtiblekh* in Dobromyl.

(As I mentioned earlier in this book, my genealogical research on my mother's side of the family resulted in my discovery that I am a direct descendant of an authentic *Chasidic* rebbe, Rabbi Chaim Joseph Gottlieb, known as the Stropkover Ruv. And while it might seem logical for me to identify more with that side of the family than my father's side, I have always had more of a connection with Dobromyl – where my ancestors were not *Chasidim*.)

When all of the singing, prayers and discourses by the Ruv were over, once again a sizable subset of the *Chasidim* reconvened in a smaller room where the line dancing and chanting once again filled the space. And, once again, when the dancing and chanting were over, the *Chasidim* made a mad rush to the corner of the room where the Ruv was situated. It was already after 1:00 A.M.

The frenzy to reach the Ruv and to obtain a personal blessing resumed, just as it had the week before. *Chasidim* were pushing and shoving and even climbing over each other, trying to get to the Ruv. I was totally surrounded and sandwiched in by beards and *streimels* and highly aggressive men and boys. Before I even got near the Ruv, I was able to inch my way out of the crowd, disheveled by the mob-like activities. Once again, I walked back to my apartment.

It was two o'clock in the morning, and the streets were almost empty, except for an occasional *Chasid* also making their way home. No doubt, they had all received their sought-after blessing while I went home without a blessing, and with a mixture of high feelings and low feelings. My ambivalence was physically and emotionally painful. On the one hand, I was high as a kite, knowing that this second experience with the *Chasidim* was more familiar and therefore more comfortable. The communal sense that I belonged somewhere – and not just somewhere but like a real scene out of authentic *shtetl* life – was exhilarating. On the other hand, the mad dash to make contact with the Ruv had me almost physically bruised and certainly emotionally wounded. It just didn't seem to be a place for me. At home, I slipped into bed almost brokenhearted. As I fell into a deep sleep I decided I would not go back.

But as foolish or unconscious as it might sound, on the next Friday night I actually found myself walking to Bobov again. Looking back, I was almost in a trance, although I didn't speculate (until much later in my life) about my possibly being a victim of some kind of mass hypnosis. I enjoyed putting on my black suit and Stetson hat. I enjoyed passing by many other men who were dressed somewhat similarly (except for the streimels) and who were also walking to one synagogue or another, about to participate in a time-honored *Kabbalat Shabbat* experience.

I met up with Tuvia, though I had not shared with him any of my negative feelings about the frenzy that so offended me. I don't know if I was protecting him or exactly what was going on between us. He and I found spots on the bleachers, ready once again for an evening of authentic *Chasidic* experiences. And once again, the procedure for the evening (into the night) was the same. The singing, the chanting, the listening to the Ruv teach Torah in Yiddish, the chanting to the angels by the Ruv, the waiting for any little scrap of food originally from the plate of the Ruv. And though it went on for hours, it never seemed long. Even standing in the same spot for all of that time did not deter me or anyone else.

And then came the mad rush to get a blessing from the Ruv. But it was different this time. I decided that rather than just being tossed around and almost bruised, I would push back, not to get to the Ruv for a blessing, but to protect myself from the onslaught. At one point the guy next to me almost elbowed me in the face and I shouted, "What's wrong with you people? You act like animals. All of this push- ing and shoving and aggression. What the hell is going on here?" And the guy looked back at me. While he was still actively pushing toward the Ruv, he turned to me and said, "We have a saying around here: when it comes to your *neshamah* (soul), there are no gentlemen."

With those words, the entire experience suddenly flipped for me. I realized that there was only one person in the room who was offended by the activity, only one person who was getting banged around. And that was me. *Everyone else was just like a salmon, swimming upstream to reach his goal, which was a blessing from the holy Bobover Ruv.*

After that night, I went back to Bobov almost every few weeks for the next ten years.

One day, Tuvia suggested it might be time for me to have a private meeting with the Ruv. The idea of an intimate conversation with an authentic *Chasidic* rebbe would be quite an opportunity for me, but at first I wondered what I would even talk about.

Tuvia suggested that I have some question or questions in mind when I was with the Ruv. So I spent several days trying to think of what to ask. I figured if this was to be the important experience that I anticipated it would be, I better make it meaningful. My first question – to Tuvia – was, "How do I get to see the Ruv privately?" Tuvia explained that every evening after the evening prayer session (known as *Ma'ariv*), the Ruv goes into his office to receive people. "What you do is get on a line," Tuvia said.

I discovered that the line of people actually forms even before the Ruv returns to his office. But then Tuvia explained that first I must see the *gabbai*. While *gabbai* can mean different things (e.g., a person who helps to run a synagogue service), in this context a *gabbai* is the assistant to the rebbe. Tuvia explained that before a person gets on the line, he (or she) must see the *gabbai*, who writes the names of people for whom you are requesting a blessing from the rebbe on a piece of parchment (known as a *kvitl*, which means "little note"). I knew that in some *Chasidic* groups, the *gabbai* (or the individual himself) actually writes the question or problem wanting to be asked or discussed. But in Bobov, the custom is to write the names of people who the petitioner knows is in need of a blessing. Then, when the person's turn comes, he walks into the office, stands before the rebbe who is sitting at his desk, and hands the parchment with the names to the rebbe. Tuvia suggested that I also hand some small amount of money along with the parchment, into the hands of the Ruv. I included a five-dollar bill.

I approached the Ruv's *gabbai* and asked him if he would just put the names of my children on the *kvitl*. At that point, I had two daughters; my son had not been born yet.

As was my habit, I got on the line early one evening and was actually the first person there. But within minutes a little *Chasidic* boy who looked to be about ten years old came to me and said, with tears in his eyes, that he needed to see the Ruv, so could he get in front of me? I agreed of course. But then, within another minute or two a man wearing a suit and holding an attaché case approached me and asked if he could get ahead of me, seeing that he had to catch a flight at the airport but needed to consult with the Ruv first. I consented.

Suddenly the Ruv appeared and went into his office. The *gabbai* followed him and then came out a few moments later, ushering the little boy into the Ruv. The boy was only in with the Ruv for about ten minutes, but it seemed like longer to me. I was quite anxious to get my turn. In the meantime, a few other *Chasidim* approached me, asking if they could get ahead of me. Since I was really a stranger there, I agreed. The man with the attaché case went in next and he was in for about fifteen minutes, hardly the brief consultation I was expecting. I settled into the line, knowing that sooner or later it would be my turn. I took a few deep breathes, held on to my *kvitl*, and was able to wait patiently. Eventually it was my turn. The *gabbai* ushered me in and left me alone with the Bobover Ruv.

The Ruv had an extraordinary face. His white beard and long *peyos* framed his face that quite literally shined with light. I am not exaggerating. Many people who I have spoken to since have confirmed that in some uncanny way, it seemed as though a beam of light came out from the Bobover Ruv's face. When he looked at me, it was as though a spotlight shined on me.

I walked to the Ruv's desk and stood before him. I then handed him the kvitl and the five-dollar bill. I had prepared quite a bit beforehand to ask my questions (I had three questions on my mind; I had not told anyone what they were.) But I found myself to be tongue-tied. I stood there in silence.

By the way, when I gave the *kvitl* and cash to the Ruv, he continued to hold my hand and didn't let it go.

Fortunately, the Ruv broke the silence in a way that I would never have anticipated: he read my mind!

My first question *was going to be*, "Why am I here in your office? Why did my path lead me to the office of a *Chasidic* rebbe?" "And why Bobov? Why not some other rebbe in some other *Chasidic* court. I was thinking that, after all, I grew up in a rather assimilated Jewish family, I essentially had almost no Jewish background, and yet there I was standing before a *Chasidic* rebbe with questions on my mind. In my brain I heard my own voice saying, "Why am I here?" But I had been thinking this; I said *nothing*.

Suddenly, the Ruv said to me (still holding on to my hand), "So, you are wondering why you are here?" I was stunned. But the Ruv continued, "You're wondering why you are here. And why in Bobov? Why not somewhere else?"

The Ruv then let go of my hand and began to pound loudly on his desk. He said firmly, "I want to tell you something very important." He then paused for a few moments and looking at me with his beam of light shining on me and said, "There is no such thing as a coincidence!"

On his desk sat a book called *Mikrahot Gedola* ("the Great Scriptures"). It is a very large book containing the text of the Five Books of Moses with vowels (there are no vowels in a Torah scroll), and several major commentaries surrounding the text. The Ruv pulled the book in front of him and opened it to the place in the Torah where Abraham sends his servant (Eliezer) to find a wife for his son Isaac. The Ruv scanned the page with his eyes and pointed to one of the commentaries.

"Here it says, 'They planned to meet by chance.'"

The Ruv continued: "What does it mean that they planned to meet by chance? Either it was a chance, or it was part of a plan!" He then looked at me and said, "You see, to you, things seem like they happen by chance, but there is a plan." He was referring, of course, to my thinking of my question of why I was there in the Bobover Ruv's office that evening.

Did the Bobover Ruv read my mind? Did he know what I was thinking? Or could this remark by the Ruv have been meaningful regardless of what was on my mind? I had done enough E.S.P. tricks in my life to be a little skeptical. But then the Ruv blew me away.

I had three questions I was planning to ask the Ruv, and I did not tell anyone what they were. The first one ("Why am I here in your office?") was basically answered by the Ruv ("There are no coincidences.") but my second question was more specific and not readily answered by a general answer. I wanted to ask the Ruv the question, "What do I do with my growing collection of sins?"

It seemed to me at the time that I had a large collection of sins, and it was growing by the day. For example, one sin that I committed regularly was gossip. I liked talking about other people, but I was not proud of it. But then there were the myriad religious sins that I committed every day – sins of non-observance of Jewish law, from breaking the Sabbath to neglecting my prayers to countless other failings. I was quite conscious of these sins, and I felt that with each passing day the list of those sins was growing steadily and rapidly. So, I simply wanted to ask the Ruv, "What do I do with my collection of sins?"

Though one could possibly think that the Ruv's response to this thought was also a stock answer, the possibility was more remote. The Ruv looked at me (I had still not gotten a word out of my mouth since entering his office) and he said emphatically, "And stop worrying about your *averas* (sins)!" The Ruv continued. "Stop worrying about your sins. Don't worry about your past; don't worry about your future. Just worry about your *mitzvos* in the present. Your *mitzvos* will take care of your past and will take care of your future. Stop worrying about your sins."

I was stunned. The Bobover Ruv had truly read my mind, I thought. I was worrying about my sins, and he told me to stop worrying about them. It was as simple as that. Of course, thinking back on it, the Ruv's remark about not worry about one's sins could also have been a stock answer. After all, who goes into the office of a *Chasidic* rebbe for a private meeting other than someone who, among other things, was worried about their sins? Who, for that matter, is a believer in God and fails to worry about this at least from time to time? Nevertheless, thus far the Bobover Ruv was, in my mind, two for two.

As I said, I had three questions on my mind that evening. The third question could also be considered a stock question with a stock answer. But the way the Ruv phrased it led me to believe that he was indeed reading my mind. My third question *was going to be*, "Can you give me some advice about my life?" The Ruv hardly missed a beat when he once again looked me squarely in the eyes with the light that shined from his face and he said to me, "And I'd like to give you some advice."

The Bobover Ruv then offered me some concrete advice. I don't feel I can reveal the advice he gave me because I never followed it, but rest assured it was a specific piece of advice that theoretically I could have followed. But one, two, three, the Ruv responded to my three questions without my needing to even give words to them.

The Ruv then looked at the *kvitl* I handed him and saw the names of two girls, my two daughters. He asked me if I had any sons and when I told him I did not he promised me that the following morning when he said his prayers, he would include the request that God grant me a son. And, of course, within several months, my son Moshe was born.

The Ruv then looked at me and said, "Who *are* you?"

I wasn't sure what he meant. Did he want my name and profession? Did he want to know about my relationship with God? Did he want to know of my questions and concerns? So I said to him, "My name is Avraham Abusch Kurzweil. And I am a descendant of Rabbi Chaim Yosef Gottlieb, the Stropkover Ruv."

The Bobover Ruv said to me, "Do you know that the Stropkover Ruv wrote a book? I said, "Yes. I know. It's call *Te'ev Gittin v'Kiddushin*" (on Jewish Divorce and Marriage Laws as discussed in Tractates *Gittin* and *Kiddushin* in the Talmud.)

The Bobover smiled and said, "Do you know who wrote the *Haskamah* [approbation or letter of praise] in the book?"

The Bobover Ruv dancing in ecstasy before his Chasidim,
c. 1987. The author is somewhere in this photo.

I immediately said, "Yes! It was Rabbi Chaim Halberstam, known
as the *Divrei Chaim*" [the title of his major book. In Jewish life, it is
not unusual for a person to be known as the title of a book he wrote].
I added that the *Divrei Chaim* was also known as the Sanzer Rebbe,
meaning that he was the leader of the *Chasidim* who belonged to the
Sanzer *Chasidic* congregation.

The Rebbe then said, "The *Divrei Chaim* was my great-grandfather!"

So there we were, the Bobover Rebbe and me, just as seven generations ago when the *Divrei Chaim*, his ancestor, was with my ancestor,
my great-great-great-grandfather, the Stropkover Ruv. It felt uncanny.
For me to meet with a *Chasidic* Rebbe and to find out that his ancestor and mine knew each other just testified once again to my soul's
connection to my past. My ancestors are in me and I am in them.

I walked backwards for several steps in the way I was instructed to
by my friend Tuvia. It was as if the Ruv was a king, and I owed him the
respect that I should not show him my back. Tuvia was waiting outside
for me, and when I exited the Ruv's study, he rushed over to me to
ask me how it went. I was somewhat in a daze. The meeting with the

Ruv was unlike anything I had ever experienced. I was speechless for a minute or two. I then shared the details of the meeting with Tuvia who was, it seemed, equally amazed by what I reported to have been through.

The next evening I saw the Ruv's older son in the room where praying took place and I went over to him, telling him rather excitedly that the night before the Ruv had read my mind. His son, who was next in line to be the Bobover Ruv, looked at me, shrugged his shoulders and said to me, "What else is new? I have seen this all my life."

Looking back on the meeting with the Ruv, I sometimes wonder whether I imagined all of it, or if in some way I was hypnotized by the Ruv. I certainly do feel that my Friday evening experiences at the Ruv's *tisch* (table) had at least an element of mass hypnosis to them – or if not, then some kind of mind control. I am surely not suggesting that the evenings are set up with the conscious idea of group manipulation, but there is something about the chanting (sometimes for hours) and the mob of people all desiring the same thing, that have my suspicions up. It happened once before to me – at an experience I had at Lubavitch, the *Chasidic* enclave in Crown Heights, Brooklyn, right across town from Bobov.

* * *

I can recall vividly that in 1977, when I was in my mid 20s, I had my first live encounter with Chasidism. I attended a weekend experience with the *Chasidic* group called Chabad/Lubavitch. The weekend was called a *pegisha*. A *pegisha* is, by definition, a weekend enclave, and at this particular *pegisha*, the attendees, like me, were largely assimilated Jews who were offered a taste of an authentic *Chasidic* experience and grabbed the opportunity. I don't recall who invited me nor how I found out about it, but there I was, on a Friday afternoon, in the neighborhood well-known as the home of the Lubavitcher rebbe, Rabbi Menachem Mendel Schneerson, and his thousands of followers. I was assigned to a family who provided me with a place to sleep and meals from Friday night through Sunday in the late afternoon.

After checking in with my hosts, we got ready to go to world

The Lubavitcher rebbe, Rabbi Menachem Mendel Schneerson

headquarters of Lubavitch, right next door to where the Rebbe lived. When the Friday evening service began, a room as big as two high school gymnasiums, if not bigger, was filled to capacity by *Chasidim*. I was one of twenty guys who, like me, wanted to experience, up close, the ways of today's Lubavitch *Chasidim*. Despite wall-to-wall men and boys by the hundreds and hundreds around us, some of us were pushed to the very front, where the rebbe sat or stood during prayers. I was pushed to the very first row.

Suddenly, like the Red Sea parting, the ocean of *Chasidim* split from the front of the great hall, where I was, to the very back where there is a door out of which the Rebbe comes. He walks down the aisle created by the splitting of the group on his way to his prayer station in the front of the crowd.

After the Rebbe got to his place, the split congregation of *Chasidim* came back together, recreating the sea of black and white again.

The Rebbe began the prayer session, which flowed from one fascinating part to the next. When the prayers were over, the Rebbe turned around and walked directly to me. I put out my hand to the Rebbe to wish him a good Shabbos and he returned the gesture as we shook hands with one another. The Rebbe then moved on, down the space created for him and he returned through the doorway in the back of the large hall.

Within moments of my handshake with the Rebbe, a crowd of *Chasidim* surrounded me, with people asking me who I was. I told them that my name was Arthur Kurzweil and they said, "Yes, but *who are you?* It was then explained to me that the handshake with the Rebbe was nearly unprecedented – and yet some of the *Chasidim* saw that the Rebbe came right over to me. I suspect he was going to wish me a Good Shabbos without the handshake, but when I reached out my hand he returned the gesture. I had no idea that the custom was not to shake the Rebbe's hand. The crowd surrounding me quickly dispersed, but I still overheard some of the *Chasidim* wondering who I was and looking back at me as they walked away.

Several years later I told this story to a young woman who, during the next time we met, confessed to me that she had fallen in love with me – based not on my good looks and charm but because "obviously the Rebbe saw something special in you." When I told the woman that I reached out my hand first, she said, "Yes, but he still walked *right over to you.*" And then she added, "Anyway, the Rebbe obviously knew that you would reach out your hand. He knows these things."

The rest of Shabbos was uneventful. I went back to my room in the home of my host and slept soundly. The next day – Saturday – was praying in the morning, then lunch back at the home of my host, and then Saturday evening with singing and dancing (men only). Again, I slept soundly on Saturday night, but had no idea what Sunday would bring. I slept late Sunday morning, was served a light brunch, and then walked back over to Lubavitch headquarters where preparations were in motion for the main event: the Rebbe's *farbrengen*. A *farbrengen* is the term used in Lubavitch for a *Chasidic* gathering, much like the Ruv's *tisch* (table) at Bobov. It goes on for hours and consists of singing, chanting, eating and drinking, interspersed with words of Torah from the Rebbe. Small paper cups and bottles of whiskey appeared throughout the hall like magic, and everyone who wanted one held the little cup in their hands. The bottles of whiskey circulated and as the afternoon progressed, the goal was to drink and then to keep your cup filled for the next time a drink was appropriate – which was when the Rebbe himself would raise his glass and wish a *"L'Chaim"* to the entire crowd – at which point all in attendance who had a cup of whiskey would return the words *L'Chaim"* and would drink another little cup of the somewhat strong beverage.

A *farbrengen* usually goes on for hours. What this means, of course, is that participants – perhaps a thousand of them – slowly or rapidly get drunk. Not unruly drunk, but high as a kite. The afternoon consisted of lots of singing – chanting really, with wordless tunes known as *niggunim*. A *niggun* is a repetitive chant, often wordless, where the main lyric is "ai-ai-ai." Though wordless, it is claimed that certain *niggunim*, especially those composed by a *Chasidic* rebbe, have intellectual or spiritual content, so that upon hearing or participating in the chanting of a *niggun*, specific content is communicated to the listener who is attuned to the sounds.

The basic structure of the Lubavitch *farbrengen* consisted of lengthy chanting; in between the chanting the Rebbe spoke, offering spiritual messages to those in attendance. A talk by the Rebbe seemed to be from five minutes to twenty minutes. During the chanting of the *niggunim*, the Rebbe would frequently gesture with his whole arm or even his whole body, encouraging the crowd to chant with more volume and more enthusiasm. To hear a group of a thousand *Chasidim* simultaneously chanting the same phrases of sounds not only almost demanded that everyone join in, but the repetition of the tune, over and over again, was quite hypnotic. And at the end of a *niggun*, or the end of words from the Rebbe, the Rebbe would raise his cup and say "*L'Chaim*" ("To Life") to all of those in attendance. This went on for hours.

But there was one more element to the Lubavitch *farbrengen* that demands description. During the chanting of the *niggunim*, individuals within the crowd would stand up, face the Rebbe and hold up an arm with their filled paper cup in their hand. The hope was that the Rebbe would see the person, lift *his* cup, and the two would wish each other a *L'Chaim*. At any given moment, during the chanting, the large hall with its thousand (or more) participants would be peppered with men who were standing at attention, holding up their cups, and waiting for the Rebbe to notice and acknowledge them.

I watched these silent requests for mutual *L'Chaims* with great interest. Sometimes the Rebbe would acknowledge one individual, and at other times, the Rebbe would acknowledge several people, one at a time, in a series of *L'Chaims*. Once a person received his *L'Chaim* from the Rebbe, the person would sit down. As the afternoon progressed, dozens of men, at different times, would choose to stand and wait for their *L'Chaim* (which was usually accompanied by a nod from the Rebbe). To be noticed by the Rebbe within the sea of people and to receive one's very own blessing of *L'Chaim* seem to be a highly coveted moment.

The *farbrengen* was absolutely fascinating. As with the Ruv's *tisch* at Bobov, I felt that I was transported by a time machine, back to some time and place in Eastern Europe two centuries ago. And I confess I loved being there.

Unfortunately for me, also as in Bobov, the Rebbe's words of Torah were in Yiddish, a language I don't understand and cannot speak. My father and his family spoke Yiddish back in Dobromyl, but when my grandmother arrived in America she refused to speak Yiddish to her children. She would only allow them to speak with her in English. In this way, she learned English in the new country. But it also meant that my father forgot most of his Yiddish skills and obviously was not able to pass them along to me. But at the *farbrengen* it hardly mattered to me. The chanting of the *niggunim*, the drinking, and my fascination while observing the thousand *Chasidim* in attendance, kept me occupied and alert, almost mesmerized.

And then, I'd say it was between the third and fourth hour of the *farbrengen*, something happened to me. It was during the chanting of a particularly moving, heartfelt *niggun*, that I slowly stood up, a cup of whiskey in my outstretched arm, standing at attention and facing the Lubavitcher Rebbe. Like the many dozens of men during that afternoon, I wanted a *L'Chaim* from the Rebbe. In fact, as I remember it, I desperately wanted a *L'Chaim* from the Rebbe. As I stood, the minutes rolled by. The Rebbe didn't even seem to look in my direction, and when he did, he didn't make the *L'Chaim* gesture I eagerly craved. Instead, he kept moving his glance to some other person in the crowd.

As time passed, the *niggun* continued to be chanted and the Rebbe encouraged everyone, with his body language, to continue chanting loudly, again with great enthusiasm. And there was nothing I wanted more than to receive my own *L'Chaim*. In my mind I was thinking, *Please give me a L'Chaim. Please don't overlook me. Please don't let the niggun end,* thereby ending my opportunity to receive what I profoundly craved.

At one point, the Rebbe glanced in my direction and offered a *L'Chaim*. But there was a man standing relatively close to me who sat down, as though it was his *L'Chaim*, not mine. But I offered a *L'Chaim* back to the Rebbe at that moment and I sat down also. I had a strange unsettling feeling. I was not sure whether I had in fact received a *L'Chaim* from the Rebbe.

I thought that perhaps I would return to another *farbrengen* some-day and try once again to receive a blessing from the Lubavitcher Rebbe. But I never did. Seventeen years passed and in June of 1994, the Lubavitcher Rebbe died. I had missed my chance to receive a *L'Chaim* from the holy Rebbe.

Part II

———

From Przemysl to Lvov: My First Attempt to Visit Dobromyl

The only thing we learn from history is that we learn nothing from history.

> – Georg Wilhelm Friedrich Hegel

If we look honestly at human history it shows that humans do not learn from the mistakes of our past. Some people might learn from some of their mistakes but the historic record shows that humanity does not learn from its mistakes, humanity does not learn from its past. There is no evidence that we know how.

> – Nigel Coutts, Educator

Over 100 Family Members Were Murdered

Over 100 members of the Kurzweil family, from Dobromyl and other nearby towns, were murdered during the Holocaust. Men, women, and children.

If I include all of my cousins, the numbers would skyrocket to hundreds if not thousands.

The Nazis constructed over 44,000 concentration camps, death camps, and incarceration sites, which included detention centers, forced-labor camps, and killing centers. They functioned independently. Places of torture, starvation, and mass murder.

Approximately 6 million Jews died during the Holocaust, and nearly 25% of them died within the span of 3 months during the killing campaign, Operation Reinhard.

Two thirds of all Jews living in Europe during World War II were murdered by the Nazi regime and its collaborators.

Jewish losses by location according to the *Holocaust Encyclopedia*:

- Auschwitz complex (including Birkenau, Monowitz, and sub-camps): approximately 1,000,000
- Treblinka: approximately 925,000
- Belzec: 434,508
- Sobibor: at least 167,000
- Chelmno: at least 167,000

- Shooting operations at various locations in central and southern German-occupied Poland: at least 200,000
- Shooting operations in German-annexed western Poland: at least 20,000
- Deaths in other facilities that the Germans designated as concentration camps: at least 150,000
- Shooting operations and gas wagons at hundreds of locations in the German-occupied Soviet Union: at least 1.3 million
- Shooting operations in the Soviet Union (German, Austrian, Czech Jews deported to the Soviet Union): approximately 55,000
- Shooting operations and gas wagons in Serbia: at least 15,000
- Shot or tortured to death in Croatia under the Ustaša regime: 23,000–25,000
- Deaths in ghettos: at least 800,000
- Other: at least 500,000

Six million individual Jews.

Kurzweils Murdered in the Holocaust (incomplete list):

Bennye Kurzweil
Henye Kurzweil
Saul Kurzweil and his wife
Chaikeh Kurzweil and her husband
Balka Kurzweil and her husband
Frymet Goldfarb Kurzweil
Mina Kurzweil Feldbrand
Ignatz Feldbrand
Norbert Feldbrand
Arthur Feldbrand
Chaya Kurzweil Sprung
Saul Sprung
Martha Sprung
Alice Sprung
Saul Kurzweil
Balka Apfel Kurzweil and her two sons

Joseph Baruch Pritsch
Hersh Kurzweil
Anna Chupper Kurzweil
Shmil Kurzweil
Molly Kurzweil
Mosh Kurzweil
Isaac Kurzweil
Eli Kurzweil
Dobroh Kurzweil
Hinde Ruchel Kurzweil
Gershon Kurzweil and his sister
Reisl Kurzweil Stubenhaus
Shimon Stubenhaus
Beilla Stubenhaus
Temma Stubenhaus and her sibling
Meyer Kurzweil
Ratza Kurzweil
Ida Kurzweil
Harry Kurzweil
Liah Kurzweil
Nachman Kurzweil
Moshe Schlaf
Eli Schlaf
Esther Blum Schlaf
Esther Schlaf Bodner
Zelig Bodner
Meyer Bodner
Regina Bodner
Syolemi Bodner
Sala Bodner
Saul Schlaf
Tonka Schlaf and her three children
Chaim Schlaf
Fela Schlaf
Samuel Schiffman

Bluma Schiffman
Rifka Schiffman
Sheime Schiffman
Zelda Stelzer Raht, his wife and daughter, and his brother
Mendel Stelzer, his wife, and their four children
Alexander Stelzer and his wife
Molly Stelzer
Harry Stelzer
David Stelzer
Tonka Stelzer
Solomon Stelzer, his wife, and their three children
Lonka Stelzer Greenhood
Zigmund Greenwood
Pinchas Kurzweil
Pepke Kurzweil and her husband
Szyman Kurzweil and his wife
David Kurzweil
Blima Kurzweil
Elu Kurzweil
Shmerl Kurzweil
Fagel Kurzweil
Ethel Kurzweil
Dozens of nameless children

My First Attempt to Visit Dobromyl

first applied for a visa from the Soviets in 1977, with my specific interest in visiting Dobromyl. At the time, I learned, there was a map published by Intourist, the official travel agency of the Soviet Union. Intourist dealt mostly with foreign tourists. A foreign tourist could only go to the locations on that official map; Dobromyl was not on it. Intourist told me I should apply for a visa to the city closest to Dobromyl on this map; that was Lvov. It is now spelled Lviv, which is the Ukrainian name of the city. I was told that when I arrived in Lvov, I should go to the Intourist office there and to request special permission to visit Dobromyl.

I flew from New York to Warsaw. While planning my trip to Poland and to the Soviet Union I obtained an international driver's license in New York, so I was able to rent a Polski Fiat from Avis of Warsaw with the intention of driving through the Polish-Soviet border near Przemysl. A Polski Fiat is a small car, quite popular in Poland at that time. From Przemysl my plan was to take my three-day visa to the Soviet Union with the permission I obtained to drive to Lvov. The drive from Warsaw to Przemysl was about five hours. Today I wonder where I got the courage to drive, alone, for those five hours, through the highways and back roads of Poland. But I was 26 years old and I was enormously excited to get to see Dobromyl, so my motivation was powerful.

The gate of the Jewish cemetery in Przemysl, circa 1977

The drive to Przemysl was beautiful. The natural beauty of the region is well-known, especially during the last leg of the drive when the winding roads take you through exquisite countryside. I drove straight through to Przemysl without making a stop. In Przemysl I booked a hotel room for the night. I left my small suitcase with the front desk and looked for a place to eat. After I ate, I then returned to the hotel and called it a day. It was still early but I was exhausted from the long drive. I also arranged to book a room at the same hotel for three nights later when I would return from the Soviet Union and then to drive back to Warsaw. All I packed for my visit to Dobromyl was a change of underwear, a toothbrush, toothpaste, my camera, wallet, passport and visa. I left the rest of my things with the hotel. I was quite trusting and I had no problem retrieving it when I returned three days later.

Although the drive from Przemysl to Dobromyl is only a little more than an hour, I would have to cross the border into the Soviet Union. I knew that border crossings can often take hours. Therefore, my strategy was to wake up early the next morning so I could be first in line at the border when it opened at 7:00 A.M.

When I awoke it was only 4:00 A.M. It was still dark, but I could already hear the sound of delivery and garbage trucks. I showered and gathered my things, putting the few items in my knapsack. I left my suitcase with the front desk and then got in my rental car and headed toward the border. It was a 10- to 15-minute drive to the crossing.

When I got to the border, it was not even 5:00 A.M. It was pitch black. All I could hear was the sound of barking dogs. I pulled up to the entrance where cars line up. As I had hoped, I was the first one there.

I usually love the early hours when as the sun comes up, but I was quite nervous and also eager to get through the border. I knew that Dobromyl was so close. I knew it would be a dream come true. Then, as the sun began to rise and the dogs continued barking, I could see where I was and what the surroundings looked like. It was then that I noticed the tall barbed wire fencing stretching in both directions as far as the eye could see. Barking dogs. Barbed wire fence. Crossing the border from one Communist country to another. Barely light out. Nobody around. It all added up to some uncertainty that what I was doing – alone – was safe.

My mind began to wander. I realized that nobody in the world knew exactly where I was. I could easily disappear. There were huge fields of crops, especially sunflowers, all over the area. A gigantic field of sunflowers is exquisite, but what I thought was that I could be killed and chopped up to serve as fertilizer for those flowers and nobody would ever know what happened to me. This particular border crossing, I was told, was quite small and not that popular, being in the southeast corner of Poland, with no large cities in the immediate area.

My stomach began to churn, and I was suddenly faced with a slight upset stomach. It might have been the food I had eaten the day before, but I figured it was probably just nerves. I took some slow deep breaths, trying to calm down. It wasn't working. I could hear my stomach making noise and quickly felt like I needed a bathroom.

It was around that time when another car pulled up right behind me. It startled me, but I saw, through my rearview mirror, that it was a family, so I figured they were no threat to me at all. Shortly thereafter a second car pulled up right behind the first one. My stomach was getting worse by the second. In a short time, I was desperate for a toilet.

What could I do? I am fairly resourceful, but I saw no solution. Would my stomach calm down? Would I shit in my pants? How embarrassing that would be! But I had to do something. I wondered if I could get out of the car and walk someplace private. But even if I could, if I was seen I would have a lot of explaining to do. An American, all alone, defecating out in the open. It wouldn't go well, I was sure.

As the day began to brighten, I saw that there were actually two barbed wire fences. I figured one was Polish and the other was Soviet. It seemed like there was a no-man's land in between. Other than the two cars behind me, I saw nothing. But I glanced to my right and saw a small building not far from where I was parked. It was a small cement structure. Perhaps it was for storage. I was confused and desperate. Could I possibly get out of my car and leave it by itself? Where were those barking dogs? I later learned that they were German Shepherd guard dogs. I knew I had no choice. I exited my Polski Fiat, locked the doors and walked as fast as I could walk to the building. I didn't know what I would find, but I knew I couldn't stay in the car.

It was a miracle. The cement structure was a washroom and toilet. And it was unlocked. I burst into the room, sat on the toilet, and got there just in time – which was a second miracle.

I was still nervous, but I felt much better. I wanted to finish up and get back to my car. Who knew what I would find? And who knew whether I was even permitted to get out of my car and walk to this little building?

I then discovered there was no toilet paper. This was bad news. If ever I needed toilet paper, it was then. What could I do? I opened up my wallet to see if I had any unnecessary paper. The only paper I had was Polish money. Let's just say it was the most expensive toilet paper I ever used.

By the time I got back into my car the line of cars was considerably longer. It was 6:30; a half hour until the border would open. I sat there, thinking about the miracle story I would be able to tell back in New York. From some reason, I was no longer nervous. I was eager to get to Lvov. At precisely 7:00 A.M., the lights in the office of the border guards came on, the gate opened, and a man in uniform approached my car and motioned for me to drive to where there were people waiting for me and the other cars.

I had to be checked by two sets of border control people. One was to get out of Poland, and the other was to go into the Soviet Union. It was relatively easy to get through the Polish side. I showed my passport and my visa for a 3-day visit to Lvov. My passport was stamped and I was waved to move on. It was the Soviet border guards who were not nearly as easy to please.

One of the border guards spoke some English, so when it was clear that I had come from New York, he approached me. First, I was asked to get out of the car and to hand over my papers: the visa and my passport. I offered my international driver's license, but he wasn't interested. He did want to see the papers for the rental car, so I gave them to him as well. He gave my papers to a colleague, also in uniform, who took them into an office next to the path my car was on. I hadn't noticed this office earlier; it had been obscured by some trees. I wondered if anyone had seen me go to the bathroom. Nobody mentioned it.

The man assigned to me then proceeded to search my body, finding only my wallet. I had nothing else with me. My knapsack was still in the passenger seat of my rental car. I was told to stand where I was. The man then took my car keys and opened the tiny trunk. It was empty. He then asked me to go into the car and to hand him my knapsack. He looked into the knapsack and discovered my change of underwear, my toothbrush, toothpaste and camera. It was then that he seemed to be suspicious. I speculated to myself that he was probably wondering what a young man from New York, USA was going to do for three days in Lvov without anything but these few items. He asked me if I had anything else and I answered, "No."

He got into the car, started the engine, and drove it to the side so the people behind me could go on ahead. Three men came out of the office and inspected every inch of my automobile. They hoisted the car up on a lift and took off its tires. They closely examined the entire underside of the car, looked into the tailpipe, and in the axles. They then lowered the car lift and opened the hood of the car. They examined the engine thoroughly with flashlights. This whole procedure took about an hour. I thought, *So much for an easy drive to Lvov!* Then they examined my camera. Fortunately, they didn't expose the film already in it.

The three men and the man who spoke some English then huddled closely and conferred with each other. I wish I knew what they were discussing. After a few minutes, the English speaker walked over to me and asked me why I was going to Lvov. I explained that my father was born in Dobromyl and I was told by Intourist to apply for permission in Lvov to go there. I also said that I was always interested in seeing this town and now I would have my chance. The man walked over to his colleagues and then raised the automobile lift to put on the wheels.

When the car was ready, my papers were returned to me. My passport had been stamped, and I was instructed to drive directly to Lvov as shown on the map I was given. I was not to stop for any reason and was not to drive on any roads other than the ones indicated on the map.

I suspected that the whole ordeal was due to the fact that my motive for this trip was puzzling to them. I had hardly anything with me, which probably prompted them to wonder what I was hiding. But finding nothing, I had permission to cross the border.

I was on my way to Lvov.

Request for Permission to Visit Dobromyl

The drive from the border to Lvov took about an hour. Although I was tempted to drive to Dobromyl, I had to remember I was in the Soviet Union now. I felt I needed to follow the rules. I drove slowly, or at least within the speed limit, not wanting to take the risk of being stopped by the police. Even though some would think I was brave to take this trip alone, I was pretty nervous. Ever since I was old enough to understand, I was taught that the U.S.S.R. was the major enemy of the United States.

I noticed there was a car behind me. The driver kept his distance, but I imagined I was being followed. I never learned if it was true or not, but just the thought of it made me extra cautious. Fortunately, my stomach was empty so I didn't need to worry about another upset stomach, and even though I was a bit nervous, I was mostly excited. I confess I was also proud of myself – driving alone, crossing the border, on my way to gain permission to visit Dobromyl. It was literally a dream come true. I was about to make my dream into a reality.

I found my hotel easily enough. I parked my car and entered the hotel lobby. Checking in was no problem. I showed my passport and I realized they were waiting for me. Someone showed me to my room. It was a tiny, narrow room, just large enough for a single bed, a bathroom and a standing closet. I took my toothbrush and toothpaste out of my knapsack and placed it in the bathroom and left my underwear in the knapsack. I was tempted to take a shower, especially after my experience at the Polish-Soviet border, but I was much too excited and eager to get to the Intourist office to gain permission to drive to Dobromyl. I recall looking out of the window of my room and seeing an old city with old buildings, and few people on the street.

It occurred to me that the room might be bugged. Everyone I met in Poland was convinced that all the apartments and even cars were bugged, so I suspected that it was the same in the Soviet Union. Feeling a little like James Bond, I searched the room but found no evidence of anything that would suggest the room was bugged, but I also had the feeling that even if it was bugged, they probably did a good job of concealing it.

The front desk clerk, who spoke no English, understood when I simply said "Intourist." He drew me a simple little map and I arrived a few minutes later at the Intourist office. There were two men working in this office and both of them spoke broken but adequate English. I was the only visitor. At the counter, I told one of the men, "I would like permission to drive to Dobromyl."

"Fill out form," he said as he handed me a form in Russian and in English. I sat down on a chair and filled out the form, excited that I was on my way to Dobromyl. Slowly I filled out the form as neatly as I could and brought it up to the counter.

"Come back in two hours."

Perhaps it wouldn't be so easy. But I had no choice. I expected to return to find permission granted for me to drive to Dobromyl, so I spent the next two hours casually walking in the neighborhood. As I looked at the shop windows, I had the feeling someone was following me. It was a woman who looked a bit older than me, and quite attractive. She carried an attaché case. To test my theory, I crossed the street. So did she. I then crossed back; she did the same. She wasn't too close to me, but once I saw her, it was obvious she was watching me.

The two hours passed quickly. I sat on a bench for a while, just doing some people watching. I noticed the woman had disappeared, only to see her appear again when I walked back to the Intourist office. She was smoking a cigarette.

I walked into the office and found someone else who was filling out the same form I had filled out. I approached the counter and was disappointed to learn from the man that I needed to come back in two more hours. There was no apology, no sign of regret, just a matter-of-fact statement of the delay. Not wanting to seem angry or upset, I left the office slightly annoyed. I suspected they were doing some kind of background check on me. I also speculated that they were contacting Dobromyl's office (if there was one) to see if they were comfortable with a visitor driving to the town.

It was noon and I was actually getting hungry. I saw a restaurant and went in and was seated right away. It was a real surprise to see the woman who I felt was tailing me enter the restaurant as well. She sat down at a table across the room from me. When I looked at her I noticed she was looking at me, but she turned her head away quickly.

I asked the waiter if he had a menu in English. He didn't understand what I was asking.

"English?"

"English? Nyet."

Luckily a person sitting at the table just behind me overheard this brief exchange and offered to translate for me. He spoke broken English but enough to help me to order potato pierogies with sour cream. In the meantime, I noticed that the woman I suspected of following me had ordered tea and a roll of some sort. I waited a rather long time for my meal, and I actually surprised myself by getting off my chair and walking over to her.

"Excuse me. May I ask you a question?

"Of course." Her Russian accent was pleasing to my ears.

I decided to get right to the point. "Are you following me?"

She blushed slightly. It was not the blush of an attractive woman who was being approached by a man, but rather a disappointed blush for being discovered.

"I am afraid so."

"Why?" I asked.

"This is my job today."

"And why are you following me? Did I do something wrong?"

"No, but I must keep track of you today. This is my job."

"Why me?"

"I do not know," she confessed. "You are my assignment for today."

Once again, I shocked myself by asking, "Would you like to come to my table and join me for lunch?"

"I am so sorry, but I cannot."

"Why, may I ask? I am harmless."

"Mister, I am not able to sit with you. I am working."

I laughed and she smiled, trying to hold back her grin.

I returned to my table. My pierogies had arrived. I sat down, looked across at my new "friend," and nodded to her.

After I finished a delicious plate of pierogies, I ordered some hot tea. I really don't care for tea, but I still had time to kill before I needed to return to the Intourist office. I figured that the tea might be good for my stomach; the fried pierogies and sour cream might not have been the best choice after my recent digestive problems. But the pierogies and sour cream had no negative effect on me, leading me to conclude that the incident at the Polish border was a case of nerves. I was feeling fine.

My two-hour wait was just about up when I headed to the Intourist office once again. When I arrived, I was told it would be one more hour! I was now nervous that I would not be successful. But I left the office and once again sat on a bench, looking at my watch every few minutes. The woman who was keeping an eye on me was across the street, trying to look as though she was window shopping. The hour went by fairly quickly for me, probably because the two-hour waits were so much longer. I didn't go back after the hour. Instead I gave them ten extra minutes. I went to the counter and was told to have a seat. Finally, I was making progress. I anticipated learning that permission had come through. I sat for 10 minutes when the same man I originally saw called my name.

I approached the counter and the man handed me a paper in Russian.

"What is this?"

The man looked right into my eyes and said, "Permission denied."

"Permission denied?! But why?"

"I am sorry. Permission denied." He sounded like he was stating a final decision.

My stomach started churning again. I left the office feeling miserable. As if the entire trip from my home in the U.S. hadn't been long enough, the five-hour wait really threw me. I left the office expecting the woman who was following me to be there. She was nowhere to be seen. I never saw her again, even though I stayed in Lvov one more day. I suspect they – whoever *they* were – decided I was harmless. Or perhaps someone else was tailing me. I didn't look around much to even notice.

I was depressed and disappointed. My lifelong desire to visit Dobromyl had slipped through my fingers. I was so close but still so far. I spent the next day just walking around and stopping for meals. I had a three-day visa; I figured I might as well use it.

One postscript worth mentioning: Over the years I have had opportunities to tell people, mostly Ukrainians and Poles, about my experience in Lvov. Everyone told me the same thing: I should have offered the man behind the counter some money – maybe $50. It might have made all the difference.

The Przemysl Train Station

Disappointment ran deep within me. The Russian border guards were emphatic: stay on the road to and from Lvov and don't make any turns. When I finally got back to Przemysl after my three uneventful days in Lvov, I was eager to try to figure out what I could do to relieve my depression. My hope to go to Dobromyl was so high, and now my mood was so low.

I wanted to go to the Przemysl town archives with the hope that I could find some records of my family's existence. I knew we came from Przemysl, I knew the Kurzweil family – at least a few branches of it – lived there, but all of my concrete evidence was based on the recollection of some of my older relatives, as well as a few references on the passenger lists I was able to obtain from the National Archives in Washington, D.C. I also had a copy of my great grandparents' wedding photo, with the word Przemysl on it. It is clearly printed on the lower right-hand side of the photograph.

My great-grandfather, Avraham Abusch Kurzweil, and my great grandmother, Hinde Ruchel Lowenthal, posed behind a fancy chair, probably the chair my great grandmother used for her *badeken*. The *badeken* (which means "covering") is part of the traditional Jewish wedding ritual. Just prior to the ceremony, which takes place under the *chuppah*, the groom approaches the bride, who is sitting on a chair. The groom covers the face of his bride with a veil and her face remains covered until the end of the wedding ceremony. This symbolic act is a custom originating with one of the biblical matriarchs of the Jewish

The wedding photo of the author's great-grandparents,
Hinde Ruchel Lowenthal and Abusch Kurzweil

People, Rebecca, whose face was covered when meeting Isaac, her
groom. In the Torah, the verse connected to the *badeken* reads "Then

she took her veil and covered herself" (Genesis 24:65). A covered face represents modesty.

I asked a librarian at the Przemysl Public Library (whose building used to be a synagogue) for the address of the archives; it was just a brief stroll away. At the archives, I approached a rather friendly man behind the counter. I made it known to him somehow that my great-grandfather, Avraham Abusch Kurzweil, was born in Przemysl in 1867. He went to a back room and appeared a few minutes later with an old book labeled "Jewish Births (in Polish) 1863 to 1874." I carefully flipped through the pages until I found it – the birth record of my great-grandfather! I had found real evidence that my branch of the Kurzweil family originated in Przemysl. I was thrilled.

My entire mood changed. While there was still some lingering disappointed at my failed mission in Lvov, to be able to see my own Hebrew name sitting in a record book in Przemysl, Poland was a major discovery. I was permitted to take pictures of some of the pages, as well as a photograph of the archivist and me – holding the record book. The records also indicated the name of my great-great-grandfather, Saul Kurzweil, after whom my father was named.

It occurred to me later in the day that I should have explored other records in the Archives, but I left quickly, walking the streets of Przemysl alone, with a grin on my face. My satisfaction was the reflection of true delight. The mere listing of the birth of my great-grandfather, Abusch, brought me a step closer to him, to finding him, to finding myself.

During my walk, I found the Przemysl train station. While I couldn't be certain, I imagined that my grandmother and her three children (including my father) took a train from Dobromyl to Przemysl and then on to Warsaw at the beginning of their immigration to the United States. Despite my uncertainty, I stepped back in order to get the whole train station in one photograph and snapped a picture. I then asked a passerby if he could take a photograph with my camera of me standing in front of the station.

Within moments, two Polish policemen approached me, grabbed

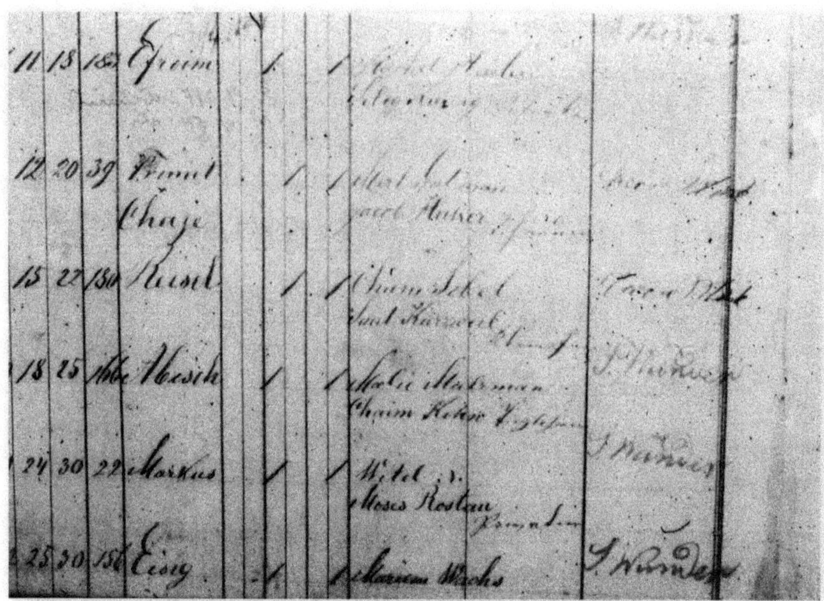

A page from the Przemysl, Poland birth records, showing
the birth of the author's great-grandfather

The author, with the Przemysl archivist, holding the book containing
the birth record of his great grandfather, Abusch Kurzweil

A then-forbidden photo of the Przemysl train station, 1977

my camera, asked for my passport, and took me to the Przemysl police station.

As I remember it, I was too high from my archives discovery to be nervous about what had just happened. We arrived on foot at the police station and I was asked to sit down in a chair next to a desk. One of the two policemen took my passport to a back room and a third policeman, who spoke some English, came out holding the passport and approached me. He then began my interrogation. He stood while I remaining sitting.

"What brings you to Poland and to Przemysl?"

I replied that my family came from Przemysl, so I decided to visit the place from where the family came.

"You family lives here?"

"No, but before the Second World War several branches of my family came from Przemysl."

"I see you also came from Lvov earlier today. Why did you go there for two nights?"

I explained that I was in Lvov for two nights in a failed attempt to visit Dobromyl, the birthplace of my father.

"Why didn't you go to Dobromyl?

"The Soviets would not permit it. I don't know why, but they didn't allow me to go."

"Why did you take a photo of our train station?

"When my father went to America in 1928, I assume that he went to Warsaw from this station. I thought it would be nice to have a photograph of the very train station he used. Can I show you a book I have in my bag?"

"What is it?"

"It's a book I published about my family history and there are photos of old Przemysl in it."

I excitedly took out the family history book I had privately published for the Kurzweil Family Circle and showed him, with great enthusiasm, some of the photos in it, including family photos from Przemysl. After showing him the pictures, he resumed the interrogation.

"Do you know it is not permitted to take photographs of train stations in Poland? It is indicated on your visa."

My Polish visa was folded and held between two pages of my passport. The policeman showed me the sentence on the visa indicating just this. He was right! I never noticed this, but it clearly stated that visitors were forbidden to take photographs of train stations in Poland.

"I am sorry. I must not have noticed this on the visa."

I wasn't fearful of the interrogation, but I was worried that the police would empty the camera of my film. I had some other photographs in it and didn't want to lose them.

I am happy to say that I was sent on my way; they did not open my camera. I later learned that Poland officially recognized train stations as military installations and it is for this reason that photographing them was forbidden.

Later that night, when I was back in my hotel room, I couldn't sleep. I was thinking about my great-grandfather's birth record sitting there in a book in the Przemysl archives. While it was not a substitute for going to Dobromyl, it was the first concrete thing I discovered in Poland about my family. The experience seemed surreal. Until that

Jewish cemetery in Przemysl, Poland, 1977

moment in the archives, my family and its life in Eastern Europe was just a story. But my great-grandfather's name, in black and white, was tangible proof that the Kurzweil family had been in Przemysl. It's not that I failed believe it; I just wanted to find some remnant of the Kurzweil family, my family, still in Poland.

I also walked to the Jewish cemetery – what was left of it – in Przemysl. It is on the outskirts of town. I searched in vain for stones with familiar names on them, but the cemetery was in profound disrepair. Stones were missing, others had sunk into the ground, and still others had tipped over. The brush was overgrown, making it difficult and sometimes impossible to walk through the cemetery. I found nothing of direct connection to my family.

Two days later, I left Przemysl for my drive back to Warsaw. But before I left, I wanted to see the Przemysl museum. Perhaps some items in the museum would bring me closer to finding the Abusch within me.

The Przemysl Museum

In 1931, of the total Przemysl population of approximately 62,000, about 18,600 residents were Jewish. By 1941, the estimated Jewish population of Jews was 14,500 – a drop from 30% to just 23%.

While I was in the city, I learned there was a museum dedicated to the history of Przemysl, so I went, expecting to find out a lot about Jewish life before the Holocaust. I was profoundly wrong. There was basically one showcase of Jewish "artifacts," with a few Chanukah menorahs, as well as a Shabbat spice box. I wasn't outraged, but I was deeply disappointed.

I hoped I would be able to fill in the blanks in my research. I don't know what I was expecting, but hardly just one small showcase with a few typical examples of pre–War Judaica. After all, I knew there was a Jewish ghetto in Przemysl during the Holocaust, as well as several synagogues. I knew that the majority of Jews living in Przemysl were sent to be murdered in death camp Belzec. Where was the evidence? Where were the photographs documenting at least some of this?

Before I left the museum, I approached a young man, a guard with a friendly face. I asked him if he spoke English. He did not. He asked me if I spoke German. I did not? He then asked me if I spoke Esperanto. Unfortunately, I did not. But I mentioned that I knew some Spanish. So did he.

What a strange sight: two young people, one an American and one a Pole, speaking broken Spanish.

"*Por favor. Otras cosas de Judios aqui?*" Were there any other Jewish things here?

"No, no mas. Pero en la casa de mi padre tiene muchas cosas judías."
No, he said but there were many Jewish things in his father's house.

This prompted me to ask him if he was Jewish.

"Eres judía?"

He laughed. *"No. Yo no soy judío. Mi padre es coleccionista."*

His father was a collector! Of Judaica?

Somehow, he communicated to me that if I met him after his workday, he would take me to his father's house – which I learned was also his house – and I could see his collection.

I took him up on his offer and precisely at 4:00 P.M. I met him in front of the museum. The walk from the museum to his house was no more than ten minutes. I had been wondering all day what I would find in his father's "collection."

On the way, I learned that his father was a retired veterinarian. Somehow the young man was able to communicate to me that before the war his father knew many Jewish people because as a veterinarian he often worked at kosher slaughterhouses in the city.

We arrived at a large, two-story house. The collector's wife met us at the door and ushered us into a large room with a table and chairs, as well as shelves around the entire room, with seemingly every inch filled with artifacts of all kinds. There seemed to be more items there than in the entire city museum! She gestured to me to sit down at the table.

Suddenly the man of the house appeared from behind me. He was tall, rather handsome, with white hair and a friendly face. He shook my hand firmly and began speaking with me in Polish. His son quickly told his father that I did not speak any Polish. His wife, who had left the room when he arrived, returned a few moments later with a tea set and a plate of cookies and cakes.

My eyes scanned the shelves. There were pieces of all sorts. Many looked quite old. They looked like many were from ancient Rome or Greece. I don't know anything about these kinds of collections, so I really wasn't sure what they all were. But, after all, I was really eager to see his Judaica items. The man reached for a few Chanukah menorahs and spice boxes, but they were not very impressive. I had seen too many of these common Jewish items not only earlier that day in the

Przemysl museum, but also in the Jewish Museum in New York and in synagogue lobby showcases where local collectors donated pieces. I'm sure he saw that I wasn't very impressed.

He then went to one of the shelves and showed me a pendant on a chain. My eyes grew wide open as I looked at one side and then the other. I held it delicately in my hand. It was about the size of a U.S. nickel. On the front was an artistic depiction of Moses holding the tablets of the Ten Commandments. It was colorful, and the tablets had Roman numerals I to X on them. And on the back, in micro Hebrew calligraphy, were the first two sentences of the Sh'ma prayer: *Hear O Israel, the Lord our God, the Lord is One. Blessed is the Name of His Glorious kingdom for all eternity.*

Many questions flooded my mind: Where did he find this Jewish pendent? Who made it? How did he come to own it? Whose pendant was this? What was her name? What did she look like? Did she survive the Holocaust? And most important . . . Could I buy it from him?

The pendant was a bit worn. I held it and kept staring at it. I was lost

Pendant found in the Przemysl ghetto area after WWII

in thought. My imagination transported me to the 1940s. I imagined a young woman wearing it around her neck.

I looked at the son and said, "¿De donde?" From where did this come?

"Mi padre encontró en el lugar del gueto después de la guerra." He knew a lot more Spanish than I did, but I understood him. His father found it on the ground where the Jewish ghetto was. He found it after the war.

And how much to buy it? "¿Cuánto para comprarlo?"

The young man asked his father, but his father did not answer him. The former veterinarian then walked over to a different corner of the room to show me a second Judaica item in his collection. When I saw it, I was stunned. It was an antisemitic ashtray!

The ashtray was bizarre. It looked like it was cast from lead. It was about the size of my open palm. The motif on it was a large pig with the head of a Jew with *peyos* (side curls), a beard, and a kippah sticking out of the pig's anus, and legs sticking out of the pig's mouth – as though the pig had eaten the Jew whole. It was raw horror. A sick joke ashtray

Antisemitic ashtray

at the expense of the Jews. It disgusted me and fascinated me. It was an authentic example of antisemitism, from Przemysl, the home of my family. For some reason, I wanted to own it. I felt it didn't belong in a non-Jew's collection where nobody saw it. And the contrast between a delicate pendant with Moses on it and this vulgar example of hatred of Jews seemed in some strange way a pair.

While I was looking carefully at the ashtray, the woman of the house encouraged me to have some tea and cake. I was hardly in the mood for it but I acted like a perfect guest. I wanted, somehow, to leave with these two items. The tea was poured from a samovar and there were cubes of sugar in a small dish next to it. I helped myself to some tea, and took two small pieces of cake. In the meantime, the collector took back the ashtray. I didn't see where he put it.

Although I was nearly overwhelmed emotionally by the two items, nothing could possibly prepare me for what happened next.

As I was finishing my tea and cookies, the veterinarian left the room and came back just a few moments later holding part of a Torah scroll. It was large but I couldn't tell how complete it was.

I was shocked and felt nearly paralyzed by the scroll. A Torah scroll is the holiest and most sacred object in Jewish life. It can take a year to write (it must be done with special ink by a trained scribe call a *sofer*). If one letter is incorrect, the entire Torah is disqualified from use until it is repaired. It is said that if a Torah scroll falls to the floor, the person or people responsible must fast during the daytime for forty days. When the Torah scroll is taken out of the *aron hakodesh*, the holy ark, in a synagogue, it is marched around the congregation and when it gets to you, the custom is to kiss it. A Torah scroll does not just lay around; it is "dressed" in fancy "garments." Yet here was this collector, holding the scroll with his bare hands and treating it quite informally.

He spread the scroll out and the black letters on parchment were hypnotic as I looked at them. I was seeing a Torah scroll in Przemysl! Where was it from? Who read from it last? In what synagogue was it before the Holocaust? From where did he get it?

This encounter was getting too intense. I think the man detected this and quickly took the Torah back into another room where he presumably kept it. He came back a moment later. He picked up the pendant and the ashtray and told his son to tell me I could buy them from him for $75 U.S. I quickly agreed. He put the pendant in a little cardboard jewelry box and the ashtray in an envelope. I handed him 75 dollars, knowing it was a lot of money by Polish standards at that time. But I wanted these two items from the town of my ancestors. It crossed my mind at that moment that my great-grandparents, Avraham Abusch Kurzweil and his wife, Hinde Ruchel Lowenthal, were married in this little city. A pendant celebrating Moses and the Ten Commandments, along with an antisemitic ashtray were bookends to the story of the fate of the Jews from Przemysl.

I stood up to indicate that I was ready to leave when the veterinarian said something to his son, and his son asked me to wait a moment. A few minutes later, he returned to the room and I saw that he had something for me. I think he felt a little guilty that he charged so much for the pendant and ashtray. I think he had expected me to bargain with him to get the price down.

Part of the museum worker's father's Judaica collection

To my complete horror, the man had cut the Torah scroll! He handed me one of its panels, wrapped in a rubber band. It was not enough that the Torah scroll was incomplete and was laying around in the house. Ironically, I think he believed he was giving me something I'd enjoy having – a kind of memento of my visit to him and to Przemysl itself. According to Jewish tradition, an old piece of a Torah scroll should be buried, if possible in a Jewish cemetery, not shredded. My head was exploding. But I took the panel from the Torah. After all, he was ignorant and I wasn't emotionally prepared to insult him by telling him it was wrong to cut a Torah scroll.

I left as soon as I could.

For the next several days in Poland, I hid the parchment in my suitcase, and looked at it every once in a while, staring at the Hebrew, a language I could not read. I wondered what part of the Torah it was from. What words of Torah were handed to me that day in Przemysl? Of all the panels in a Torah scroll, which one did I receive? It was not until I returned back to New York when I asked a friend who knew Hebrew to tell me where in the Torah this panel was from. What words of Torah were delivered to me that day when this man cut into it?

When I located a translation, a chill ran down my spine.

The words of the Torah in that single panel read:

*If you do not obey God your Lord and do not carefully keep all
    his commandments and decrees as I am prescribing them for
    you today, then all these curses will come to bear on you.*
Cursed will you be in the city and cursed in the field.
Cursed will be your food basket, and your kneading bowl.
*Cursed will be the fruit of your womb, the fruit of your land, the
    calves of your herd and the lambs of your flock.*
Cursed will you be when you come and cursed when you go.
*God will bring misfortune, confusion and frustration against
    you in all you undertake. It will destroy you and make you
    rapidly vanish because of your evil ways in forsaking My
    teachings.* (Deut. 28:15…)

Belzec I

The next morning, I went to my car for my return to Warsaw. About an hour into the drive, I had a feeling I had made a wrong turn. I pulled over and stopped the car. My map confirmed what I feared.

I saw that if I drove back to the point of confusion, and corrected my error, I could get back on the recommended route in about 45 minutes to an hour. But I also saw that if I stayed on the highway I was currently on, it too would bring me back to Warsaw. It would take more time to stay on this highway, but the idea of driving back just didn't appeal to me. If my arithmetic was correct, it would only be 1½ to 2 hours more driving. That didn't bother me. I'd get to see more beautiful Polish countryside.

Within a short time, I came across a road sign that stunned me. It said *Belzec*.

I knew of Belzec, Poland. It was the site of one of the most notorious Nazi death camps. It was one of the places where many Jews from Dobromyl and vicinity were sent to be murdered. Many of my relatives perished there.

I feel that in some way all of the Jews of Dobromyl were my relatives. I suspect that given the time, I could show how, through marriage, each Jewish family had some family connection to every other Jewish family. Nevertheless, I also know that many of my blood relatives were sent to Belzec.

Reinhard Heydrich, a high-ranking Nazi, was the chairman of a secret meeting of Nazi leaders to design a mission named after Heydrich himself. It was called Operation Reinhard.

The road to Belzec

Operation Reinhard was a major piece of the "Final Solution" or "The Final Solution to the Jewish Question," another name for the Nazi plan of genocide: the murder of all Jews in the world. Operation Reinhard was essentially the plan to destroy Polish Jewry.

Belzec extermination camp was built by the Nazi Secret Service (SS). "Operation Reinhard" included the construction of the Belzec death camp, where more than half a million Jews were systematically killed. Its years of operation were 1942 and 1943.

Death camp Belzec, located in eastern Poland, was designed to murder tens of thousands of Jews in a day. The Jews arrived by trains. They were squashed into cattle cars, and those who didn't die of suffocation were murdered shortly after their arrival at Belzec.

The Nazis included deception as a tool. In order to avoid riots, the Jews were told they would be examined medically and then relocated. In reality, the Jews were told to take off all of their clothing, after which they were murdered in large locked chambers filled with other Jews. Those chambers were then filled with lethal gas. When the screaming stopped, the Nazis knew the Jews in the chamber were dead. Workers would clear the chamber of the corpses for burning and pulverizing and then the next batch of Jews would be forced into the chamber.

Belzec, built by the German Nazi SS, was not designed to house people, but to murder them and to destroy the human remains. All evidence needed to be erased. The extermination camp burned corpses on five open-air grids. Bones that did not break down during cremation were put through a crushing machine designed specifically for this gruesome task.

Belzec operated from March 17, 1942 to the end of June, 1943. In that time close to a half million Jews were murdered.

Many of my great aunts, great uncles, and cousins were put on trains, destination Belzec. The relatives who were not shot by Nazis in Dobromyl and other nearby towns and villages were literally destroyed in this Nazi extermination camp in eastern Poland.

During the Holocaust the two major death camps were Treblinka and Auschwitz. Belzec was the third deadliest extermination camp. Only seven Jews somehow survived Belzec. Israeli historian David Silberklang writes that Belzec "was perhaps the place most representative of the totality and finality of the Nazi plans for Jews."

Jews from the towns and villages surrounding Przemysl were often sent to the Przemysl ghetto before being sent to their death at Belzec.

The ghetto in Dobromyl was designated in October 1941. On July 29, 1942, 5,000 Jews from Chyrow and Dobromyl were sent to their death in Belzec. Two hundred Jews were burnt alive in Dobromyl's grand synagogue. The last Jews in Dobromyl were shot in December, 1942. The mass execution took place on the left bank of the Wyrwa River.

The Przemysl ghetto was liquidated in August 1943. In all, more than 6,000 Jews were deported to the death camp at Belzec.

On August 3, 1942, more than 3,000 Jews were deported to Belzec.

On August 4, 1942, a further 3,000 were sent to the same place.

Train cattle cars were the major way Jews were sent to Belzec. Stuffed into these cattle cars, many Jews died of suffocation before arriving at the death camp. Those Jews who arrived at Belzec were forced, naked, into the gas chambers and were whipped to squeeze as many Jews as possible into each chamber.

As I looked at the road sign *Belzec*, I knew from my research that in 1978 there was no memorial built at this site. The Nazis exhumed bodies, pulverized bones, and dismantled the entire operation to hide the evidence. Fir trees and wild lupines were planted on the site. It was not until 2004 that a memorial museum in Belzec was built.

I sat in my car for about ten minutes, and I felt quite numb. How can it be possible for humanity to sink so low? How can I even grasp the size of a half million innocent Jews who were sent to horrible deaths? Who worked at this extermination camp? How did they go home at night? How did they describe what they were doing?

I got out of my car and took a photo of the sign. I was disturbed by how tranquil it was there. Lush greenery and silence. At one moment I wondered: if I remained silent, could I possibly still hear the echoes of this death camp's operation?

And then, suddenly, as quickly as I could, I drove away from this quiet little town. There was nothing to see there, and even if there was, what did I need it for? I felt numb for at least another hour of my drive back to Warsaw. Or perhaps a part of that numbness has never left me. I wondered how many people in the surrounding villages, close to Belzec, knew what was happening there. But I also wondered – what could they do about it? The Nazi reign of terror must have intimidated most if not all of those living nearby. How could local civilians fight against the viciousness of the Nazis?

Auschwitz

The first time I went to see the former death camp Auschwitz, I found the process itself to be somewhat bizarre. I was in Krakow and found that I had to ask someone, "Where do I buy a ticket to Auschwitz?" And once I had my ticket, it was equally bizarre to ask, "Excuse me, but where do I get the bus to Auschwitz?"

There was no good way to say it.

A building in Auschwitz where Nazi medical experiments took place

The year was 1978; I was 27 years old. Old enough, I suppose, to try to grasp the immensity of the place. The death camp had morphed into a museum. One does not visit the death camp, but rather a museum dedicated to the horrors of the place. Auschwitz was the largest and deadliest of the six extermination camps run by the Nazis and their collaborators. 1.3 million individuals were brought to Auschwitz; 1.1 million of them were Jews; 960,000 of those Jews were murdered there.

The largest group of prisoners came from Hungary, followed by people from Poland and France. On one single day, October 10, 1944, 800 children were murdered there.

Inmates were housed in barracks designed to hold 700 people, but in reality, there were 1,200 to each two-story structure. During the time it was functioning, 8,400 people worked in death camp Auschwitz.

I took a tour which began at the gates of this infamous death camp, with its sign in German, *Arbeit macht frei* ("Work makes you free") and ended at the site of the ovens (for burning bodies). Of the people in the tour group I was with, I remember in particular one Jewish family.

They were standing directly behind me when we arrived to see two of the ovens. Surrounding the ovens were colorful flowers. While it

Ovens in Auschwitz where bodies were burned

Auschwitz gas chamber

is not the custom of Jews to set flowers on a grave, one sees flowers at Christian cemeteries all of the time. The couple were offended and they let everyone knows by their (snide and loud) remarks of how it was "inappropriate and offensive" to put flowers there. "Jews don't put flowers on graves," they said, in fierce objection.

The fact is I was embarrassed by *them*. They were totally ignorant of the fact that many non-Jews were also murdered at Auschwitz and people were probably placing flowers because some of their family members also perished there. The couple seemed to be claiming Auschwitz as theirs; they saw the flowers as a desecration. They weren't aware how Polish Christians suffered greatly during the Holocaust. Jews do not have a monopoly on suffering. I walked away from them, not wanting to be associated with these foolish Jews. They were American Jews who had as their goal in visiting Poland to tell them what "*you* did to *us*."

Part III

Dobromyl: Making Contact

For me the Holocaust was not only a Jewish tragedy, but also a human tragedy. After the war, when I saw that the Jews were talking only about the tragedy of six million Jews, I sent letters to Jewish organizations asking them to talk also about the millions of others who were persecuted with us together – many of them only because they helped Jews.

– Simon Wiesenthal

Facebook 1

One day in 2016, on a whim, I searched for "Dobromyl" on Facebook. To my great surprise, Dobromyl has a Facebook page. I actually trembled when I saw it. The town of my imagination suddenly came to life. It seemed incongruous to me. For so many years I had an image of Dobromyl with no technology. Dobromyl, in my mind's eye, was just a little old *shtetl*.

I knew from my research that Dobromyl had less than 5,000 inhabitants. It was still a little town to me. I imagined Dobromyl to be a little village with horses and wagons and old houses with small subsistence vegetable gardens.

When I finally arrived in Dobromyl for the first time, I realized I was not too far off. While some families had a car, there was still an occasional horse pulling a wagon with, typically, an elderly person driving it. And many of the houses did indeed have vegetable gardens. Much of Dobromyl consists of families who truly count on their backyard vegetables, their egg-laying chickens, and an occasional pig or a bunch of chickens running around the yard to raise and then to slaughter.

For years I imagined that the reason the Soviets would not let me go to Dobromyl was because of the poverty I would have seen. I imagined dirt roads, and many abandoned shops that once upon a time were occupied by Jewish artisans such as tinsmiths, blacksmiths, locksmiths, plus tobacco sellers, butcher shops and vegetable stands.

It never occurred to me, for example, that some homes would have running water. My father had often told me that my grandmother went outside their little house to a communal well for their water.

I never thought there would be a Facebook presence. After all, to have a Facebook page meant to own a computer and to have internet access. It seemed impossible to me. I stared at the Dobromyl Facebook page with confusion. Could it be I was wrong about Dobromyl, and that modern life had reached the little *shtetl*? Was my father's little *shtetl* really connected to the internet?

The Dobromyl Facebook page was written mostly in Ukrainian, which uses a Cyrillic alphabet and seemed to be dominated by religious drawings and paintings. There were references to Christmas, Easter and what looked like other religious Christian postings. Using Google Translate, I was able to discover that many people were wishing each other holiday greetings.

After my first encounter with the Dobromyl Facebook page, I went back to it *several times a day* for a few weeks, glancing at it with disbelief. *Dobromyl has a Facebook page* I repeated to myself, wondering if I would wake up from a wild dream. For me, Dobromyl had just flipped on its switch and was now alive.

A few weeks after my discovery I wondered if I could actually join the page and write on it in English. But what I would say? What do I have to say to the current residents of Dobromyl? Would I say that I was Jewish? What would be my purpose? I couldn't imagine having a Facebook friend from Dobromyl.

Every time I thought about it, I got nervous. Dobromyl was alive but I was not a part of it. It seemed impossible for the page to exist and equally impossible that I would add my name to its list of members. For weeks, I kept wondering what I would write. What approach would I take? I couldn't even imagine that I would do it.

But I also thought about all the things I have of interest – at least of interest to me – from Dobromyl:

- Old photos of Jewish life in Dobromyl from before the Holocaust
- Family photos to remind citizens of Dobromyl that Jews were once 50% of the population

- Old envelopes with the return address of one of the rabbis in Dobromyl who used to correspond with my great-grandfather in New York

And then there was the Dobromyl memorial book with lots of photos, and a little map of the town center. I could show them on the map where my family's house was!

An envelope addressed to the author's great-grandfather, from a rabbi in Dobromyl. "Abusch" is spelled with an "i", reflecting an alternate pronunciation of the name.

I knew these were just dreams, pipe dreams. What would a Christian Ukrainian, from a town where no Jews had lived for decades, want with a descendant of old Jews from Dobromyl?

But I finally concluded that I must, somehow, contact people in the town. I tried to compose some introduction. But what would it say? How would I explain who I was, or why Dobromyl was so important to me?

And even if I were able to write something, then what? It seemed quite inconceivable that I would strike up a conversation with someone from my father's town. Not only would language be a barrier, but what does a Jew from New York, who was never in Dobromyl, say to them?

I wondered if they knew of the destruction of the Jewish community in Dobromyl? Would I be a terrible reminder of the past? Would they simply ignore me if I wrote on the Facebook page?

I grew up in a mostly Christian, and mostly Roman Catholic and Lutheran, suburban neighborhood. Almost all our immediate neighbors were Catholic, and the children of those households did not go to public school as I did, but rather to the Catholic parochial school in town. And I knew that after decades, we and our neighbors hardly ever spoke to one another – except for friendly "hellos" from time to time. If I thought I had little in common with my neighbors in New York, what connection would I have with Christians from Dobromyl?

Then, one day, I went to the Dobromyl Facebook page and without thinking I spontaneously wrote, "Hello. My name is Arthur Kurzweil.

The author's grandfather (right) with his gutter-making metal press

Dobromyl building with old gutters, probably
made by the author's great-grandfather

My father and grandfather were born in Dobromyl. My great grandparents lived in Dobromyl. We are a Jewish family. *Am I welcome here*"?

Before I had time to think about it, I pressed *Send*! It took a few hours at most to begin receiving at least a dozen responses including:

"Of course, you are welcome here."

"Dobromyl is just as much your town as it is our town."

"Jews lived in Dobromyl for hundreds of years."

"We don't know our own history. We need you to teach us!"

I was blown away by the reception I received.

A few people said they would be quite interested in old photographs of Dobromyl. I scanned a bunch of family photos taken in Dobromyl, as well as several photographs that I scanned from the Dobromyl Memorial Book, and shared them on the Facebook page. They were enthusiastically received, with some photos prompting speculations as to exactly where the photos were taken.

When I made it known that my great-grandfather was a tinsmith in the town, someone sent me a few photographs of an old building with rain gutters. I was told by the sender that the gutters were undoubtedly made by my great-grandfather! Here is a photo, taken in Dobromyl, of my grandfather, Yudl (on the right), with his metal bending machine – designed to make rain gutters. Unfortunately, I don't know who the other man and boy are.

But I had finally made contact with Dobromyl – thanks to Facebook. While so many people seem to be critical of Facebook, for me it was the means by which I was able to connect with people who live there today. This was an amazing development. How I wished my father was alive to know that I have actually had Facebook chats with current residents of Dobromyl.

The Wall of Memory

Sometime in 2015, an article appeared in a Polish newspaper reporting that over 100 Jewish gravestones were found behind a house in the town of Dobromyl, Ukraine.

The gravestones were not just found behind the house in question. In fact, they had been used to build a sidewalk for the Gestapo. When the Nazis took over Dobromyl, they confiscated one of the Jewish homes and turned it into Gestapo headquarters.

There is no record of how exactly the huge gravestones got there.

Jewish home seized by the Nazis for use as Gestapo headquarters. The walkway outside the house was paved with Jewish gravestones.

Originally, they were up on a hill, on the other side of the town, in the centuries-old Jewish cemetery. Somehow, probably with slave labor provided by the Jews in the town, the gravestones were dislodged from where they stood and brought down the hill and across town to the house, and placed on top of the dirt and mud – to make a sidewalk to protect the boots of the Nazis. The gravestones were both right side up and facedown. The Nazis walked over them each day.

The newspaper article reported that one Mr. Moshe Rubinfeld, a resident of Brooklyn, New York and a former resident of Dobromyl, knew about the fate of these gravestones and contacted a Polish organization that, among other things, restores Jewish cemeteries.

Mr. Rubinfeld had been trying for ten years to get the attention of someone – anyone – in authority in Dobromyl, in an attempt to do something about the situation of these desecrated gravestones. He periodically wrote letters to the mayor of Dobromyl, but never received an answer. It is important to mention that Mr. Rubinfeld wrote to a different mayor than I eventually did. The previous mayor had seemingly no interest in the matter, while the new mayor offered to do anything he could to cooperate with the effort to dig up the gravestones. His name was Yurij Petryk. He has since passed away after a brief bout with cancer.

The Polish organization referred him to a Ukrainian group, the Lviv Volunteer Center, led by Mr. Sasha Nazar, a native of Lviv, and after ten years of failed attempts, Mr. Rubinfeld finally connected with people who could handle the situation. He also was in direct contact with the new mayor in Dobromyl who promised total cooperation. All that was needed was money to hire laborers to proceed with the daunting task of digging up the gravestones and taking them back to the land that was the former Jewish cemetery. The plan was to use the gravestones to construct a monument in memory of the former Jewish residents of Dobromyl, including victims of the Nazis.

As I mentioned, the gravestones were huge. They were not little footstones as we often see in the United States. They were tall, heavy headstones, and each took the strength of more than a few people to lift them on to carts and to pull them by tractor up a few long and steep hills to the Jewish cemetery.

Walkway paved with Jewish gravestones

Mr. Rubinfeld's phone number in Brooklyn was easy to find, so I called him, introduced myself as a descendant of a Jewish family from Dobromyl, and requested to meet him. My wife, Bobby, and I drove to Mr. Rubinfeld's apartment, about an hour from where we lived. We found that Mr. Rubinfeld was an elderly man with a great spirit. He told us of all of his failed attempts to do something about the sidewalk made of Jewish gravestones, and also told us that he finally made contact with the Lviv Volunteer Center. Even though they had not been able to collect all of the money needed, the task of digging up the gravestones had already begun.

"We don't have enough money," Mr. Rubinfeld told us. They only had a third of the amount needed, donated by anyone Mr. Rubinfeld could convince that it was a worthy cause. I later learned that Mr. Rubinfeld had raised enough money to have the gravestones dug up and transported to the land of the Jewish cemetery, but they did not have the money it would cost to build the monument – later called the Wall of Memory.

The Dobromyl Facebook page announced that the digging had

From the Jewish cemetery, looking down on the town

begun, with the help of the Lviv Volunteer Center and local residents of Dobromyl. Around the same time, I posted an inquiry on the Facebook page, asking if anyone knew the fate of the house where my father lived. I received a message from a young woman named Marika that the house was now a shop owned by her mother. She also owned the hotel directly across the street. Marika, a journalist, ultimately wrote an article for her online publication about the discovery of the gravestones.

I called Mr. Rubinfeld when I learned that the gravestones had all been dug up and relocated. Bobby and I then went to visit Mr. Rubinfeld once again, and this time I brought money with me.

"Mr. Kurzweil, we need money to build a monument" Mr. Rubinfeld said.

"How much do you need?"

"I don't know," he said.

I handed him twenty 100-dollar bills. "Here's $2000," I said.

"It is too much," Mr. Rubinfeld insisted.

"Please tell me how much you think you need," I replied.

Mr. Rubinfeld said, "I will take $1,500." He handed me the pile of hundreds and I took five bills and put them in my pocket, handing him the $1,500 that he requested.

I saw that Mr. Rubinfeld was elated, but he held most of his emotion inside. Nevertheless, I could see from his eyes and his smile and his posture that his dream could finally become a reality. Mr. Rubinfeld was able to arrange for my money to be transferred to Dobromyl. A monument, built from the remnants of the Jewish gravestones, would occupy part of the space where the Jewish cemetery once stood. Mr. Rubinfeld was able to locate a man, Mr. Lubomir Jacynicz, who was a resident of Dobromyl and qualified to be the main engineer of the monument. He and his helpers did a magnificent job. It was officially named the Wall of Memory.

Once the monument was built, in June of 2016 a ceremony was scheduled and occurred. It was planned quite quickly – too quickly for me to attend. And I really didn't want to go to Dobromyl when there was a crowd of people there. I felt I needed to explore Dobromyl in solitude. Or perhaps I needed to appear there and feel special – which led me to writing a letter to the mayor of the town.

Wall of Memory

Dedication plaque at the Wall of Memory

A Letter to the Mayor

In addition to my great desire to see the house where my father was born and to discover anything else of interest in Dobromyl, including, of course, the Wall of Memory I had helped to fund, I wanted to meet the mayor of the town. I didn't want to just stumble into Dobromyl one day as an anonymous tourist or visitor. I wanted to be noticed; I wanted to feel like a Jew from Dobromyl who has returned to the home of his father, his grandparents, his great-grandparents.

Through the internet, I located a woman who was offering her skills as a Ukrainian/English translator. After a few email exchanges, we settled on a fee for her service and I emailed her my English letter to the mayor of Dobromyl. I also paid her to mail the letter to the mayor by registered mail, translated into Ukrainian, addressed to "The Mayor of Dobromyl, c/o Town Hall, Dobromyl, Ukraine." She agreed.

In my letter, I explained who I was: a descendant of a Jewish family in Dobromyl. I explained that many people in my family were murdered during the Holocaust, but my father, as a boy, left the town before the Holocaust, with his parents, and went to America.

I told him I was interested in working on a project in Dobromyl – although I didn't know what it would be. I wanted to brainstorm with him and to do something appropriate. I thought – correctly – that this would be the perfect way to catch his interest. I included my email address in the letter, as well as the date I planned to arrive, and I waited for a response.

Two weeks later, I received an email from the mayor. It was in

Ukrainian, so I once again sought the services of my translator. We negotiated a price and she promptly sent me a translation of the mayor's email. The email said he would like to meet with me. He would be waiting for me on the date I told him I would present myself at his office.

I want to make something clear to readers of this book: I had no intention of bringing up the Holocaust when I went to Dobromyl. If it came up in conversation, I would participate, but in no way did I want to come across with a "this is what *you* (or *they*) did to *us*" attitude. I made sure of this by keeping my focus on the children of Dobromyl. I didn't want to add to the curriculum in the school. I didn't want to ask older people where their parents were during those horribly dark days. I didn't want to push it into everyone's face. I merely wanted to be one person who went back to Dobromyl to see what it was like.

When I wrote the mayor, I had no idea what kind of project I could propose. I had vague thoughts of organizing a tour of Dobromyl, or a donation of books to the Dobromyl library – if there was such a thing. Or perhaps I would photograph the town for one reason or another. I spoke of the Holocaust's impact on my family in my letter to the mayor because I wanted to get his sympathy, and I mentioned some unnamed project to entice him. I wanted to ensure that the mayor would greet me warmly and with curiosity. But once I arrived, my focus would be on the present and the future, not the past.

Elie Wiesel once wrote that when he returned to his town of Sighet many years after the war, he felt most at home in the Jewish cemetery. Just about everything else had changed. The Dobromyl I wanted to visit was the home of my ancestors and I wanted to see the place, regardless of how it had changed.

Of course it had changed! There were no longer Jews living there. No more hustle-bustle of Jews working or shopping in the market. It also remained a mystery to me how my great-grandfather maintained his tinsmith business. Did he work out of his home? Did he by some chance have a shop? I really had no idea what to expect the town to look like or be like. What would I feel walking down a street in Dobromyl? What would the place without Jews feel like? What would it be like to stand before the little house where my father lived? Was it still a house? Was it torn down and replaced by something else? Once Dobromyl was a thriving Jewish *shtetl*; now it was a basically Christian town. How would that Christianity display itself?

As soon as I received an email from the mayor of Dobromyl welcoming me, I made my reservation to fly, once again, to Lviv, Ukraine. The mayor's email closed with a P.S. He wrote, "Holy be the Memory of the Jews living in Dobromyl in the last century."

My First Dreidel

When I arranged for my first actual trip to Dobromyl, I decided to first stop in Warsaw, spend a few days, and then fly on to Lviv. In particular, I wanted to see the amazing new Jewish museum focusing on the history of the Jews in Poland. The name of the museum is POLIN Museum of the History of Jews in Poland. POLIN is the Hebrew word for Poland.

I also found my way to the area in Warsaw where, on weekends, there is a huge, sprawling street fair. The fair consisted of what seemed like a few hundred vendors, selling everything from new kitsch Polish souvenirs and "I Love Warsaw" T-shirts to old coins, crucifixes, old glass, antique magnifying glasses, antique chess sets, Matryoshka dolls, original paintings, lots of Ukrainian religious icons, used clothing, used tableware and more. There were thousands of things to buy, and each vendor seemed to specialize in one or two kinds of items. I confess it was very funny to see a booth selling toilet paper with Putin's picture on each sheet.

The aisles were crowded at the Warsaw street fair; sometimes it was too crowded to even see what the vendors were selling. But I caught sight of what looked like a pair of old Shabbos candlesticks sitting on wooden shelves at one stall. Next to the candlesticks were a few antique-looking Chanukah menorahs.

The majority of items, being offered by the same vendor who displayed the menorahs and the candlesticks, were antique coins. I edged up to the front of the crowd and, with a smile, I greeted the vendor. He was an elderly man with an all grey goatee. He spoke a little English.

I asked the man if the menorahs were old? They certainly looked old and tarnished. He surprised me; he said "No, they are copies." With these few words, the man earned my respect. Other vendors might have claimed they were original and would steal money on the sale. If you saw these Chanukah menorahs they would look quite worn, old and tarnished to you.

"They did a good job. They look real."

"Of course," he responded.

The man then reached into his pants pocket and retrieved the first small, handmade dreidel made from lead I had ever seen. It was an emotional moment for me. As he displayed the dreidel on his flat palm my first thoughts were, *This dreidel was once owned by a child and played with by a child in Poland before the Holocaust*. It seemed sacred. The man handed the dreidel to me. Just touching this precious dreidel was heartbreaking. Where is the owner of this dreidel? Did this child perish? After all, this might be the only thing left from the life of some Jewish child.

"Is it real?" I asked.

"Absolutely," he replied emphatically.

"How would I know?" I asked.

"I am telling you it is real. Trust me. I have seen them before."

"Where is it from?"

"An old woman who lives in the same building where I live came to me. She said she found it in her flat. Under a broken floorboard. She didn't know what it was. She knows I sell old things. I gave her 20 zloty and she was happy. The building is within the old Jewish ghetto."

Twenty Polish zloty is about five U.S. dollars.

"How much are you selling it for?" I asked the man.

"Fifty U.S. dollars," he responded.

Fifty dollars. It seemed low, and reasonable, and high at the same time. The dreidel was quite small, about the size of a U.S. quarter. But it was apparently an authentic Jewish artifact, a Jewish artifact from Warsaw, from before the Holocaust.

I knew how I'd feel if I didn't buy it. I would walk away thinking someone else would purchase it from this man and the person would own a real Jewish object from before the Holocaust.

But maybe he was a fraud and used the menorahs to gain my confidence. Maybe this dreidel was also a copy. How could I just basically throw away fifty bucks on a piece of junk?

I am somewhat familiar with scams, probably because I've been a victim of a few small scams in my life. I developed an interest in the phenomenon of scams, and I have several books on the topic. So, maybe the dreidel seller was just one more scam artist. How would I know?

I made the purchase, thanked the lovely man, and walked away. And in my pocket was a dreidel. I felt I had no choice. I wanted – I needed – that dreidel. A child's dreidel from the Warsaw Ghetto.

I kept my hand in my pocket as I walked away, feeling a piece of tragic Jewish history between my fingers.

In anticipation of my trip to Ukraine, I went to the Ukrainian Museum on East 6th Street in Manhattan. While it is a lovely museum, there wasn't a trace of anything Jewish in the place, despite the fact that Jews have been in Ukraine for over 1,000 years. For many years, half or more of the population of Dobromyl was Jewish.

The museum has a lovely little gift shop, so I went in and browsed around. In the gift shop, I struck up a conversation with a Ukrainian man who said he grew up in Lviv. I was delighted to meet him. I asked him if he knew the town of Dobromyl. He said he knew of it but was never there.

When I told him I was planning a trip to Lviv and Dobromyl, he became extremely interested in me. He knew I was Jewish from my grey beard and black yarmulke. He also told me his maternal grandmother was Jewish. This called for a cup of tea in a local café. We exchanged names: I said my name is Arthur and he said, "Call me Joe."

Over tea, I kept wondering if I should tell him about the matrilineal descent law in Jewish life: In a mixed marriage, if the bride is Jewish, all offspring are automatically Jewish, making his mother Jewish, and if his mother was Jewish, he was automatically Jewish as well.

I decided to tell him, and he said, "You know someone else once

Dreidel the author purchased from a Warsaw market vendor

told me that, but I thought he was full of shit – forgive my language. You're the second person who said that."

We had a pleasant conversation, with him asking me questions about my life and family, and me asking him questions such as how to get a ride from the airport in Lviv to my hotel, the Swiss Hotel, in downtown Lviv. He told me of a friend of his in Lviv who is an Uber driver and he would drive me there for 50 U.S. dollars. I took the man's name (Ivan) and phone number. When I arrived in Lviv, flying there from Warsaw, I called the number as soon as the jet landed, and Ivan was at the airport within about 10 minutes.

"Where are you from?" Ivan asked, in fairly good English, as he lifted my suitcase and put it in the trunk. I said New York City and the driver's face registered with curiosity and excitement. "I want to go to New York City," he almost shouted.

It was bumper to bumper traffic in Lviv. I was sure to have a long drive and a long conversation with the driver. He asked me about my family and I asked him about his family. He asked me about my work and I asked him about his work. But then he asked, "Why are you in Lviv? Business?"

I told him I was going to Dobromyl, where my father was born.

Then I had an idea. I asked Ivan if he would be my driver to Dobromyl the next day, which was when I would meet the mayor of Dobromyl. We agreed to meet at 8:00 the next morning. I would stay in Dobromyl for two days, so we agreed that he would pick me up two days later.

On the way to my hotel, I kept touching the dreidel I had purchased in Warsaw. Occasionally I would take the dreidel out of my pocket to inspect it carefully. Ivan noticed me holding the dreidel and was prompted to ask, "What is that?"

The stop-and-go traffic allowed me to hand Ivan the dreidel for a moment. "Be careful," I warned him. He replied, "I'm watching the traffic, don't worry."

"I'm not worried about the traffic; I'm worried about this object."

I explained how I visited a large street fair in Warsaw, and I bought it from one of the vendors.

"I know this object," Ivan said to me. "I have one similar at my home. I don't know what it is." I explained to him that a dreidel was a spinning top used to play a game on the Jewish holiday of Chanukah.

"Why do you have one?" I asked him.

"I found it in a field when I was using my metal-detecting device. It was a Jewish area before the war. Now a forest has grown there. I searched in this area, looking for something valuable. I found nothing but this – spinning top."

"Do you do metal detecting? I asked.

"I used to do it a lot. I had lots of time so I went for a treasure hunt. Sometimes a person can find just one valuable coin, so the whole day of searching suddenly becomes worthwhile. One day I found this spinning top."

"So you no longer do it? I asked.

"First of all, we never know for sure if it is legal. Some say it is, but others say you must not keep valuable historical items found during a metal detecting expedition. Some say the legality has to do with the value of the item. Again, items of historical valuable items must be given to the government office dealing with historic artifacts. But nobody follows these laws, whatever they may be.

"So, when I find something, I don't sell it at a street fair. I sell my finds to someone who is looking for valuable finds. And this person sells at the street fairs, or sells it to someone at a street fair. A find may go through four sets of hands before a customer buys it at a street fair. So, I have found several guys who do metal detecting. I buy the items from them and I then sell the items to the street fair vendors. I am a middleman. The vendors don't care for getting muddy in the fields, but for others it is an exciting and potentially quite profitable activity."

The driver dropped me off at the Swiss Hotel and we agreed that he would pick me up and get me to Dobromyl the next day. I felt like I was dreaming.

Part IV

Dobromyl At Last

Parents are not to be put to death for their children, nor children put to death for their parents; each will die for their own sin.

– Deuteronomy 24:16

In general the sages rejected the idea that children could be punished, even at the hands of heaven, for the sins of their parents. As a result, they systematically re-interpreted every passage that gave the opposite impression, that children were indeed being punished for their parents' sins.

– Rabbi Jonathan Sacks

On the Road to Dobromyl

The road was about 70 miles long, and it had thousands, perhaps a hundred thousand, potholes. Maybe more. Some were as small as a baseball; others were large enough for even the most cautious and skilled driver to do serious damage to their automobile. In some places the pock-marked road was more pothole than pavement, and although the cab ride was more or less straight, vehicles needed to navigate cautiously, trying to avoid the bigger holes in the old black asphalt.

My driver from the airport to the Swiss Hotel couldn't make it but he sent someone else to take me to Dobromyl. Unfortunately, this new driver didn't speak English. We zig-zagged our way for over two hours, from Lviv in western Ukraine to Dobromyl near the Ukraine-Poland border. The cab driver was unphased by the condition of the road, which in the United States would surely be labeled *Caution: Closed for Repairs*. He seemed to be relaxed behind the driver's wheel, while I sat tense in the back seat. As the road cut through the rural countryside we passed dozens of villages and towns with lush farms and an occasional cow grazing by the side of the road.

I felt like one of those rodeo stars trying to stay astride a wild bull. I was shaken, but surprisingly I didn't get carsick with all the bouncing and swerving. I was much too excited, knowing I would soon reach Dobromyl for the first time. It had been my dream for most of my life. I just sat in the back seat and I let the cab, like a car on a fierce roller coaster, bounce and jerk its way to our destination.

My journey to Dobromyl was not a straight one: not then, at age 64, nor years ago, when I was about 10 and first became aware my father was born there. Depending on the year, Dobromyl (the Ukrainian spelling), which was spelled Dobromil (the Polish spelling) when my father was just a boy, changed hands several times. Prior to being located in western Ukraine, it was once in eastern Poland, and before that in the Austrian-Hungarian Empire. It was also one of hundreds of small Jewish towns and villages in what was called the region of Galicia, which included the largest population of Jews in the world – before the Nazis came and changed all of that.

I remember searching through the atlas in our home. It was a separate volume of the multi-volume World Book Encyclopedia, decades before the internet. I hoped to find some dot on a map indicating the precise location of Dobromyl. My father laughed, knowing that his tiny town would probably not appear on any map, perhaps not even in the largest atlas in our public library.

I was fourteen when I rode my bike to my hometown library, about two miles away from home. In those days, most young teenagers in the suburbs never hesitated to mount a two-wheeler and go wherever they reasonably wanted. I snaked my way through the smooth streets and neighborhoods and finally reach my destination. I locked my bike in the place where bicycles parked, and I ran into the library.

The largest atlas in the library was heavier than I could carry single-handedly, so a librarian helped me transport the huge World Atlas to a nearby desk. It was then when I learned libraries not only had books but also had librarians who helped people to find what they were looking for.

The librarian looked in the index to this huge atlas and found a map with Dobromyl on it. Just to see the dot on the map was statisfying. I rode my bicycle back to my home feeling content. Dobromyl exists.

Mr. Adelman, the head librarian, eventually became a hero of mine. He seemed to know how to find the answers to everything. Ten years later, I became a professional librarian. It was always thrilling to search for the answer to questions from people who visited or called the library's reference department.

The first question I was ever asked, after earning my master's degree in Library Science and locating a job, was from a man who asked "Can you help me to find out how to make home-made sausages?"

I have never eaten a sausage. Sausages are generally made of pork meat, which means it is not kosher. I wound my way around the high stacks of books in the library where I worked, and I located just the kind of book the person was looking for to answer his question.

Before the Holocaust there were about 5,000 people in the little town of Dobromyl, and about half of them were Jews. Today, in the 21st century, there are still about 5,000 people in the town, but no Jews. Yet there I was, a Jew, headed toward Dobromyl, the home of my ancestors for hundreds of years.

The Road Sign

"Dobromyl," the driver said as he pointed to a road sign. I didn't speak Ukrainian, and he didn't speak English, but I made it known that I wanted him to stop the car. Could this be Dobromyl? Have I really arrived at the home of my ancestors?

"Stop," I shouted, as I held up my hand like a traffic cop would gesture when he or she wanted a vehicle to halt. He heard me and saw my gesture in his rearview mirror. The road sign was in Ukrainian, so I pointed to it and asked, "Dobromyl?"

"*Yes,*" he said in Ukrainian. Yes, this was the edge of the town of Dobromyl.

Was it possible? Had I finally arrived in Dobromyl?

The driver put his car in reverse, and we slowly went backwards, riding over dozens of potholes, until we arrived in front of the sign. When the cab came to a halt, I opened the door and signaled the cab driver to do the same. I wanted a photograph of me with the road sign. I gestured with my iPhone and easily communicated my desire.

Until then, the driver had no idea what I wanted with this little town of Dobromyl. But suddenly he knew. I knew that he knew by his broad smile and by the careful way he positioned me for the best possible photo. He insisted on taking three or four shots. Suddenly he seemed to be invested in the success of my visit. I was frustrated by the fact that we didn't have a common language. I wanted to tell him my whole story, starting from the first time I learned of Dobromyl as the birthplace of my father. I wanted to tell him everything. How I

Road sign to Dobromyl

tried to visit Dobromyl in the 1970s; how I dreamed of the town; how I had daydreamed thousands of times about this very moment.

I'm here, I shouted silently in my mind. *I'm in fucking Dobromyl*!

And then I started to cry.

At first, I covered my face, trying to hide my tears, but then I revealed myself; I had no reason to mask my emotions. I wanted to be fully present. Until that point, Dobromyl was either in the past for me or in the future. But now it was in the present, and my ecstatic celebration had just begun.

We got back in the car and continued to drive toward the center of town. We passed a few small houses on this rural road but had not yet arrived at the heart of the town. I carefully looked at both sides of the road, my head rotating back and forth, trying not to miss a thing. I saw two people on bicycles. Both were elderly, a woman and a man. The woman wore a kerchief and peasant clothing; the man had some wood tied to the back of his bike. They looked like elderly grandparents. I could never imagine my grandparents riding bicycles.

We passed a man riding on the seat of a horse-drawn cart. The cart was empty. We passed a few houses; some were abandoned and falling apart. We passed a miniature chapel, and a dramatic larger-than-life statue of Jesus dragging a large cross. For a moment I thought about Jesus, a Jew, who had to carry the wooden cross used by the Romans to kill people. When the controversial film, *The Passion of Christ*, was released, someone asked a friend of mine if he had planned to see the film, to which my friend answered, "I don't need to see a film about one more Jew who was tortured to death."

We drove over a tiny bridge going over an equally tiny river. I was sure this was the river my father told me about, where people would go swimming. My father would say, "If you go out of the door of the house where we lived and turned to the right, the river was just a short walk away." And right over the bridge, on the left, was the structure that was my father's house. It was now a shop. I was sure of it – and later learned I was correct.

In the Dobromyl memorial book there was a map of the center of Dobromyl, and I had studied that map carefully for years. I already knew where my father's house was, and I knew he was born in that house. On the map, the house is #51. When we approached the town, and when I saw the house, I knew it was the right one. In relation to the central square, it was exactly where the map said it was, but I wasn't absolutely certain, so I didn't ask the driver to stop. I had an appointment with the town's mayor, and I was already an hour late.

The author's father's childhood home

It felt surreal. After so many years of imagining this moment, it was finally here. I was in Dobromyl. My mind was racing. I thought about my deceased father and how much he would have loved to travel with me to the place of his birth. I thought about the absence of Jews. I imagined that at one time the streets in Dobromyl would be filled with Jews, beards, *yarmulkes, sheitles* (head coverings for women). There would be butcher shops, a fish market, shops selling freshly baked pastry and bread, *yeshiva* students holding the books they were studying, pious-looking rabbis and *yeshiva* teachers, old Jewish women out for a walk – and somewhere my great-grandfather Abusch would be in his metalwork shop, creating something for a customer. But now the town looked like an abandoned movie set, and the Jewish actors had not yet arrived. Where were they all? Where was the land soaked with Jewish blood? Where were the borders of the ghettos the Nazis established? Where were the bodies lying dead in the street?

But I was actually breathing the air of Dobromyl. I felt like dancing for joy and weeping at the same time. These extreme emotions caused me to be numb. And I was already late for my appointment with the mayor.

I showed the driver a piece of paper with the mayor's name and the address of the town hall on it. The cab driver stopped his cab right in front of town hall. I paid the driver 50 U.S. dollars, and he left a moment later. I would have to arrange for a different ride back to my hotel in Lviv, but at that moment it was not of concern. I'd work it out.

I walked through the doorway of the decidedly rundown town hall and immediately encountered a woman who I later learned was the mayor's secretary and assistant. I showed her the piece of paper, but she already knew who I was. She signaled me to follow her.

The building was quite old, and the stairway was narrow and dark. In the middle of each step was a slight depression worn into the wood, indicating decades of wear and tear. Did my great-grandfather ever have cause to walk those steps?

I walked up and around the winding staircase, on the deeply worn steps, to the third floor. The secretary had me follow her to one of the offices at the top of the stairs, and she knocked on the door. We walked

A Dobromyl street in 2017, with homes built before the Second World War. Some of these houses are empty and abandoned.

in. It was the mayor's office. He was a young, handsome man in his 40s. He wore a suit and tie with a white shirt and greeted me with a warm handshake and immediately began speaking to me in Ukrainian. He stood up straight and tall and it looked like it was a ceremony. He was officially welcoming me to Dobromyl.

I shrugged my shoulders and shook my head, from which the mayor knew I could not understand him. He immediately picked up his phone and said something to someone. Within five minutes a woman walked into the mayor's office.

The author with Dobromyl Mayor Yurij Petryk

Her name was Olexandra, an English teacher in the school, and while I didn't know it at the time, she was to become my interpreter for the next few days. Finally, I was able to speak and communicate with the mayor, Mr. Yurij Petryk. The mayor spoke with her, and she then turned to me and said, "The mayor would like to welcome you to Dobromyl." It was almost 70 years since the Jewish population of the town was murdered. I was probably the first Jew who had returned to receive an official welcome.

Oh Dad, how I wish you were here with me. We could walk to the river together. We could stroll up and down the streets of Dobromyl. We would go to the Wall of Memory together – and I would declare that nobody has a better memory of Dobromyl than you do. You knew it was true and I knew it also.

A painting of Dobromyl from the 1920s in the Przemysl museum

A picture postcard of a street in Dobromyl, circa early 1900.

An old picture postcard of part of the market
square in Dobromyl circa early 1900.

The author by a sign for Dobromyl

For some people in Dobromyl, this is the only means of transportation

Kippah

Forty years ago, I decided to wear a *kippah* (*yarmulke*).

I didn't grow up wearing one. My family was not religiously observant, we rarely went to synagogue, and our kitchen was not kosher. But, as Rabbi Adin Steinsaltz has written, returning to religious practice is not an all-of-a-sudden act but rather "a series of small turnings." And at a certain point, I made a decision to cover my head full-time. I was already wearing my *kippah* when I studied holy books at home, but before I went outside, I took it off. Wearing a *kippah* was a momentous decision.

At first, I thought everyone was staring at me. They weren't. And over time, I simply forgot about it as I went on my way. Since wearing a *kippah* or a hat is supposed to remind the wearer of God above, it's ironic that when you wear one, after a short while you forget it's on. Once I went into the shower with it.

One day, a friend of mine called me to ask if I'd like to have brunch with her. It was early on in my *kippah* wearing days. When I walked to the restaurant where we were to have brunch, I wore my kippah for most of the way, but a block before I arrived at the destination I took off the *kippah* and stuffed it in my pocket. I chickened out. I had known this woman for many years, but not with a *kippah*. I became self-conscious, and I wanted to avoid a conversation about it. In fact, I knew, at any given time, which of my friends and acquaintances had or had not seen me under my new head covering.

At brunch, my friend quickly told me that she was a lesbian. She was willing to come out of her closet, but I was still stuck in mine. From that day on, I have worn my *kippah* with pride. That is, until I travelled to Dobromyl, when I made a very conscious decision not to wear it.

There were a few reasons for my decision. One was that I was simply nervous travelling in Eastern Europe with an announcement on my head that I was Jewish. It was just one less thing I had to worry about. Antisemitism is alive and well in the world, and I didn't want to be a target of stares, glares, or anything else. My jean jacket, old jeans, and full beard make me look more like a hipster than a rabbi. By the way, I was told that everyone in Dobromyl knew I was Jewish.

But I did not want people to think I was a rabbi. I wanted to relate with people as informally as possible, and I knew from experience that when a person thinks you're a rabbi, they act differently, unnaturally. Since one of my main missions in Dobromyl was to meet children, I was particularly aware that a *kippah* can be a heavy symbol. I wanted to be as neutral a person as possible. I knew I would indicate to people that I was a Jew, but the *kippah* just seemed to me to be a bit too much – especially in a place like Ukraine.

Other than in the Jewish cemetery in Dobromyl and in other Jewish cemeteries that I visited, I travelled bareheaded.

My First Conversation with the Mayor

Mayor Yurij Petryk and I sat at a long table in his office. His secretary asked me if I wanted coffee or tea, but I asked for my favorite drink: a glass of cold water. Was I sure? I said, "Yes please." From that meeting on, over the years, we've met many times at that table, and there was always a glass of cold water waiting for me – along with some cookies.

Other than the long conference room table and the mayor's desk, there was little else in the big room. There were a few file cabinets, a bookcase, and a few decidedly religious (Christian) pictures on the wall. There seems to be no separation of church and state in Ukraine. Ukraine is a Christian country. Period. In the town hall as well as the public school, Christian pictures are everywhere. They are in every classroom and every hallway.

I had the memorial book of Dobromyl with me, and lots of family photos. At first, I showed the mayor the memorial book, specifically the street map of Dobromyl, indicating where my father's house was. The mayor studied the map for a few moments to get his bearings.

He located the town hall first, and then I pointed out the location of my father's house. With his finger, the mayor traced the road leading to the house from town hall. When his finger landed on the house he said in Ukrainian, "This is Kopika."

I asked what Kopika meant and I was told the word was based on a form of Russian currency, the kopek. It is equivalent to our penny – a

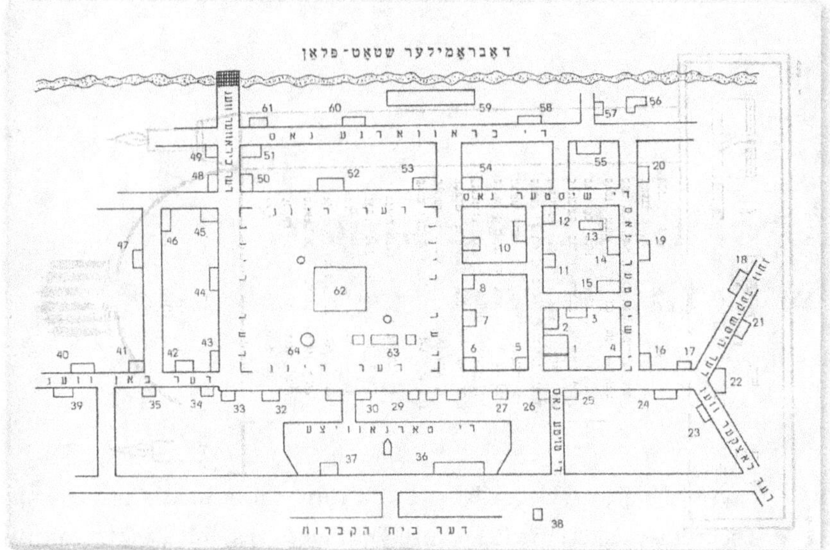

A street map of Dobromyl, in Yiddish, published in the Dobromyl memorial book in 1963. Number 62 is the town hall; number 51 is the house where the author's father was born and lived; the hotel was built on the site where the house at number 49 stood.

small coin, indicating good prices to be found there. One hundred kopeks equals one ruble in Russia or one hryvnia in Ukraine.

Kopika was a small shop, similar to a Seven-Eleven, with a little bit of everything. My father's house is now a general store. The mayor told me that the hotel in Dobromyl is across the narrow road and is owned by the same person who owns Kopika. I would be staying in this hotel for the next few nights.

After we looked at the map, I showed the mayor the family photos I had brought with me. All the photos were taken in Dobromyl. I showed him every photograph and I told him who survived the Holocaust and who was murdered. Most had been murdered.

I had made a conscious decision not to dwell on the Holocaust during any of my trips to Dobromyl, but I wanted to give the mayor a general idea of the fate of my Dobromyl family. I was not visiting Dobromyl to teach them or remind them of their terrible history, the outrageous events of World War II. I was there to see the town and

The author's father's childhood home is now
home to Kopika, a convenience store

to help its children. Why did I care about these Ukrainian children, many of whose grandparents and great-grandparents were possibly anti-Semites?

I asked the mayor, "Is there a children's playground in Dobromyl?"

"No," he said with a disappointed look on his face.

"Are there playgrounds in any of the villages surrounding Dobromyl?"

Again, he said, "No." And then he said, "I wrote a proposal to the government for funds to build a playground, but it was rejected,"

He then jumped up from his chair and hurriedly went to his filing cabinet. He pulled out a thick folder and brought it over to the long table. Up until that point, the mayor had been sitting across from me, but now he took the seat next to me. He opened the folder and showed me the plan for the playground he had proposed. He also pulled out a brochure from a playground equipment company located in Lviv, with photographs of various pieces of equipment: a slide, a see-saw, monkey bars, and other typical playground items.

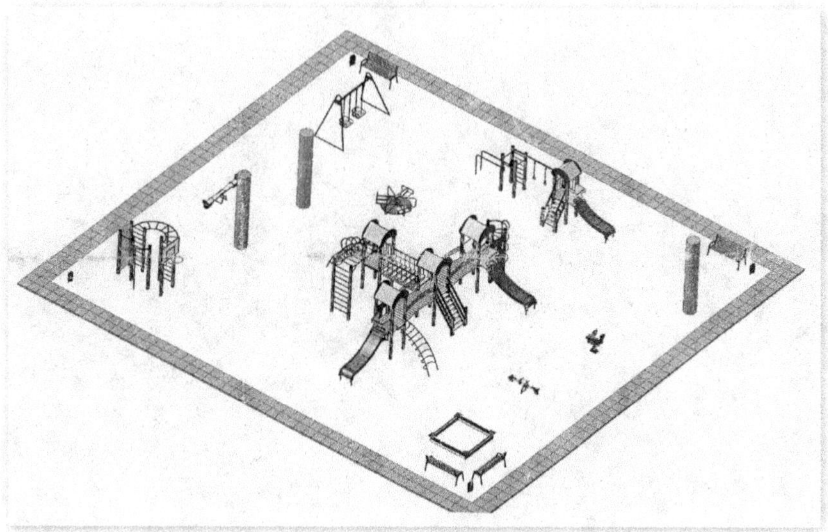

Playground plan

"Is this the playground you would build today if you had the money for it?" I asked.

The mayor nodded, again with a disappointed expression on his face.

"Does it include soft material for the ground, to cushion a child if they fall?"

"No, it is not necessary," he replied.

"And how much would it cost?" He showed me the amount: 289,485 Ukrainian hryvnia.

I laughed at the large number. "And what would that be in U.S. dollars?"

The mayor went to his desk and brought back a calculator.

He showed me his calculation. It was $11,000.

I suddenly found myself saying, "Build it. I will pay for it."

The mayor and the English teacher who continued to interpret for me were shocked.

And so was I. It was spontaneous. I did not plan anything. But I already had a picture in my mind of children playing on the equipment. The plan also included some benches where parents could sit while their children played. I had visions of a busy playground where families could go and enjoy themselves. I already imagined it would be a source of pride for the town. I also imagined how people from the surrounding villages will say to their children, "Let's go to Dobromyl to use their playground."

The mayor's facial expression changed from disappointment to shock.

"You will pay for the whole playground?" he asked.

"Yes, I will go back to the United States and I will bring you the money. Eleven thousand dollars." I reached out and shook the mayor's hand.

Two months later, I returned to Dobromyl with $11,000 in cash.

The Wall of Memory II

It was a short walk from my hotel room to the Wall of Memory. Both the mayor and Olexandra offered to take me there, but I told them I much preferred to go there alone. They understood, and they pointed me in the right direction to the land on which the Jewish cemetery stood. I walked across the town square to the other side, and then I made a right turn up a hill. I was told I would eventually see a sign on the right side of the road pointing in the direction to the cemetery.

Walking across the town square, I felt the eyes of the residents on me. Most of them turned away when I looked at them, presumably not wanting me to think I was being stared at, but others waved to me. It was the older people who turned their heads and the younger ones who made the friendly gestures. Not many strangers come to Dobromyl, and I felt conspicuous with my large beard. Everyone knew I was a visitor.

I wondered who they thought I was. I felt like a Jew. But I had no fear. I walked proudly but modestly. Although I had decided not to wear my kippah during my trip to Dobromyl and the Ukraine, I kept it in my pocket and put it on when I arrived at the cemetery land.

I would need to walk uphill the entire time, huffing and puffing. First there was a paved road right off the main road cutting through the main square, and a steeper one to get to the small, narrow dirt road bringing me to the foot of the cemetery and, finally, to the path leading up to the heart of the cemetery's land. Each road or path was steeper than the one before it. On the second road, there was a handmade sign attached to an electric pole. It read "Jewish Cemetery," in English and Ukrainian, with an arrow pointing the way. When I reached the top, I realized the Jewish cemetery was situated on the tallest hill surrounding the town. It looked over the entire expanse of Dobromyl.

Sign pointing to the Jewish cemetery

Walking these roads, while my mind and heart were mainly in the present, I also thought again about how surreal it all was. After decades of thinking about Dobromyl, I was walking alone to Dobromyl's Jewish cemetery. But I really didn't feel alone. I felt like a representative of every Jew who ever lived in Dobromyl. I knew my ancestors, my grandparents and great-grandparents, must surely have walked these same steps.

When I arrived at the cemetery, I recited in a whisper, in Hebrew, the *shehechiyanu* prayer:

Blessed are You, the Lord our God, Ruler of the universe, who has kept us alive, sustained us, and permitted us to reach this moment.

Looking upward, I saw the Wall of Memory in the distance.

Once the gravestones were brought to the cemetery, it must have been clear that they couldn't be placed where they once stood, Undoubtedly, I was standing on graves with each step, but it couldn't be helped. Where there were once graves, there was now just grass. Acres of grass. No graves had been there for several decades. The decision was made, by Mr. Rubinfeld and Lubomir, to use the stones to build a monument. Lubomir was the chief engineer and builder on the project. The result was truly magnificent.

As I walked up to the monument, it became more and more clear. The huge gravestones were used as giant bricks to create a wall. The gravestones were placed back-to-back, so one can look at the faces of gravestones on either side.

I walked up to the wall and kissed it, as one often does when approaching the Western Wall in Jerusalem, a remnant of the Holy Temple. At the center of the wall, situated at its base, is a plaque with the names of the people who funded the wall. To my great surprise, my name was there too! I stood before this massive wall and spent some time in meditation. I also recited the traditional Mourner's Kaddish. It's supposed to be said with ten people, but I made an exception. I don't recall what my meditation consisted of. I might have spent most of the time just standing still and breathing. At one moment, I began to cry. I knew I was not the first Kurzweil to be present at this cemetery. I felt I was part of an unbroken chain of generations. I wiped my tears with my sleeve.

The wall was constructed from over one hundred gravestones. Starting at one end, I examined each stone as I translated the surnames engraved on each one. I found two stones containing surnames in my family: Lowenthal and Pietnizer. They were related to me by blood or through marriage. There were, I'm sorry to say, no specific Kurzweils to be found. Of course, these gravestones were just a fraction of the stones originally in the cemetery before the Holocaust. (It was later discovered that the foundation of the bridge from Dobromyl to Chyrow was built with hundreds of gravestones piled on top of each other. But one would have to dismantle the entire bridge to rescue them. It would be virtually impossible.)

A bridge in Dobromyl. Its foundation was made from Jewish gravestones.

There was no place to sit. And after the trek up the hills to the cemetery, my feet needed some rest. When I finally returned to town, I rested for a while in my hotel room. I was invited to dinner that evening by the mayor and his wife, at which time I suggested that there be two benches next to the Wall of Memory for pilgrims to sit and rest their feet and to meditate. Lubomir built the two benches, costing me $400. It was well worth the investment.

I had spent about two hours at the Wall of Memory. Sometimes I took photographs, trying to show how large and dramatic the wall was. And I looked down at the town, locating the approximate place where the sidewalk had been paved with Jewish gravestone by the house the Nazis used as a headquarters. Transporting the huge stones up to the cemetery land must have been difficult at best. I felt profoundly grateful to the volunteers from Lviv who orchestrated the job with the help of some paid laborers.

The long path leading to the Wall of Memory

At one point, I stood still for about 10 minutes, trying to hear voices from the heavens or from the graves. All I detected was silence. What was I hoping for? Crying corpses? Old deceased relatives who wanted to tell me something? I was anticipating some mystical experience,

Dedication marker for the Wall of Memory

The Wall of Memory overlooking the town of Dobromyl

but all I heard was silence. There were no cars in the distance, no machinery to drown out the voices. Just silence.

After a while, I left the cemetery, promising myself I would return there before I left Dobromyl. When I walked back to the center of town, I enjoyed the downhill roads. I noticed that across the main road was the Christian cemetery, with gravestones as far back as my eyes could see. I had not noticed it when I first walked up the hill. There were fresh flowers placed on many graves, testifying to the number of present-day visitors. The contrast between the two cemeteries was extreme.

I walked back to the hotel. But first I stopped at Kopika for a bottle of cold water and a few cookies. I fell asleep, and I had a good nap before dinner. I woke up in the middle of a dream about the cemetery. It was crowded. There was standing room only. Some great rabbi had just died. But we couldn't find the coffin or the grave.

The Globe

For some reason, it particularly bothered me that there wasn't an up-to-date globe in the school. During the Soviet influence on Ukraine, from the end of the Second World War until 1991, Ukraine was not really an independent country. But in 1991, after the breakdown of the former Soviet Union, Ukraine reasserted itself as its own nation. Nevertheless, Dobromyl is filled with remnants of the Soviet influence and control of Ukraine. One piece of evidence of this was the globe in the school.

I remember Olexandra pointing this out during our very first meeting. It was not possible for a student in Dobromyl's school to go to the globe and locate the country in which they were living. As a kid, I often looked at the globe my brother and I had in our bedroom. It was on a stand allowing me to spin the globe freely. I can't imagine how many times I spun the globe and pointed to somewhere on it as it spun. Sometimes I would imagine that one day I would travel to the country my finger landed on – sort of my own kind of divination.

So, one afternoon when I was in Lviv, I wandered around, looking for a new globe. I found it easily. A few streets away from the hotel was a bookstore with three or four globes on display in various corners of the shop. I selected a medium size globe, but I first made sure that Ukraine was clearly represented on it. I must have been quite a sight as I walked back to my hotel carrying a colorful globe. And I reminded myself that in Greek mythology Zeus enslaved Atlas to hold up the earth on his shoulders for all eternity. It hadn't occurred to me that the reason a book of maps is called an atlas is because of this Greek myth.

The next day, when I went to Dobromyl, in addition to my small suitcase, I carried the globe to the school and was truly proud to bring the first accurate globe to Dobromyl.

The headmaster of the school (left) in Dobromyl
sitting with the town's mayor

A month later, I returned to Dobromyl with $11,000 in hundred-dollar bills. After arriving at the hotel and stopping again at my father's house – at Kopika – to purchase some cold water, I walked to the town hall and up the three winding flights of worn stairs. The mayor was waiting for me, but this time his office was filled with most of the people from the town council – about 15 people. They were there, I imagined, for two reasons. One, they wanted to meet their new playground benefactor. And two, the mayor wanted everyone to see the cash I was bringing so that there would be no question that the money was all accounted for. After shaking each person's hand, I sat and counted out the 110 hundred-dollar bills. It was an odd feeling. I felt like some kind of rich philanthropist. I suppose I was, as I was making 11 piles of hundred-dollar bills. After counting it all carefully, I put all the bills into one pile and handed them to the mayor. He said something in Ukrainian but Olexandra didn't interpret. She didn't need to. I knew it was an expression of heartfelt thanks.

The mayor's assistant handed the mayor an envelope into which he put the money, wrapping it with several rubber bands. The mayor then gave the envelope filled with $11,000 to his assistant and said

The author presents the funds for the playground to the
Dobromyl mayor, with town council in attendance

something to her. I imagined it was directions for where to put the cash. All of these actions were very out in the open for each town councilperson to see. I knew that Ukraine suffered from a lot of corruption in the past – and possibly in the present. I'm sure that the mayor, and everyone else in the room, wanted to assure me that every last dollar would be going to the correct place – to purchase a playground for Dobromyl's children.

I said goodbye to all of the town council people, again with firm, sincere handshakes, after which Olexandra announced, "Now we shall go to the school."

It was a short walk from Town Hall to the school. Was I really in Dobromyl or was this a dream? After years of daydreams and imaginings, I was really in Dobromyl. And I was actually getting to know the place. While I generally had a very bad sense of direction, I felt as though I had lived in this neighborhood at one time.

I carried the guitar I had purchased in Lviv, along with the globe.

It took less than ten minutes to get to the school. When we had walked up three flights of stairs, Olexandra said, "First we will go to the school's headmaster."

We walked down the hall and I was greeted warmly by a man whose father was headmaster before him. He started to speak to me in Ukrainian, oblivious to the fact that I didn't understand a word he was saying. Olexandra pointed this out to him and then she told me the headmaster welcomed me to the school.

Olexandra suggested we go to see some of the classrooms. I left the globe and guitar in the headmaster's office. I didn't know she was buying time for the students who were planning a party for me in one of the larger classrooms.

To my great surprise, a teacher who sat alone in his classroom was Oleh, a computer science teacher and the first person I ever spoke with in present day Dobromyl. We had met on Skype. He had made contact with me on the Dobromyl Facebook page some months before. When we spoke on Skype, I was ecstatic. It was wonderful to speak with someone who lived in Dobromyl. I was thrilled to meet him in person. I embraced him; and while he was slightly shocked at my intimacy, he knew my affection was genuine.

"Let us go to see the students," Olexandra said. I asked her if I could bring the guitar with me. We returned to the headmaster's office and retrieved it.

We entered the room and before me were about forty students. They stood up, as they did each and every time I entered a classroom. It was a sweet gesture, but it also made me uncomfortable, and I signaled them to be seated. I wanted my meetings with the children to always be informal.

I put the guitar case down and said hello to the room filled with students. A young teenage girl approached me, holding a loaf of bread with salt on a cloth with Ukrainian designs embroidered on it. This is a Ukrainian tradition when greeting someone.

The tradition was familiar to me. It is a well-known Jewish custom to bring bread and salt when visiting a new home. The girl who gave me the bread and salt also memorized a few sentences – in English – formally welcoming me to their school.

Then the party began. One girl sang a song in an extremely heartfelt manner, in Ukrainian. She had the voice of an angel. Then a teenage boy played a guitar they already had and sang a song in English.

Then in walked the mayor and the headmaster, each of whom spoke with the students and told them about the playground that I would pay for. The students applauded.

These children were young and innocent. To me they were just children who happened to be born in this nearly impoverished town. They were innocent souls; sweet young people who had probably not been taught that at one time half of the town was populated by 2,500 Jews, most of whom were murdered by Nazis or even possibly by some of their great-grandparents or relatives.

Many people with whom I've shared my relationship to the children of Dobromyl have asked me if they knew the dark history of their town, of all of Ukraine. Did they know that not only were the Jews murdered but that some of them were burned alive in the town's main

The author accepts a gift from a Ukrainian student of
bread and salt on a traditionally embroidered cloth

synagogue? They did not know. Nor was I the one to tell them. It was not my goal to educate the people of Dobromyl, and especially not the children, of the past and the wickedness and the evil.

I was there to make friends.

I had thought quite a bit about the question. What would my posture be as I got involved with the children and the adults in Dobromyl?

I certainly felt that the Holocaust was a lot to dump on the young people in the school. And the more I learn about the history of Ukraine, the more I understand the complexity of it all. Frankly, it's difficult to keep track of all the strands of history running through Dobromyl. And certainly the Holocaust, the Nazi "war against the Jews," was a huge part of the story of Dobromyl, but it is not the only story. Nazis murdered many Ukrainians, Russians murdered many Ukrainians, Ukrainians murdered Jews, Nazis terrorized the town, and I can easily imagine how every person or family experienced the terror in some way or another. Yes, I know half of the pre-war population of Dobromyl was Jewish, and that most of these Jews were terrorized, tortured, murdered. But I also know that I was not going to be the person to tell an innocent 12-year-old girl that it was not entirely unlikely that her Ukrainian family in some way had blood on their hands.

Opening Day at the Playground

watched on my computer as the playground was being built. It was thrilling for me. One of the things purchased with my donation was a security camera. The camera was, and continues to be, amazing. I can watch the playground from my home in the U.S.!

One day I received a message from the mayor that the playground was just about finished. Would I be able to come for an opening ceremony? I immediately responded and said I would let him know when I could come to Dobromyl. A few messages back and forth and we had a date.

I had an idea. I looked online for a Ukrainian organization in order to find someone who could help me with the Ukrainian language. My idea was to create a T-shirt that I would distribute to the children. I found a Ukrainian school in my county, called them, and discovered to my delight that the principal of the school lived in my town, less than a half mile away. I told her my idea to have the sentence, "Meet me at the new Dobromyl playground" printed on blue and yellow T-shirts (the official colors of Dobromyl and the colors of the Ukrainian flag). We made an appointment, and I went to visit her. Mission accomplished. She provided me with the correct spelling, and I emailed it to a T-shirt company that was able to ship 100 T-shirts of mixed sizes to me in time.

When I packed my suitcases, I used one extra-large suitcase for all 100 T-shirts.

When I arrived in Dobromyl, I checked into the hotel, looked at my

Olexandra Mrachynska, English teacher, giving out T-shirts
that say "Meet me at the new Dobromyl playground"

father's house, and walked to the playground. All of the equipment was shiny and new – and quite colorful. The center square was pretty drab and colorless, but the playground changed the look of the entire center of town. When Olexandra arrived to once again to be my interpreter with the mayor, she kept repeating how colorful it was. The official opening was planned for the next day. The mayor would speak, then Olexandra, and then me – with interpretation by Olexandra. I would then distribute the T-shirts.

It seemed like the whole town came out for the opening ceremony. The mayor began:

We have a very joyful day today. A great day for the children. I am very glad to stand here in the place of the playground, to see happiness in the children's eyes, to hear their voices of delight. I walk here every day and I see all of this. It's an amazing thing! There are a lot of kids in our small town in Ukraine. Our children are very grateful for this gift, which they received from a man whose father was born here. Mr. Arthur Kurzweil and his family privately supported our town in many ways. There are many more projects he is doing in Dobromyl. Mr. Arthur Kurzweil, I thank you sincerely for this wonderful gift. We wish you and your family God's providence, good health, and the strength and inspiration to complete all the good things you are doing. The greatest gift for all of us is to see the children's happy eyes and their joyous faces. Please take this plaque from our community as a sign of our gratitude for all of your support in Dobromyl.

I thought a lot about what I would say with the whole town of Dobromyl listening. It may have been the only time in the history of Dobromyl when a Jew had an opportunity to deliver a message to the citizens of the town. With Olexandra interpreting phrase by phrase, I told a story found in the Talmud. But rather than say the story was from the Talmud, I said that my father told me the story. Imagine: I gave a talk to the population of Dobromyl, quoting from the Talmud! I told them:

One hundred years ago my father was born here. When I was a boy he taught me something that I would like to teach you.

We know from the Bible that God made Adam and Eve. So, my father said to me, "Why only two people? Why did God not make people all over the world?" And he said the reason is because all of us are really one family. Nobody can say, "My family is better than your family" because we are one family.

Some people said to me, "How can we thank you?" So, I am thinking: how can you thank me? And there are two ways you can thank me. One is by being gentle to each other. And the other is to make sure that when you come here to the playground please, please, please have fun!

I love you all.

Dobromyl residents gather for the playground dedication.

The playground in winter

The Dobromyl playground

160
150
140
130
120
110
100
90
80
70
This
playground
is a gift
from
the Kurzweil
family
to
the Children
of
Dobromyl

Цей
дитячий
майданчик
є дарунком
для дітей
Добромиля
від
родини
Курцвейл

АПТЕКА

The Park

Once the playground was complete, the mayor asked me if I would pay for a sitting park adjacent to the playground. The mayor told me it would have benches, winding paths, trees to be planted, and a wrought iron fence for three of the four sides. It would cost me another $11,000.

I immediately said yes. I could already picture it (the plan was completed when he proposed the project). I later learned that the park was designed by the mayor's wife.

Work on the park started immediately, and I was able to watch its progress by watching the playground security camera, which the town purchased when construction began on the playground. To this day, I look at the park every morning while I skim the day's headlines.

During each of the several times I've visited Dobromyl, every morning I would walk from the hotel across the street to my father's former house, now the convenience store Kopika. I'd purchase a bottle of cold water and make my way to the park, right in front of Town Hall. The playground and sitting park look great. I'm told that although the park is called "The New Park," among the children in town it is referred to as "Arthur's Park." It warms my heart to watch as children play while their mothers and fathers keep an eye on them while chatting with friends and neighbors.

I have been told that the park and playground have changed the course of the town of Dobromyl. Not only does it attract children and their parents from surrounding villages and from Dobromyl itself, but it also provides a space for neighbors to speak with each other. I have watched the park's camera many times when I see small groups of adults sitting on benches in the park, hours at a time. The park is also quite attractive, and the playground is colorful, adding to the pride that people are developing in Dobromyl. For so many years, Dobromyl had been going downhill, with young people leaving and younger people planning to leave. I wouldn't be surprised if more people stay, not because of the small park I sponsored but because the playground, park and other improvements I supported offered the town a jumpstart.

GoFundMe

After opening day at the playground, the headmaster of the school and Olexandra accompanied me back upstairs to the headmaster's office. I was walking with the headmaster mostly in silence; sometimes he would speak to me in Ukrainian, seemingly oblivious to the fact that I didn't understand a word he was saying. Olexandra and another English teacher were behind us, having a conversation in English. They could easily have spoken Ukrainian with each other, but I'm sure it was out of respect for me that they chose to speak English. They probably had another motive as well because at one point I overheard Olexandra say, "If only we had a projector so we could teach all of the students the same page at the same time."

When we arrived at the headmaster's office, I asked Olexandra to repeat what she had said about her desire to have a projector. She explained to me that it is often quite difficult to teach when the students can't see the lesson at the same time.

I had just purchased a projector for myself back in New York a few weeks earlier. It cost $75. I said to her, "I'll buy one for you." I then added, "What else do you need for the school?"

"Oh, Mr. Kurzweil, we need everything. We want to be a modern school, but we don't have the tools to teach."

The school, I was told, was built by the Soviets before Ukraine became independent. Once Ukraine was no longer a part of the Soviet Union, it was on its own. This, as I understand it, is one of the reasons some Ukrainians are not nationalists: in some ways they were better off when they were not independent. After the Soviet Union broke apart, Dobromyl had little support from the "new" country of Ukraine. So, while the school was an impressive building from the outside, and while the inside had classrooms and offices, there were hardly any tools – such as projectors, tape recorders, gym equipment, educational posters, computers, and more. Basically, it was a school without the modern tools found in most educational institutions in the West. The school was working on a shoestring budget. Some starting teachers were earning little more than the equivalent of $100 U.S. per month.

"Do you have tape recorders? Tablets?"

"We have one tablet for four teachers to share. It's impossible."

"What else?" I asked.

"I would have to think about it. And what are you thinking about, Mr. Kurzweil?"

"I have an idea. There is a website called GoFundMe. People ask for donations and people donate money to the cause. I will raise money for this school!" When I returned home to New York, I signed up on the GoFundMe site and sent a plea to my closest friends by email.

Every few minutes I looked at the GoFundMe website and was overjoyed by the tally increasing dollar by dollar. It was exhilarating.

I must report that I received two letters from people on my list who were far from pleased by my request. I anticipated more than two such letters, and I have a hunch there were others who donated but who only did so out of friendship and trust in me. In fact, one old friend donated but sent me a letter saying she didn't really support what I was doing, but out of friendship she would participate. She donated $100.

The two letters of protest registered deep anger for what I was doing. Phrases like "How can you support people who murdered our fellow Jews?" and "Aren't there better places to put your effort and money than in Ukraine of all places?" and "My father's family suffered profound suffering at the hands of these people!" and "Why not donate to Israel?!"

These people. This phrase echoed in my brain. Was there really a *these people?* Am I to hate all Ukrainians? I was told by one of the email writers that the "Ukrainians were worse than the Poles, worse than the Nazis." And, "they betrayed us," and, "My father survived and told me of unspeakable, vicious actions on the part of the Ukrainians who were once – supposedly – our friendly neighbors," and, "I could not possibly give a penny to anything in that country," and, "I am shocked that you, Arthur, of all people, would do this project of yours. You should know better than to help Ukrainians."

These writers were outraged that I could call my GoFundMe project "Love Thy Neighbor."

One of the writers wrote, in big bold letters, "NEVER FORGET!!"

Shopping in Lviv

At a certain point, the donations on the GoFundMe website came to a halt. Everyone who intended to contribute to my effort had made their donation. The total came to $23,273.

I wrote to Olexandra and gave her an assignment. I asked her to make a list of what the school needed along with the cost of each item. In short order, I received a long list from her:

Computer Equipment

- 13 desktop computers and monitors
- 13 notebook computers w/ DVD players
- 12 sets of speakers
- 12 headsets
- 4 multimedia projectors
- 4 portable screens
- 2 printers

Physical Education

- 1 exercise machine with multiple stations
- 4 ping-pong tables
- 10 ping-pong paddles
- 25 volleyballs, soccer balls, and basketballs
- timers
- gymnastic mats
- gymnastic parallel bars

- gymnastic horses
- 1 lawnmower

Sound System
- 1 keyboard
- 1 keyboard stand
- 2 12″ speakers
- 2 speaker stands
- 1 12-channel mixer
- 2 microphones
- 2 microphone stands
- Digital camera w/ tripod
- 6-camera security system
- 2 acoustic guitars w/ cases

Now I needed someone to place orders in the places in Lviv where such items are available. I found the perfect person. Marika, who wrote the original article about the Jewish gravestones used as a sidewalk, and who knew some English, had a friend named Halia Lutsyshyn who was fluent in English and was simply a delightful and intelligent young woman. Halia and I corresponded back and forth until she was able to order everything. Since then Halia and I have become good friends.

It was finally the right time to return to Lviv and Dobromyl to pick up our orders – with cash in my pocket! I arrived in Lviv and the mayor arranged for a school bus to pick me up at my hotel there.

Shopping in Lviv was quite an experience. We were quite a team. Our group included Halia Lutsyshyn, two physical education teachers from Dobromyl, the headmaster of the school (Andriy Kernytsky), Olexandra Mrachynska, and me. I doubt that any of us went on a shopping spree before this day, with $20,000 to spend. Halia made it easy; she had ordered most of the items before we got there. But we had a wonderful time selecting a 33mm camera, a lawnmower, and some gym equipment. We loaded up the bus with most of the items. Some things, like the ping pong tables, were just too big for us to lift and fit, as were the pieces of gymnastic equipment, so we made arrangements to pick up the oversized items the next day. Piles of boxes almost filled the entire bus.

The leaders of the shopping committee at the computer shop: the author with school headmaster Andriy Kernytsky, interpreter Olexandra Mrachynska, and volunteer Halia Lutsyshyn

Seven of us squeezed in, with the piles of boxes all over the place. We then headed to the road where the potholes, once again, resulted in a long, swerving, bumpy ride. I was fearful that at least a few of us would get motion sickness along the way. But I think we were all too high from the shopping and the anticipation of the reception we would receive when we finally got back to Dobromyl.

When we arrived in Dobromyl, the bus drove to the school. Olexandra and the headmaster went into the school where they found several of the older students eagerly anticipating the delivery, waiting at the school's entrance. Some of the students helped unload the bus,

Ping pong tables set up in the gym

with the headmaster overseeing the process. The school bus emptied out and I just stood there and smiled, content with the success of the day. I was profoundly satisfied. We had put the money to good use. Dobromyl's students now had some modern tools and equipment to help them thrive.

The next day the physical education teachers traveled to Sambor (between Dobromyl and Lviv, and the birthplace of my great-grandmother) to pick up the gym equipment. When they returned, my mission was accomplished.

I often think of the impact our fundraising effort may have had on the students. Have the computers altered the trajectory of the lives of some of the students? Has the state-of-the-art gymnasium equipment added to the health and confidence of the young people? Have the tablets and projectors for the teachers changed the way they teach?

Who was Stepan Andrivovch Bandera?

Each time I have walked into Dobromyl's main school, I have been conscious of the fact that a portrait of Stepan Andrivovch Bandera hangs in the school lobby and elsewhere in the school (classrooms, etc.). In fact, the school is named after him!

Stepan Andrivovch Bandera (1909–1959) is a Ukrainian hero for so many. He was also a Nazi sympathizer whose major enemies were Poles and Jews. Bandera was the leader of the Ukrainian national movement in western Ukraine. He fought for the creation of the Ukrainian state. A Ukrainian radical politician, it is said that Bandera was also a fierce anti-Semite. In June of 1941, leaflets were found in the name of Bandera, advocating the destruction of Moscow, Jews, Poles, and Hungarians. Bandera's followers, in small bands of men, searched for Jews and Communists. These Ukrainian nationalist groups murdered thousands of Jews, working with Nazi death squads and on their own. During this time Bandara was in prison, so he was not directly involved, but it was clear that he led the fight to advocate that Jews and Poles did not belong in Ukraine. During the Holocaust, one-sixth of the Jews murdered by the Nazis were from Ukraine.

Bandera belonged to the far-right Organization of Ukrainian Nationalists. He was first its chief propaganda officer; in 1933, he became head of the organization. Bandera was considered to be an "ultranationalist." Jews were murdered by Bandera's followers, who were greatly influenced by his philosophy and his leadership.

Bandera became a folk hero.

Was Bandera a fascist or a nationalist?

In October 2007, Lviv displayed a statue dedicated to Stepan Bandera. On October 18, 2007, the Lviv City Council established a "Stepan Bandera Award." The largest stadium in Lviv was named for him.

The town of Uman, Ukraine is an important pilgrimage location for many Jews because the *Chasidic* master, Rabbi Nachman of Breslov, is buried there. It was proposed that the town be renamed "Bandera City" but fortunately this did not occur.

In 2010, the outgoing President of Ukraine, Viktor Yushchenko, posthumously awarded Bandera the title of Hero of Ukraine. This was condemned by many in the Jewish, American, Polish and Russian communities. The award was officially canceled in 2011. There are, however, many monuments to Bandera throughout western Ukraine.

Some say that while Bandera and his men were responsible for killing Jews, technically, Bandera's ideology wasn't antisemitic. It was pro-Ukrainian, and against all others.

Many people in Russia hate the memory of Bandera. Russian president Putin called him "Hitler's accomplice."

Basically, the celebration of Bandera today was based on his belief in an independent Ukraine. Unfortunately too many Ukrainians forget or ignore that he and his followers cooperated with the Nazis.

Bandera is seen by many as a hero, and as a leader who fiercely advocated Ukrainian independence. Others see him as a war criminal because his followers cooperated in the murder of countless Jews and Poles in World War II.

Some surveys indicate that a third of Lviv's residents consider themselves to be followers of Bandera. To others, particularly in eastern Ukraine, Bandera is a villain who cooperated with Hitler.

In 2016, a major street in Kyiv was named after Bandera. The street happens to lead to Babi Yar, where over 33,000 Jews were murdered by Nazis and collaborating Ukrainians.

During one of my visits to Ukraine, I had a brief conversation about Bandera with a young Ukrainian friend of mine who lives in Lviv:

AK: Is Bandera a hero for most Ukrainians today?

H: For those who support nationalism – yes. But part of the population is pro-Russian population. They have a different opinion.

AK: In this case, is a Ukrainian nationalist someone who wants an independent Ukraine?

H: It is a person who is against any kind of foreign occupation and puts national interests of their country in the first place.

AK: Would you think that most Ukrainians who live in east Ukraine are pro-Russian and those in western Ukraine are nationalists? Or is it more complex than that?

H: I think it is more complex than that. It is a general assumption that people in the east are "friendlier" with Russia. However, I think it's not obligatory. People in different parts of Ukraine can have different opinions.

AK: Why would a Ukrainian want Russian domination? Why would some people be against an independent Ukraine? I know this must be a big question.

H: Yes! I think there is a part of people who lived in USSR, and they think that life there was better. They had jobs, etc.

AK: I understand.

H: I think more young people lean to the idea of an independent country. I often hear from older people that life was better back then.

AK: The school in Dobromyl is named after Bandera. If there were pro-Russians in Dobromyl, would they be against it?

H: I think there might be some people like that but especially in western Ukraine they are not numerous. Basically, nationalism is not only about Russian occupation. It concerns any foreign influence, for example Polish, etc. Ukraine has a tragic history of being torn into different directions.

AK: Yes, I have been reading about this. Ukraine is in the middle of Poland and Russia and has suffered because of this.

H: The main thing is to learn lessons from this history.

*　　*　　*

I have been trying to sort out my feelings about Bandera. Of course, there is really nothing to sort out. He inspired and prompted the murder of thousands of Jews. But every once in a while, I get a glimpse of the underlying reason for the support of such a man as Bandera. At the core of his belief – I believe – is a man who believed in his nationality: Ukrainian. Ukrainian history is filled with the repression of Ukrainian culture, language, and independence. Surely the Soviet Union made every attempt to crush Ukrainian identity. Poland did the same.

As I write this, I imagine that critics and historians who know far more than I do would say I am profoundly naïve. I have spent months reading the history of that region and I confess I am no closer to understanding the situation than I was before I began. In fact, I may be more confused than ever. Perhaps it is my preconceived notion of there being good guys and bad guys in every conflict. Once I abandon the search for these heroes and villains, I begin to drown in the details, in the claims and counterclaims.

When I was an undergraduate, I attended an innovative school called New College at Hofstra University. During the first year, the required classes included History, Mathematics, Art, Science and Anthropology. Those were the titles of the classes – nothing more specific. The history class was taught by an historian, whose goal it was to teach us how an historian works at his discipline. Likewise, we were taught mathematics by a mathematician. Art was a class called "Art," and the instructor was an artist, and so on. The object of each class was not to teach us content but rather the process of each discipline. How does an historian work? What does a mathematician do? What are the role and methods of a scientist?

My history professor was Dr. Robert Sobel. He was the most published professor on the Hofstra University campus. He wrote many books including *The Big Board, A History of the New York Stock Exchange; The French Revolution; Herbert Hoover and the Onset of the Great Depression, 1929–1930,* and dozens of other volumes. He was mainly an historian of the world of business. In our class, his task was not to teach us about any topic or era in history. His task was to teach us how to be an historian. What tools does an historian use? What sources does an historian use? How does an historian decide how to approach their subject?

I remember our midterm and final exams. Both were take-home exams, both consisted of one question, and we were given three or four days to complete them. The midterm exam was "What Were the Causes of the American Civil War?" Our final exam was "Was Lenin a Marxist?" We had not covered either topic in our classes that semester. Instead, as Dr. Sobel stated, we were to take a position and defend it. There were no right or wrong answers. The exams were evaluated based on our ability to write clearly, and to defend our views with reputable sources – because that is what an historian does! For example, the answer to the question, "Was Lenin a Marxist?" does not have a yes or no answer. Rather, each student would have to read and research enough on the subject to establish a point of view, and then to support it through strong, highly regarded sources. Some students said yes, Lenin was a Marxist. Others disagreed. The point was that it didn't matter. What mattered was how well we defended our thesis.

This class convinced me that regarding the study of history, there was no objective "truth" when it comes to the complex pathways of history. I was, of course, not about to decide who Bandera was or try to defend my position. Sometimes historical research seems like an endless abyss of claims and counterclaims. So, when I walked into the school named for Bandera and saw his portrait hanging in the lobby, I was able to avoid any knee-jerk reaction based on the little knowledge I had. Rather, I merely kept my attention on the innocent children, who had no responsibility for the views of their parents or grandparents or great-grandparents. Perhaps most importantly, I don't assume that everyone who supports Bandera's memory is an anti-Semite.

I don't want to give the impression that I have no points of view about anything. Perhaps it sounds like I have simply thrown up my hands and given up any kind of understanding about history or any other subject for that matter. In fact, I have plenty of opinions on lots of things, past and present. It is simply that I made a choice in my relationship with the children of Dobromyl to remain ahistorical. The dictionary definition of ahistorical is "not concerned with or related to history, historical development, or tradition." This became my truth. On the one hand, I was steeped in history in my travels, but while I was in Dobromyl and relating to their children, I was purely ahistorical.

What Was I Doing There?

Why am I writing about my travels to Poland and Ukraine? I am confident when this gets published I will receive severe criticism.

I know that relatively speaking, I am a rich philanthropist to the citizens of Dobromyl. This is, of course not true, and while I was almost 70, I had not prepared too well financially for my old age.

But the joy of my activities was based on the fact that I could make a real difference in Dobromyl. For example, I proposed a playground to Dobromyl's mayor. He said yes with great enthusiasm, and within days the workers from the playground manufacturers were already busy constructing the playground on the site. This would be impossible in the U.S. or in Israel. There would be meetings, public testimonies, referendums, and debates on where to put the playground or whether a playground was necessary. Who knows what other red tape would be involved?

But what was I doing there, in this town of Dobromyl, the town of my father's childhood, the town where Jews were tortured and murdered, the town where half of the population was Jewish but now no Jew remains?

What was I doing there, when there are so many other things to do with my time and money, when none of my relatives have the same obsession as I have, when I could be taking a real vacation – to Las Vegas or Spain or Israel – when I could write about life and not death?

What was I doing there, in a tiny border town in Ukraine, where the land is soaked with Jewish blood?

What was I doing there, when there is so little to see, when most of the points of interest represent death, when the Jewish cemetery was destroyed, the great synagogue was destroyed, and the previously Jewish-owned shops were destroyed, and where there are just a few people who can speak English?

What was I doing there, when I know that most of the young people in the town have no knowledge of the atrocities inflicted on the former Jewish residents, where the younger people there have almost no knowledge of the former Jewish community itself?

What was I doing there, where Jews who come to sight-see are mostly looking at empty spaces where Jewish things used to be?

What was I doing there, when I don't know where my great-grandfather prayed, where I don't know where my family went to take a walk in the otherwise beautiful countryside, where I don't know where my great-grandfather's metal-working shop was, where I don't know where my grandmother bought food for the family, where I don't know where my grandparents' wedding took place, where I don't hear the *klezmer* music, where I don't hear the Yiddish being spoken, where I don't know where to buy a *tallis*, or a *yarmulke*, or a new prayer book?

What was I doing in the Jewish town that is no longer a Jewish town, where I can't find a rabbi, where I can't find a *chazan*, where I don't know who the *mohel* was, where I can't locate the kosher butcher, where I don't know where the Jewish children played?

What was I doing there?

Jesus In Dobromyl

On the road from Chyrow (the birthplace of my grandmother) to Dobromyl, there is a larger-than-life statue of Jesus of Nazareth dragging a wooden crucifix and wearing a crown of thorns. It is quite dramatic, and I was moved by it each time I passed it by.

I am aware that the people who erected the statue surely meant it as a Christian symbol. But for me it is not a Christian statue but a Jewish one. For me it is, in a sense, a symbolic Holocaust memorial.

There stands Jesus, a Jew, with a humiliating, painful crown of thorns on his head, carrying a crucifix, on his way to being tortured in the year 33 C.E.

It never happened to me, but I was prepared that if I were to meet a Christian Ukrainian who told me that "the Jews killed Christ," I would respond by saying, "The Jews" didn't do anything, any more than "the Ukrainians." I'm so tired of these generalizations about entire groups of people.

I'll admit that I had to get used to the sheer quantity of Christian art and iconography throughout the Dobromyl of today. Every classroom, every office in the town hall, every place I looked there was something Christian. It didn't bother me. I don't assume – as some people do – that a Christian symbol in Ukraine represents, among other things, the terrible absence of Jews. (There is no Jewish census in Ukraine; estimates of the number of Jews living in Ukraine today

Statue of Jesus of Nazareth on the road between Chyrow and Dobromyl

range from 50,000 to 400,000; in 1941 it is estimated that there were 2.7 millions Jews in what is now Ukraine.) The absence of Jews is a fact, and it cannot be undone. But I don't believe this should prevent Christians from giving expression to their faith. I did not go to Dobromyl to see what was. I went to see what is. And what I found is

Digging up the Jewish gravestones used to pave a walkway

a battered, impoverished little town, still reeling from, among other things, the invasion of the Soviets and the Nazis.

I was also aware that sitting on the top of the highest hill surrounding Dobromyl today is the Wall of Memory. It is clear and visible from many vantage points in the town. I often wondered if anyone in town resented this huge Jewish symbol towering over the town, looking down upon a *shtetl* whose Jews were murdered.

What I didn't know, and still don't know, is how Jews are represented by the priests of Dobromyl. Is it still a part of a warped theology that "the Jews" killed Christ?

But I am growing tired of defending the Ukrainians. I am tired of comparing Christians to Jews. I am tired of slipping into a mood that has me trying to justify my trips to Dobromyl and the gifts I gave them. Once again, Elie Wiesel said it best: "I wish that Christians would be better Christians and Jews would be better Jews."

Crucifixion was a common way Jews were murdered by the ancient Romans. The ancient historians Josephus and Appian refer to the crucifixion of thousands of Jews during the Roman occupation.

Do the children of Dobromyl know that Jesus was a Jew? Do they know that the suffering of the Jewish people throughout history was quite often perpetrated in the name of Christianity? Will they ever know? Will my love of the children of Dobromyl do any good for this insane world of ours?

I believe the only response to outrageous hatred is outrageous love. And yes, my love for the innocent children of Dobromyl is outrageous. I have not regretted that outrageous love for a moment.

Love Thy Neighbor

One of the tragic condemnations regarding the Holocaust is that non-Jews betrayed their Jewish neighbors. Non-Jews who were otherwise peaceful and relatively cordial to Jews before the Holocaust cooperated with the Nazis, often displaying as much if not often more viciousness than the Nazi occupiers. Certainly, in Dobromyl, (and surely in hundreds of towns like Dobromyl), the violent, inhumane actions on the part of some resident non-Jews toward Jews were unspeakable. Accounts of the terror and murder of many residents are horrible. Sometimes I wish I had never learned the details of such events; I often can't get the images out of my mind.

But what happened to the principle from the Torah to love thy neighbor?

Often, I wonder what I would have done if Nazis occupied my town and threatened to kill my children in front of me if I didn't cooperate with them in destroying my neighbors. Would I refuse and watch as my children were shot dead? Would I physically attack the Nazis, which would surely result in my own death? Would I try to take one with me by grabbing a rifle of theirs, lunging toward one of them and being killed in the process? Or have I seen too many movies?

I made a pen pal email friend in Dobromyl, a high school graduate. In one message he asked me if anybody from my family still lived in Dobromyl. I told him my father left Dobromyl in 1928 and there were no other relatives in the town today. I spared him the knowledge that most of my relatives in Dobromyl were murdered, many in the town itself, and many of those by local Ukrainians.

The young man then wrote to me: "Too bad. If your father didn't leave Dobromyl, we'd be neighbors."

How naive and innocent. If my father had not left Dobromyl in 1928 with his mother and two siblings, I most probably wouldn't exist today. Surely, they would have been murdered like all the other Jews who didn't get out in time.

I can easily imagine how some readers would question my decision. Why didn't I tell him the truth about the Holocaust? Why did I omit these hard facts about our shared history? But I had decided: I would not talk about the Holocaust to the children of Dobromyl. I felt this must come from within their community, and when they get older, they will discover the wicked truth. I didn't want to be the person to bring the nightmarish facts to them. I was building a relationship with the people of the town. Discussing the Holocaust with them would surely have prevented the trust and intimacy I wanted to build. I would wait until the day they brought it up.

By coming "back" to Dobromyl, I was encountering people whose families very possibly had been our neighbors. As I walked up and down the street where my father's house was, I saw other houses occupied by people who may very well have had ancestors or relatives who were there during the Holocaust.

But the way I figured it, these were my neighbors too. I wasn't prepared to simply encounter them, look around the town, and leave with no real human contact. I wasn't there to judge them or to ignore them. I wasn't there to be a Jew who just wanted to see the place and leave. I didn't want to give out hostile vibes. These people, the children, and their parents might have been related to the very people who cooperated with the Nazis. But I consider them to be innocent. I don't want to be judged by the sins of my ancestors, and I didn't want to judge them by the sins of their ancestors.

One of the people I met in the town thanked me for coming and helping to improve the town. "We thought we were just forgotten. We didn't know if anyone cared. But you have come to see us, and you are the only one who got involved enough to help us."

The street in Dobromyl where the author's father lived as a child

But how could I not get involved? They are my neighbors. I am supposed to love my neighbor. I now had the opportunity. Was I going to blow it?

My father left Poland in 1928, so he is not considered to be a Holocaust survivor. His father and his mother and siblings left in time to survive. But before they left, they surely were neighbors and also did business with the non-Jews in town. As Rabbi Joachim Prinz once said, "Neighbor is not a geographic term. It is a moral concept."

When my father and his family lived in Brooklyn, N.Y., their apartment was on the second floor of a two-story building. And if you looked out of the kitchen window, it opened to a landing across from which was another kitchen window of an apartment occupied by Italian Christians. My father often told me about the relations between the two families. My father could often smell some delicious Italian dish whose amazing aroma floated from one open window to the other. And likewise, the Italian family could often smell the scrumptious baked goods my grandmother made. My grandmother would often give the neighbors some of the cakes and pastries she baked. But she could never accept the food our Italian neighbors offered. It wasn't kosher. I sometimes imagined that the neighbors were confused or even insulted by this.

And I think back to my knowledge of Dobromyl, when the same thing most probably happened. The history books tell me that Jews usually stayed to themselves in the *shtetl*. The strictness of the kosher laws and the fear of intermarriage and assimilation prompted Jews to build a psychological and physical barrier between themselves and the non-Jews. (This is reflected in *Fiddler on the Roof* when Tevye's third daughter becomes friends with a local Christian young man and ultimately marries him by the service of a priest.) It is also well documented that when steamships brought immigrants to the United States, the Jewish passengers did not mingle with the non-Jewish immigrants but rather stayed together in corners of the ships, particularly for fear that non-kosher food would be shared with the Jews.

I imagine that in the *shtetl*, non-Jews were probably put off by (and probably jealous of) their Jewish "neighbors" who tended not to mingle with each other. And I can easily imagine on Shabbos, when Jewish families would be together, wearing their cleanest and best clothing and walking to the synagogue or to a relative's home for a Shabbos meal, that the non-Jews would look at them with jealous eyes.

My fear is that I sound like I am justifying non-Jewish hostility towards Jews. I am not. I am merely trying to understand the dynamics between Jewish and non-Jewish neighbors in Dobromyl.

Searching for Jewish Remnants

Jews lived In Dobromyl for centuries. Before the Holocaust, over half of the population of Dobromyl was Jewish. So, one would think there would still be some evidence of this in the town. I was determined to locate something – anything – from the days when there was a vibrant Jewish community in Dobromyl.

Many towns in Poland and Ukraine still have the remains of synagogues. Often, they are just empty shells of a building. But in Dobromyl there were no signs of a former synagogue. Testimony from the few Dobromyl survivors indicates that in addition to several small synagogues in Dobromyl there was a large synagogue in town, but that it was burned to the ground with hundreds of Jews inside, all of whom perished.

There were smaller synagogues, called *shtiblekh* (plural for *shtiebel*) which were small Jewish houses of worship. Many towns had small *shtiblekh* organized by occupation, so that all the craftsmen, for example, would congregate in that place. Sometimes a *shtiebel* would be organized by members of a particular *Chasidic* group. For example, in Dobromyl there were Belzer *Chasidim* in town, so there was certainly a Belz *shtiebel.*

One day I spent most of an afternoon just strolling around the town by myself, looking for evidence of *mezuzot* on doorposts. I couldn't find even one. In most cases, the doorposts were new, or constructed post-war. The doorposts that looked old enough to be pre-war didn't have any telltale indent where a *mezuzah* once might have been.

There is one rather curious Jewish remnant in Dobromyl, but it was so subtle that it may have gone unnoticed by many passersby. There is a wrought iron railing on a balcony overlooking the market square. Part of the design of the wrought iron includes a star of David. I wondered, but have never found out, why this star of David was on this particular balcony. But there it was, looking over the town central square, and it had obviously been there for the past 70-plus years. It remains a mystery to me. Why didn't the Nazis destroy it? How was it that they let this obvious Jewish symbol remain?

Dobromyl balcony with a star of David on its railing

Of course, the main remnants in most towns with pre–Holocaust Jewish populations are whatever is left of the Jewish cemeteries, most of which have been neglected or mostly destroyed. In those towns that still have some gravestones where the cemetery once was, they are often scattered around, with most gravestones obviously missing, having been used for projects by local townspeople or Nazis during or since the Second World War. In Dobromyl, as we know, many of the Jewish gravestones were used as a sidewalk surrounding the gestapo headquarters in the town.

I made many friends in Dobromyl and one of them is Lev. Despite his Jewish sounding first name, he is not Jewish. Lev was born and grew up in Dobromyl but lives with his wife in England. He still has family in Dobromyl however, so he visits frequently. Lev had some experience using a metal detector in Dobromyl and found two wax seals with Hebrew on them.

He gave me one as a gift, a token of friendship. I was deeply moved and I cherish this Jewish remnant. Finally, I at least had *something* Jewish from pre-war Dobromyl!

But while I am thrilled to own it, I realized I wouldn't be satisfied with my search until I had found something specifically about my family in Dobromyl.

Jewishgen.com and GesherGalicia.com have copies of birth, marriage, and death records, and I was excited to find records of my family in Dobromyl, including my father's birth record. I also located the marriage records of my great-great grandparents, Saul Kurzweil and Mollie Lowenthal. Saul was the man after whom my father was named.

It has been difficult for me to keep track of the history of Dobromyl. In fact, it reminds me of when old Jewish immigrants in the United States are asked what country they came from. They often answer, "The border changed so many times. Every day it was a different country." While that statement is surely an exaggeration, it does reflect my own experience of trying to learn Dobromyl's history.

I know that before the First World War, Dobromyl was part of the Austrian Empire, and that between the two World Wars, Dobromyl was part of Poland. My father, having been born in Dobromyl (although it was spelled Dobromil – the Polish spelling) always said he was born in Poland – and he was. But by the time I got there it was part of Ukraine. During the Holocaust, Dobromyl was occupied by the Germans, then by the Poles, and then by the Russians. Between the end of the Second World War and the breakup of the Soviet Union, it was a part of the U.S.S.R. – the Union of Soviet Socialist Republics. Of course, once the Holocaust ended, it really didn't matter much to surviving Jews. There was no Jewish population. What did it matter?

My understanding is that after the Holocaust there were a few

Jews remaining in Dobromyl, but they inevitably left as well. Today, unless someone is denying it or simply not mentioning it, there are no Jews left. Therefore, it is no surprise that I couldn't find any evidence of Jewish life other than the gravestones from the destroyed Jewish cemetery.

Part V

"If You See What Needs to Be Repaired"

It is unfortunate that in most cases when the sins of the father fall on the son it is because unlike God, people refuse to forgive and forget and heap past wrongs upon innocent generations.

– E.A. Bucchianeri, *Brushstrokes of a Gadfly*

The Gymnasium

The physical education teachers seemed to be delighted to have all the new equipment that we bought as part of the GoFundMe campaign. I was eager to see it all in the large gymnasium and I asked to go for an inspection of the purchases.

When we got there, a few of the physical education teachers were waiting for us. I noticed almost all of the purchases were out in the open, ready for use: the ping pong tables, the gymnastic horses, mats, and the large multi-part exercise station were all sitting unused. The equipment was still pristine. Some of the pieces were actually still in their original packaging. Nobody had used any of it.

The trouble seemed to be that it was freezing in the gym, far too cold for anyone to use the space. I asked one of the teachers who showed us around what was going on.

"Mr. Kurzweil, we have a problem." Olexandra interpreted for me.

"Yes?" I answered with a confusing tone.

"We are afraid the wall will fall down. We cannot use the gym. Nobody is permitted to enter this room. Certainly not the students."

"Is it safe for us to be here right now?" I was worried about our own fate, standing in the cold gym, facing the large concrete wall. The wall didn't appear about to fall, but it was leaning slightly, so it was obvious there was a problem.

"Is there a solution to this problem?" I asked the teacher.

"We had an engineer and an inspector visit us. They explained to us how the wall could be reinforced," Olexandra interpreted.

"Are they sure? Do you have a plan?" I was both relieved and disappointed that they weren't using the gym. My primary concern in all of my activities in Dobromyl was the children. If a single child were to get seriously hurt because of something that I did in Dobromyl, I could never forgive myself. I was glad that they were being cautious.

"Are you sure the wall can be fixed?" I asked.

"This is what the inspector said," said the teacher.

I wondered who came to inspect the situation.

I spoke in a firm tone. "You must get another opinion, from the best, most qualified person. And let me know how much it would cost to save the wall and make its foundation secure."

"If they are correct, it would cost $6,000. We have already received an estimate." Olexandra looked a little uncomfortable. She had the safety of the children in mind. But she was not comfortable asking me for money again.

"If you get another expert opinion, and if you are told that this wall can be repaired, I will pay for it," I announced casually. I realized once again that I was giving the impression that I was a rich man. They probably thought I was a millionaire. Of course I was clearly the richest man they had ever met.

"And what about the heat," I asked in a friendly manner. "Can it be fixed?"

Olexandra asked one of the gym teachers and received a quick reply.

"They say it would be $4,000," Olexandra reported.

"I will pay for fixing the heat." They looked at each other, all with serious facial expressions. I suspect they wanted to jump for joy, but they remained businesslike.

I continued. "But I want all bills in writing, and I would like them to be itemized. I explained to Olexandra what I meant by "itemized." When I finally received the itemized invoices, they were in Ukrainian, and in Ukrainian currency. But they also showed math to convert it into dollars. The bill to repair the gymnasium wall came to just under $6,000 – $14 less.

"I don't have the money with me. Can the work start as soon as possible?"

Workers reinforcing the gymnasium wall

They had already hired the workers who would take direction from an engineer.

"I will wire the money to your bank when I return to New York next week."

When I next returned to Dobromyl, spring had almost arrived, and the reinforced wall was completed. The heat was fixed as well, and they turned it on for me to see that it worked. Warm air quickly filled the gym.

When we went to shop with the GoFundMe money, one of the stops we made was to a huge seller of lawn supplies, including power mowers. Mowing the lawn was the responsibility of the physical education department. After all, it was they who needed the grass to be mowed for the students to play soccer. I encouraged them to buy the best one they could. They were a little embarrassed by my advice, so they chose the second-best lawn mower.

I kept on stressing, at every opportunity I could, that I was an advocate for the young people in town. This was my mission. This was the basis of my philanthropy. For example, on one of my trips to Dobromyl, someone asked to see me and brought me to an unfinished room in one of the buildings right on the central square of town. I imagined that the room was some kind of Jewish shop before the Holocaust.

I had been asked if I played chess and when I said that I did, someone got the idea that I could help them to finish the room with nice walls, a carpet, and a bathroom. I was told it could become the town chess club for the young people in town – and that it would be named after me: the Kurzweil Chess Club. When I asked them how much it would cost, I was told $3,000 would be enough. When I asked the mayor and Olexandra if it was a good idea, they told me in no uncertain terms that it was not a good idea. The room would become a hangout for unemployed men in the town to play chess, smoke cigarettes and drink vodka. I never spoke with the chess player again. I suspect the mayor had a word with him.

The Soccer Stadium

One afternoon, the mayor wanted to show me the Dobromyl soccer stadium. It was the pride and joy of the town. The Dobromyl team was a successful one. If I understood correctly, the town team was the champion of a large league of teams from many surrounding towns and districts. I was also told that other teams used the Dobromyl stadium for competitions due to its quality. Huge bleachers ran along both long sides of the field.

I confess I have little interest in sports, and I hardly appreciate the value of them. I don't like the "our team-your team" business. In the U.S. I have heard some baseball fans say, for example, that they hate the New York Yankees. Hate is a strong word to use, and the idea of the fierce sports competitions remind me of gladiators fighting each other in ancient Rome.

When I was young, every four years, my family would watch the Olympics on the television, and every four years I would hear my father – who also had no interest in sports – question why it was assumed because we were Americans that we would root for the United States teams or individuals in all competitions. My father would say it made more sense to watch the competition and "may the best team win."

My father was shot and wounded severely during the Second World War. Because he had only partial mobility of his arm, he was never able to participate in sports, and subsequently he and I never threw the ball around in the backyard when I was growing up. Nor did we ever get involved with any teams. I may have gone to only one Yankees game in my entire childhood.

Not being sports oriented, I never learned to appreciate being a fan or a player. During recess in school, I was much more interested in hanging out and talking to the girls than I was in playing any sports.

The mayor brought me to the outdoor stadium to show me how good it looked – except for the overhang in one corner of the bleachers. The original fabric was of poor quality and a severe rainstorm had ripped it apart. Its remnant was hanging down and was an eyesore. The mayor somewhat meekly asked me if I could pay for a new awning for the stadium bleachers. The cost would be $7,000 and would be made from quality material that would not fall apart.

I saw that the soccer stadium meant a lot to him. I assume that the main reason people from other towns would visit Dobromyl was because of the soccer schedule, and the mayor wanted to make a good impression when out-of-towners visited.

Even though the soccer field is used by young people in Dobromyl, fitting my criteria, I also knew that it is mainly used by the adult team participating in competitions with other towns. But I shared the mayor's feelings: I wanted people to see a growing town with a quality soccer field, so I consented and said I would pay for it. I asked if it could be done quickly, and the mayor said he would get the project rolling that very day. Within a few months it was completed.

And when I visited again, the mayor took me to see the new awning. It looked great! It also happened to be raining that day, so I was able to see the awning effectively in use.

Later that evening, the mayor and I went out to dinner. His wife joined us, as did Olexandra. At that meal, the mayor brought up the subject of the soccer stadium and asked me again if I liked it. I said I did like it a lot and that I was going to be happy to imagine the new awning during games. The awning would cover people if it rained and also protect them from the sun on very sunny days.

The next day, the mayor invited me to watch a match between two teams of high school students, both from Dobromyl. They started a game, but I wasn't watching them too attentively. My eyes wandered.

The mayor told the manager of the stadium that the boys didn't need to play any longer.

New awning at the Dobromyl soccer field

On the way back to his car, the mayor brought up another subject. He showed me some literature discussing the idea of converting the stadium into a field with artificial grass. I told him immediately that it was not of interest for me to sponsor. He accepted my refusal very graciously. He didn't want to press his luck with me. I had already given a lot of money to the town, but artificial grass seemed like a luxury to me. Also, it was a stretch to purchase artificial grass for the stadium since I made it clear every chance I could that my interest was in the children of Dobromyl.

And once again, I found I was asking myself, *Why?* Why would I want to pay for anything having to do with a sports stadium? I did it mainly out of respect for the mayor. It was important to him, and I wanted to show him that I valued his point of view. Through various side discussions I understood that the powers that be in Dobromyl were conscious of the fact that healthy, strong bodies are the way to build a healthy, strong nation. Ukraine is struggling with its identity. The typical person in present-day Ukraine wants an independent Ukraine, not a Ukraine dominated by foreign culture. They've had enough of Russian/Soviet domination, and enough of Polish domination. They are in the process of reclaiming their cultural identity.

As I write this, a war between Russia and Ukraine is raging. It began with an unprovoked major attack by Russia. It is my prayer that the fighting will end and that peace will return to the region. But once again the world is watching an attempt by Russia to dominate Ukraine and to destroy its national identity. The president of Russia has gone as far as saying that there is no such entity as Ukraine!

And what of the Jews of Ukraine? Where do they fit into the nation's identity?

Time, I suppose, will tell.

The Bathroom

Months later, when I once again visited Dobromyl, the mayor took me to see the school for the younger children.

Part of the building was unfinished, which was one of the reasons he wanted me to see it. The teachers were desperate for more space. The classrooms were cramped and there weren't enough of them. The mayor told me the town of Dobromyl was eligible for a grant from a government matching fund to expand the school. The mayor said they were short a few thousand dollars to meet the matching fund, and the mayor asked me if I could help.

I am quite certain that most if not all the children in the town did not know that before the Second World War half of the town's population was Jewish. My research led me to understand that Jews have been the target of prejudice and hatred largely based on what they have learned in church, *but I didn't even want to go there.* Ignorance and stupidity were not going to get in the way of the help I wanted to provide Dobromyl's children. Fortunately, I was able to help with the matching fund, and the building was expanded and completed by the following year.

During my next trip to Dobromyl a few months later, the mayor brought me back to the school to show me the progress that had been made. School was in session, so I was treated to watching the young children sing Ukrainian songs as they danced around in a circle. I could have watched them all day. I love watching young children filled with song and innocence and joy. But the mayor seemed to be in a bit of a rush, and we were probably being a little distracting to the classes.

Before we left the school, I needed to go to the bathroom. I asked where the bathroom was located.

I was told, to my horror, that there was no bathroom in the building. Both the teachers as well as the young students were required to use an outhouse while school was in session. I couldn't believe it, but I was assured that this was the case.

Even in the *winter*?

Yes, even in the winter.

Did they mean to say that these little children needed to go outside in the freezing Ukrainian winter weather to get to an old, cold, cramped outhouse? I was assured, despite my disbelief, that this was indeed the case.

I asked if there was a location inside in school where a bathroom could be built. We walked to a place in the building where there was an empty room. The mayor told me that this space was earmarked for a bathroom to be built one day, but there were no funds for it and many other priorities. I indicated that for me this was an unacceptable situation. I said to the mayor that I refused to imagine the young children of Dobromyl having to cope with no indoor bathroom.

My father had told me there was no bathroom in his house in Dobromyl when he was a boy. But that was in the 1920s. In his family's little house, there were just two rooms, one for his family in the front and one for another family in the back. They had an outhouse. I suppose that we humans can get used to almost anything, especially if one has never had an indoor bathroom to begin with. The things we take for granted are astonishing. I often imagined how my father, as a little boy in Dobromyl, would have to relieve himself during the cold winters.

The very moment I learned there was no indoor bathroom, it became as clear as ever that I was deeply connected to all the children in Dobromyl. They were precious to me, and I even had the *chutzpah* to think they needed me. I loved them all. I loved their innocence. I loved the fact that their world could be wide open to so many possibilities.

While in Dobromyl I often thought about my Jewish ancestors

and their Jewish friends who probably would have thought I was out of my mind to build a bathroom for little Ukrainian children in Dobromyl. For the most part, I didn't dwell on the probability that these adorable children were the great-grandchildren of Ukrainians who very possibly pointed out and identified Jews to the Nazi S.S. who then arrested the Jews and murdered them. My mind bounced back and forth, sometimes being preoccupied with the fact that I was a Jew but mostly just seeing them as fellow human beings. When it comes to little children and their need to go to the bathroom, we were all human beings, and I knew I could help them.

I asked the mayor if he had any idea how much a bathroom would cost. He didn't know but said he could easily find out. I asked if he even had a ballpark idea of the cost. He told me he suspected it would be no more than $10,000, so I asked him if he could please give me an accurate figure. By the evening, when I had dinner with the mayor and his wife and Olexandra, he had a cost, slightly less than his original guesstimate of $10,000.

The next morning, we went back to the school and to the space reserved for a future bathroom. The mayor even had a preliminary design sketched out. Word had spread overnight about my interest in the fact that there was no bathroom, so several parents joined us in that empty space.

"Let's do it," I said. "As soon as possible. I will pay for it. These children – and their teachers – must have indoor facilities."

By the time I returned to Dobromyl several months later, the bathroom was completed. It was a bright, beautiful room, with a sink and two stalls for the teachers. The other part of the space included a sink and four spaces for the children. The room also had heat. I was more than satisfied, and I learned that the children and their teachers were tremendously grateful to me. They didn't know that I was the grateful one. It is not every day that a person gets an opportunity to really change the quality of life for children.

Teaching English in Dobromyl

The English students in Dobromyl

It is common knowledge that throughout the world a young person has a better chance of a successful future if he or she has a working knowledge of English or some other foreign language. English or German are therefore required subjects in Dobromyl's schools. Olexandra is one of only a few teachers who are English instructors in the town.

One day Olexandra asked me if I could help with the students' English. I wondered how I could help, so I said yes, not immediately understanding that her request was mostly about money. At first,

The author teaching the English Camp students the song
"Where Do the Children Play?" by Cat Stevens

The author shows the English Camp students a magic trick

The students of English Camp

The author with interpreter & English teacher Olexandra Mrachynska

Olexandra explained to me that they wanted to buy textbooks that were better than the ones they were using. The books she had in mind included workbooks for the students as well.

But after I purchased these books and workbooks for the students, for supplemental after school learning sessions, then came the cost of paying the teachers for their time. After all, Olexandra could not expect the teachers to give their time for free. After a long day in the classroom, the motivation for staying after school was extra pay – which the school itself did not have. I agreed, and periodically over the years Olexandra has asked me for money to pay three teachers to participate in these after-hours, supplemental English sessions. I have been assured that my contributions are paying off, but I have no way of knowing to what extent the additional study is effective. I have come to trust Olexandra.

In addition to these after-school classes, Olexandra invented what she calls "English Camp." It consists of one or two weeks during the summer when any students who desire to participate can join and can enjoy some fun games that help them review English vocabulary. Olexandra does this for free. One year I went to Dobromyl and spent one week participating in the camp. Mostly I watched as Olexandra, in a much more informal setting, got the young people to speak English.

I prepared a little for my week with the students. I photocopied the lyrics to a song by Cat Stevens called "Where Do the Children Play?" and gave a copy to each student. We sat in a semi-circle, with me in the center. First, I reviewed the words with them, skipping some of the more obscure terms like *cosmic* and *slot machine*. Then I took one of the guitars that I had purchased for the school and I played the song for the students. I was a little surprised that I had no embarrassment while singing. My singing voice is not great, but the students respected my sincerity. After I sang the song solo, I invited the students to sing along with me. Their sweet voices carried the song through to the end. They also understood that I chose this particular song to sing to fit with my sponsorship of the playground in the center of town.

After we sang the song, I presented a slideshow using one of the projectors and a screen I had bought with the GoFundMe money. My slideshow consisted mostly of old family photos taken in Dobromyl, although I added a few photos of the same people who came to America. During the slideshow I brought up a subject that I never spoke of at any other time during any of my visits to Dobromyl: the fact that most of the Kurzweil family from Dobromyl were murdered during the Second World War. I was hesitant about it, but I felt that at least once I needed to mention this. Frankly, I don't know if my words registered with the students. Most of the students have no knowledge that their town was once more than 50% Jewish, and that most were murdered. They also have no awareness that for some of the students, the houses they live in were once occupied by Jewish families.

I thought long and hard about this decision. My basic approach was not to be the person to come into the town to teach the young people about the Holocaust. The adults know full well that Jewish families were decimated, and that the entire population of Jews was destroyed. They know that the Jews of Dobromyl lived in the town for many generations. They know that the Jews were humiliated. Tortured. Shipped to death camps. Shot on the street or in their homes. Betrayed by some of their neighbors. Murdered by bullet or by sledgehammer.

That was the only time I mentioned anything about the fate of my family and other Jews in Dobromyl. My primary goal was to make friends and to help fellow human beings in their struggle to live.

Another activity I participated in with the young people during English Camp was my presentation of a magic show. I had brought some tricks from home (as I usually do) in case there was an opportunity to perform. My little magic show was a great success, and I topped it off by bringing enough of one magic trick and teaching it to the whole class. The trick is called "Two Card Monte," and one of the advantages of this trick is that all you need is two special playing cards. So each of the children was able to go home with a trick to perform. It was a special treat for them.

I've been interested in magic tricks since the third grade. One day my third-grade teacher announced that we were going to put on a play for the school about George Washington, and that we needed a three-cornered hat for the production. I raised my hand and told the teacher that my father could make one.

When my father retuned home that evening, I told him what I had said to the teacher, and he asked me why I suggested that since he has no skills as a hat maker. I don't know how I answered him, but I am quite certain that at the time I believed my father could do anything.

My father located a costume store in a nearby town and we drove there. When my father saw a three-cornered hat at the store, he concluded that he could make one. As we were walking around the shop, I noticed there was a section of magic tricks, and I urged my father to let me look there.

It was then that my father purchased my first trick. It was called "Penny into Dime," allowing me to take a penny, put it on a small block of wood and transform it into a dime! It was simple to perform, and it began my lifelong interest in performing magic tricks. When we arrived at home, my father also did a kind of magic trick: through the aid of his seeing a three-cornered hat at the store and looking at a picture of one in our World Book Encyclopedia, my father was able to create, from cardboard, a perfect three-cornered hat!

Over the years I have purchased hundreds of magic tricks as well as many books on how to perform as a magician. In recent years, I have been performing a one-man show called "Searching for God in a Magic Shop," where I discuss some heavy ideas within Jewish theology while performing some rather cool magic tricks. The basic premise of my show is that every trick works the same way: the audience is fooled because they do not see everything. And so it is with our lives: we can say "*Gam Zu L'Tova*" ("This too is for the best") because we don't see everything. Only God sees everything. We trust in God that there is a reason for everything, however terrible it might seem to us. It is a profound challenge to develop this kind of faith, but it is exactly what Jewish tradition demands of us.

By the way, the Talmud (*Avodah Zara* 18a–b) describes a sleight of hand magic trick performed by none other than Rabbi Meir. The

Romans were searching for Rabbi Akiva, claiming that he was guilty of rebelling against Rome. The Talmud says, "One day Romans saw Rabbi Meir and ran after him, and he ran away from them...Some say he escaped captive because he saw food cooked by gentiles and dipped one finger in the food and tasted it with another finger, and thereby fooled them into thinking that he was eating the food which they knew Rabbi Meir would not eat."

The author discussing the sleight of hand move described in the Talmud with Rabbi Adin Steinsaltz

The children also prepared a play for me that they performed in costume. It was based on a Ukrainian *Vertep* show, which was originally a puppet theater but is now performed by children as well. The play presents the story of the birth of Jesus. There are various versions of the play, both religious and secular. Sometimes the play makes fun of current national customs, and the plays often have a variety of characters including "a Jew." While I did not follow the play – it was, after all, in Ukrainian, I am fairly certain that one of the characters was a Jew, or possibly a Romani. He seemed to be the villain of the

Dobromyl students out for a celebratory lunch

story. I don't think the children or Olexandra identified the character as being Jewish.

Another activity I planned for English Camp week was inspired by *Foxfire*, a magazine published in Appalachia. *Foxfire*, started in 1966, was a project where young people living in Appalachia wrote articles based on local research. The students conducted interviews with local residents, thereby creating oral histories and recording craft traditions, ultimately creating a magazine and some books that anthologized the magazine's contents. I wanted to do the same thing in Dobromyl. My idea was to send the students into their community with the goal of recording, ultimately in print, the local culture. They would collect recipes, oral histories, folk traditions, stories, and anything else that would explore the culture of Dobromyl.

I ultimately thought the idea was too ambitious for me to tackle, and I didn't have the courage to suggest it to Olexandra, who had plenty on her plate already. But I did realize a part of my vision. I asked each of the students to go home and to ask their parents or grandparents for a recipe. The recipe had to be written in English, in a standard cookbook format: ingredients, measurements, and a

Cover of cookbook written by the students

description of the method for creating the dish. I told the students that we would create a book and that I would pay each of them one U.S. dollar for their work. All of the students participated and the result would be a cookbook which I would publish back in New York. The next day, each student arrived at English Camp with a recipe. They lined up and one by one they gave me their written work as I handed each of them a one dollar bill.

At the end of the week, I took the whole class out for lunch. There was a new café in town, which for me was a clear sign that there was some growth in Dobromyl. I suspect it is probably rare for a young student in Dobromyl to go out for a meal. But for me it was a real celebration to end a wonderful week with Olexandra and her students.

Facebook II

A lot has happened since I first made Facebook contact with the people of Dobromyl. For example, in August of 2021, on the occasion of Ukraine's day of independence, I posted this message on the public Dobromyl Facebook page:

Happy 30th Anniversary to all of my friends in Dobromyl. Tomorrow I will lift my cup and make a toast in celebration of your 30 years of independence. You are in my prayers for good health, prosperity and continued success as you build and rebuild. And may you receive God's blessings on this important occasion.

In response, I received over 150 reactions (all positive) and 30 comments, this one being typical:

Thank you for everything you have done for us…Many years to you.…

It was written in Ukrainian but, of course, a simple click and it was immediately translated.

I can't deny it feels wonderful to be appreciated. But it also prompts me to think, once again, about my motives. Why did I donate so much to the people (mainly the children) of Dobromyl? I would like to think my motives have been pure, but I know they aren't.

For example, I know my ego has something to do with it. I am aware that my writing and lecturing for the past 40+ years has brought me a considerable amount of attention. Chances are somewhat likely that if you are reading this book now, you knew of me before this reading, either from one of my previous books or from my – quite literally – hundreds of lectures across the country over the years. My books have done well, and my lectures have been well-received, so I should feel that I have gotten more than my share of attention and praise.

This brings to mind something Kurt Vonnegut wrote. Vonnegut once explained that writers shouldn't lecture because the typewriter doesn't applaud. That immediate gratification is so addictive. The warmth and appreciation of an audience is far more tempting than the cold stare of the keyboard looking back at me.

To keep my ego in check a bit, I am reminded of something Heinrich Heine is reported to have said: "I am very famous among the people who know me."

And then there is the quote from satirical writer Paul Krassner who said, "The biggest ego trip is worrying if you're on one."

I can't deny that when I walk around the market square in Dobromyl, I am aware that everyone who sees me knows me – probably as the philanthropist or rich man whose Jewish family came from Dobromyl. It is a trip to know that almost everyone in the town both knows me and appreciates me.

It was also an ego trip to walk into the mayor of Dobromyl's office and say that I would pay for a playground and a park. In the United States, I am not particularly rich, but when I am in Dobromyl, I am probably the wealthiest person for miles around. After the playground and park were built, each time I visited, the mayor asked me for something else. I didn't always say yes, but I consented enough of the time to know that a rush of an ego boost arrived immediately.

Walking into the school in Dobromyl also fed my ego. Every child, every student and teacher, knew who I was when I was there – and they particularly knew I was a big donor (perhaps the only donor) to the school. Everyone treated me like a king. Even though I sincerely tried to discourage it by joking and relating to everyone in an informal way, I still knew that everyone was on their best respectful behavior when I was in town.

Frankly, I feel I was somewhat successful in earning true, sincere affection from the people of Dobromyl. But I can imagine cynical voices saying, "When we were poor, defenseless Jews in Dobromyl, we were eventually tortured and murdered, but now that you have given them money you have bought their respect." Of course, I don't know, nor will I ever know, what kind of antisemitism may be hiding beneath the surface. But I feel that the affection and friendship I have received is genuine. I don't think I am being naïve.

Another moving phenomenon has occurred on Facebook. On the occasion of *Rosh Hashanah* and Passover, I receive, each year, holy day messages from some of the people in Dobromyl. I believe that many of the Ukrainians who know of the terrible, tragic Jewish history of the place look for opportunities to reach out to me in authentic friendship. Yes, I am probably, in many cases, their only "Jew," but I am the person they want to use to show that the past is gone, that a new day has arrived. It is a part of their *teshuvah*, their expression of regret and repentance.

Dobromyl offered me an experience I probably never would know elsewhere in my life. To them, I am a philanthropist and a hero. But many times, people in Dobromyl thank me for my "big heart." I have given them more than just money. I have given them friendship and genuine warmth. On a certain level, I am just one person reaching out to others – who wants them to reach back and embrace me as a friend.

A Note About the Mitzvah of Tzedakah

I need to say something about money. The reader who has gotten this far the book has come to know that I donated a considerable amount of money to the town of Dobromyl. Let me put it in context:

According to Jewish law, one must give 10% of one's earnings to *tzedakah,* or charity. For most of my adult life, I did not do this. When I added up my earnings throughout my adult life, I saw that I had neglected a considerable amount of *tzedakah* giving. I decided I had to make up for that neglect! I therefore set aside enough money to be able to make up for this failure. If I add up the amount of money I invested in Dobromyl, I realized that I was able to retroactively perform this important *mitzvah.* As Maimonides taught: "We are required to be more careful in fulfilling the *mitzvah* of *tzedakah* than any other mitzvah." And as it is taught in the Jerusalem Talmud, "*Tzedakah* and acts of kindness are the equivalent of all the *mitzvot* of the Torah." (Pe'ah 1:1)

Shabbos in Dobromyl

I did not grow up in a Jewishly observant home. We did not observe the Sabbath; we did not observe the kosher laws; we did not go to synagogue except a few times each year on the high holy days. But in my mid to late 20s, I was becoming more knowledgeable about Judaism to the point of obsession. I am not sure I can explain why. I'm not sure I know. I just knew I felt a profound pull in the direction of my family's spiritual heritage.

When I was in the first grade, one day I refused to eat the ham being served in the school cafeteria. When the teacher asked me why I was not eating my lunch, I explained that I was Jewish and that ham in not kosher. After that day I continued to eat non-kosher food all the time. But something got into my head, so for that one day, I kept kosher.

After my Bar Mitzvah, when most of the kids my age finally stopped going to the synagogue (and really hated how boring it was), I decided to go every Shabbos (Saturday) morning. This lasted for about a year. But I look back on it as one more blip on my Jewish radar.

I also know that when my father's father died, my father went to the synagogue twice a day to recite the Mourner's prayer (*Kaddish*) for eleven months. From time to time, I accompanied my father, and I was often moved by his dedication.

Then in college, I heard a lecture by Theodore Bikel, sponsored by the campus Hillel organization. At that time, I didn't know who or what a Hillel was, but I learned that it was the name of the Jewish club on campus. Hillel was one of the great Jewish Sages and whose wisdom is recorded in the sacred Jewish book, the *Mishnah*. One of his most well-known statements is, "If I am not for myself, who will be for me? And if I am only for myself, who am I? And if not now, then when?" At the time, I was more interested in ending the war in Vietnam than I was in getting involved in a Jewish club. A poster on the wall of the university announced that Theodore Bikel, a Jewish folk singer, would be on campus that afternoon caught my attention because, like him, I also played the guitar. When Bikel entered the auditorium, he had no guitar with him. It was then that I found out he wasn't on campus to present a concert but rather to give a talk to the Jewish students.

Bikel began his talk by saying that he had been meeting a lot of Jewish Buddhists on college campuses lately. My ears perked up. I was not a Jewish Buddhist, and I was never a member of any Eastern religious group, but like many young people in those days (the late 60s and early 70s), I was reading a lot of books about eastern meditation and philosophy, and I was influenced by the Beatles and their interest in meditation and Eastern stuff. Bikel had one message that day: If you want to reject Judaism, reject it. But don't reject it until you know something about it, so you know what you are rejecting.

I walked out of the lecture hall with my friend Richard Carlow thinking that Bikel had a point. I really knew very little about Judaism – and it was time to change that. I called a Conservative rabbi in a town near the university and asked if we could make an appointment. When the appointment arrived, Richard and I said to the rabbi, "We know nothing about Judaism. Can you help us?" The rabbi apparently had little time for us, two late 1960s scruffy college students, so he handed us several booklets on Judaism and suggested we read them. We took them home. They were boring, superficial, and basically convinced me that Judaism had nothing to offer me.

But by the late 70s I found myself, once again, with more than a curiosity about Judaism. I concluded that Judaism could not be as meaningless as those pamphlets were. So, I began to systematically read just about every book in the Judaism section of the local public library (296 in the Dewey Decimal System. Melvil Dewey, the inventor of the Dewey Decimal System, certainly had his biases: all of human knowledge is classified between 000 and 999. The 200s is "Religion" and most of it concerns itself with Christianity. Judaism got one number: 296). I found most of the books to be as soulless and uninteresting as those horrible little pamphlets, but slowly a more meaningful Judaism began to take shape in my mind. By 1980, I was reading about Judaism almost exclusively. And I discovered a book that changed my life: *The Thirteen Petalled Rose* by Rabbi Adin Steinsaltz of Jerusalem. It remains my favorite book. It is an introduction to Judaism but unlike any introductory book on Judaism you will ever encounter.

I decided to wear my yarmulke whenever I was home. When I was outside, I took it off. This made me, in a way, a Marrano, a hidden Jew who was not Jewish very publicly, only privately.

I needed to make two decisions before leaving the U.S. for Ukraine and Dobromyl. One was how I would eat without kosher food, and whether I would wear my yarmulke as I do every day in New York – inside and outside.

The decision about keeping kosher was quite simple. I mostly ate salads, but the one animal I ate was a fish – salmon to be exact. The salmon is delicious in Ukraine. Although eating on a plate that was not used exclusively with kosher food is also contrary to the laws of *kashrut,* I felt comfortable doing this. The more complicated decision was whether or not to wear a yarmulke. My normal daily practice includes wearing one all the time.

Ultimately, as I wrote about earlier in this book, I decided not to wear my yarmulke in Ukraine, unless I was in a cemetery. It was a difficult decision. And it may have been the wrong decision. I don't know exactly what I was thinking. I didn't want to wear a costume or a mask. I wanted to just be a person who came to visit. Of course, I was told that everyone in the town eventually knew of me and knew that I was Jewish. But I didn't want there to be any barriers between me and everyone else. I didn't want my first impression to be "Jew" any more than I wanted my first impression of people in Dobromyl to be anything other than human. I didn't want to be a ghost from the past. Nor did I have some need to make a grand public statement that I am a Jew. I just wanted to be a friendly neighbor.

OK. Perhaps I was naïve. It may have made no difference. But I was thinking mostly about the children. I didn't want children to ask their parents why that man was wearing a black cap. But now, looking back on it, I think, *why not?*

Of course, I wasn't just some guy. I was, after all, a descendant of the Jews from Dobromyl. But I wanted to make it easy for them to embrace me. As I think back on it, I may have made the wrong choice. But in reality, I was mostly concerned about my own safety. There are crazy people in the world, and some are crazy and antisemitic. During my trips to Ukraine and Poland I was often alone, and while I also sometimes feel vulnerable in the United States while wearing my yarmulke, there is no comparison between the safety I feel in the U.S. and the safety I feel outside of my country.

During one of my trips to Dobromyl, I was there on a Friday and planned to stay through the night. Shabbos was coming.

Early in the day, I asked Tatiana, the woman who owns the hotel (and the building that was my father's house) if she had candlesticks and candles and matches and salt. I would like to light two candles with my dinner that evening. She said yes without hesitation.

I spent the day walking around town, spending time at the Jewish cemetery, taking a nap, reading, and shopping for two loaves of challah (easy to find; it is a traditional bread in Ukraine) until it was just before sundown. I took a shower, dressed in my black jeans, white shirt – and my yarmulke. And I went down to the dining room. In the otherwise empty room, my table setting, the candles and matches and salt were waiting for me. Tables for eating should always have a salt shaker. This is because there was salt on the altar in the Holy Temple in Jerusalem. Eating in Judaism is raised to the level of ritual, and the salt on the table helps in that transformation from table to altar.

I felt it was some kind of historic moment. Who knows when the last member of the Kurzweil family – or any Jew, for that matter – lit Shabbos candles in Dobromyl? I was looking out the window, staring at my father's house, and then I recited the blessing for lighting candles on Friday night to usher in the Sabbath.

I recited the blessing, and then salted (part of the ritual) and tasted the delicious, fresh challah. Many people erroneously think that reciting a blessing before eating the challah is somehow "blessing the bread." In Judaism, there is no such thing. Similarly, many people

Fresh bread is easy to find in Dobromyl

Salmon, the author's preferred choice for dinner

think that kosher food is food that has been blessed by a rabbi. This is also far from the truth. A blessing is an expression of gratitude:

Blessed are You, Lord our God, Ruler of the universe, Who brings forth bread from the earth.

As I sat and ate my meal of fresh salmon, I was thinking of other things I was grateful for:

Blessed are You, Lord our God, Ruler of the universe…
…Who found my wife, Bobby, for me.
…Who allowed me to fulfill my lifelong dream to visit Dobromyl.
…Who gave me a healthy body and mind.
…Who provided me with new friends, young and old, in Dobromyl.
…Who didn't allow hatred or bitterness to get in the way.
…Who gave me a mind and heart free of bigotry.
…Who helped me to learn how to read.

…Who gave me a personality capable of openness and
  friendliness and generosity.
…Who gave me the ability to love all children.
…Who prevented me from feeling superior to anyone.
…Who provided me with the ability to laugh and to cry.
…Who led me to learn about the profound ways of Judaism.
…Who gave me parents who encouraged me to pursue my
  interests.
…Who helped me to obey the command to love my
  neighbor.
…Who allowed me to remember.
…Who provided me with the ability to forget.

It was probably the first time since the Jewish people of town were all murdered by the Nazis and their collaborators that something like this happened. I was alone, praying in Hebrew, welcoming the Sabbath. I added a *shehechiyanu*, the blessing that expresses gratitude for being alive and having reached this moment. And then I asked Tatiana to take my picture. I wanted a record of this moment.

As I said the blessing, I sobbed. I am sure Tatiana knew what those tears meant.

Honorary Citizenship

On one of the days that I was in Dobromyl, the mayor asked me to meet him in the early afternoon at his office. Once again, I worked my way up the worn winding staircase to his office in Town Hall. Each time I walked those steps I wondered whether my grandfather or great-grandfather had any reason to walk those same steps. Perhaps they had to register their tinsmith business or one of the organizations they belonged to. I knew that my great-grandfather had been the president of the Dobromyl *Yad Charutzim* ("Hand of the Diligent"), a craftsman association. Perhaps he needed to go to Town Hall on some official business for the association.

I had no idea I was in for quite a surprise from the mayor. He took me to his car, and we drove no more than a few minutes to Dobromyl's music school. I had learned that the music school in Dobromyl had an excellent reputation in the region. When we arrived at another cramped and somewhat dilapidated building, I was met by the staff of the school and perhaps one hundred children. *They were there to offer a concert in my honor.*

For me, it might as well have been Carnegie Hall. And I was, as always, so moved by the beautiful face of each child. I was also quite impressed by the voices of the singers and the chorus, and the music performed by the children.

At one point, I recognized the piece they were playing. It was *Hatikvah* ("The Hope"), the Israeli national anthem. One of the female music instructors looked at me during the playing of the piece. She caught my eye and smiled. I knew what her smile was about. She, and the school, were saying "This one's for you." Hearing this song in the little town of Dobromyl brought tears to my eyes.

I had naïvely wondered many times whether the people of Dobromyl knew I was Jewish. One of the men in town, who I became friendly with, at one point said to me privately, "Arthur, everyone in town knows you and knows that you are Jewish."

I was also told of the poor condition of the instruments. They were in desperate need of new musical instruments worthy of the school's reputation. The director of the school pointed this out to me, and I thought that this was the motive for the concert in my honor – to buy new instruments for the school. And, in part, it may have been. But the next thing that happened was something the mayor knew would please me: I became an official honorary citizen of Dobromyl!

Perhaps I am crazy. Why would honorary citizenship in a small town in Ukraine where its Jews – 50% of the town's population before the Second World War – were destroyed, mean so much to me? It doesn't offer me any special rights or responsibilities. It is not something I would put on a resume or brief bio of myself. And it was not publicized, not even in Dobromyl, although I had learned that news travels quickly by word of mouth in this little town. I suspect there were very few, if any, other honorary citizens of Dobromyl, and if there were, I was almost surely the only Jew.

For many reasons, I thought so highly of the mayor. In this case, he knew just what would mean something to me. He knew there was no better way to acknowledge my generosity than to make my honorary citizenship official.

I ate a brief dinner with the mayor that evening and then went back to my room at the hotel. As always, I looked out my hotel window and looked at Kopika, the general store that was once my father's home. I would wonder what life may have been like for my father as a boy, and my uncle, aunt, grandmother, and grandfather.

On occasion, I would wonder just how many people I know who would think I was crazy – to be thrilled to be honored by the people of

The mayor of Dobromyl

a tiny, impoverished town where Jews were murdered, sometimes in the most horrible ways (is any murder not horrible?) a little more than a generation ago. It never crossed my mind that they were buttering me up to prepare for their next request for me to pay for something the children in town needed. I am convinced I was truly being honored. Yes, I have no doubt that part of the honor was due to my monetary

Looking out the window from the hotel to the
author's father's childhood house

contributions. But I also believe the people of the town were moved by my dedication to the children.

I believe something else was also going on. One of the people in the town, I believe it was Olexandra, said something to me one day that rang with truth: the people of the town were deeply moved that someone "out there in the world" remembered them. While the town had occasional visitors who had some family connection with Dobromyl, I was the only person who not only looked back but also forward in time. The children of Dobromyl needed a future, and I was someone who had decided to try to help make that happen. Before I came along, Dobromyl was just one of hundreds of towns in western Ukraine whose people felt isolated and forgotten. Now they had me – and everybody I knew – thinking about the poor people of Dobromyl and some of their needs. It was not much to offer me, but honorary citizenship acknowledged that I felt I was actually one of them.

I went to bed that night and slept soundly, drifting off to a deep sleep. But I woke up with a faint memory of a nightmare I had. I was on trial somewhere. A tribunal of three old Jewish men were deciding whether I was innocent or guilty of something. But during the nightmare I didn't know what the charges were against me. Lying in bed, trying to recuperate from the troubling dream, I was sure I knew: was I guilty for helping the Ukrainian people of Dobromyl?

After I showered and dressed I went downstairs to the empty dining room and sat at the table already set for me. My chair faced the window, where I could see my father's house, framed perfectly by the flowers around the dining room window. I sat and ate breakfast and savored every moment, both the fresh bread and butter and fresh fruit, as well as the view of my father's house.

And I was thinking about that tribunal. The image from the bad dream lingered. It was a tribunal of ancient-looking wise men who were judging my motives for my love affair with Dobromyl.

Why am I even thinking these things as though I'm on trial for treason? I don't need to stand in front of a tribunal. I knew that as much as the love affair with the town persisted, I felt a pull toward the grandchildren and great-grandchildren of very possibly some Ukrainian, Polish, and Russian murderers during the War. But the children are innocent. They are my neighbors.

Part VI

Searching for My Murdered Family

When we come to the other world and meet the millions of Jews who died in the camps and they ask us, "What have you done?" there will be many answers. You will say, "I became a jeweler." Another will say, "I smuggled coffee and American cigarettes." Another will say, "I built houses." But I will say, "I didn't forget you."

– Simon Wiesenthal

A Few Inches Below the Surface

We met on the lower level, the breakfast room, in the Swiss Hotel in Lviv. The Uber driver, Jerzy, gave me his contact information, so I called. He seemed friendly enough on the phone. I told him I was in Lviv, and I suggested perhaps we could meet. Lviv is the nearest airport to Dobromyl, and this was my second trip.

A charming hotel, with a friendly staff, the hotel also has a wine cellar and offered tours and tastings by appointment. I took advantage of this opportunity and booked a tour and tasting for that afternoon. I had recently learned of Gewürztraminer, an aromatic wine grape, white, slightly sweet, and delicious. And I was in luck. The wine cellar included excellent Gewürztraminer, and its marvelous taste prompted me to have it with dinner that evening. Wine, as I've learned, is not a beverage; it is an aesthetic experience.

I was sitting at a table in the breakfast room, listening to the classical music from the speakers around the room and sipping a glass of freshly squeezed orange juice taken from the far more than adequate buffet breakfast offerings. Precisely at 9:00 A.M. my guest – actually guests – arrived. I was only expecting a man, Robert as he identified himself, to meet me, but Robert brought his girlfriend, Jadwiga.

"I met Jadwiga while metal-detecting several years ago," Robert said while we got comfortable and introduced ourselves to each other at a relatively private corner table. "I saw her on the same field where I was searching, but we didn't know each other. All of a sudden Jadwiga let out a shout of joy. I ran over and saw what Jadwiga had found; it was a small pile of a dozen old coins. They had probably been in a pouch of some kind. There was a little evidence of that, but the coins were all in a small pile." Robert and Jadwiga spoke surprisingly good English.

Jadwiga took a small, leather-bound photo album out of her shoulder bag and showed me two photos of the coins. One photo was of the coins in the hole where they dug and found them; the other was a photo of all of the coins, cleaned off and spread out. Jadwiga said, "I sold the coins to a collector here in Lviv for $300 U.S. The buyer has an antique shop in Lviv."

When I asked Robert for his surname, he said he would rather not mention it. The laws concerning the legality of metal collecting are either ambiguous or rarely enforced, but to stay safe from any hassles, Robert was simply Robert. In fact, he later told me his name was not really Robert. To this day I do not know his real name. We each helped ourselves to the buffet breakfast and sat back down for the purpose of our meeting.

What does Robert sell? He is the middleman between people who metal detect and people who want what the metal detectors find. Mostly, Robert deals in coins. The Jewish items he finds or receives are now saved for me. Sometimes he gives me them as gifts and sometimes he charges me. I have become a good customer, and he doesn't have to look for buyers of Jewish items too often. He has me as a loyal purchaser.

"Do you do any metal detecting yourself now?" I asked Robert.

"I did several years ago, and I still go out searching from time to time. But people know I have a lot of customers, so they would rather sell what they find at a lower price than to take the time to find a buyer."

In addition to coins and jewelry, metal detectors also find their share of junk —mostly odd scraps of metal. Robert told me how a metal detector will generally toss pieces of scrap metal into a jar or can, separating the junk from the possibly valuable coins and other potential finds.

Robert then said, "I don't know exactly when it happened, and I certainly don't know who found it first, but at some point, someone discovered lots of 'junk' to actually be Jewish items." Word spread among many metal detectors, and those who knew Robert sold these items for a very low price.

"Were you able to bring any of these items this morning?" I asked Robert. He smiled sheepishly and then said, "Yes!" quite enthusiastically.

Robert then looked at Jadwiga and said, "Show him what we brought."

Jadwiga reached into her shoulder bag and withdrew a purple velvet drawstring bag. She handed the bag to Robert, who proceeded to dump the contents of the bag onto one of the napkins on our breakfast table. There were six items: five dreidels and what looked like a miniature chair about an inch high.

I knew about these dreidels. And I could easily see why someone not familiar with such an item might mistake it for a piece of lead junk. I was quite excited, and both Jadwiga and Robert saw the emotion on my face. My eyes were bulging, my face felt red from my excitement, and I couldn't take my eyes off the dreidels. I already owned one little dreidel, but five more would be a spectacular addition to my little collection.

"How much?" I asked.

"Nothing. It is a gift from us to you," Jadwiga said somewhat seriously.

Jadwiga and Robert were delighted by my reaction to their gifts. I now had a total of six lead dreidels. I held each of the five individually, examining them closely. Then I held all five in my hand. I laid them out on the table and then I almost went numb. I didn't know what to feel. Should I be happy to have these tiny remnants of Jewish life? Or should I be depressed to learn that the evidence of Jewish life I am looking for are little metal relics found by treasure hunters, a few inches underground?

I felt both joy and sadness holding these tiny dreidels. I was thrilled to see evidence of Jewish life in Ukraine, even if was from many decades in the past. But with each dreidel I held, I knew that it represented a life, probably a young life that had been snuffed out by the Nazis.

Since my emotions are usually not dictated by what I think I should

Miniature chair, part of an oil menorah

be feeling, I knew that I had a range of emotions simultaneously. At one extreme was my absolute fascination with these little items. These dreidels were, after all, held by Jewish hands, most probably children who played the dreidel game on Chanukah.

On the other hand, these Jewish "finds" under the ground represented a whole Jewish civilization. I came to Ukraine looking for evidence of Jewish life, and these little artifacts certainly testified to the Jewish life that once was. Of course, any way I looked at it, the whole thing was quite depressing, but for some reason I felt a dose of joy as I held these artifacts.

I then held the miniature chair and I was pretty sure I knew what it was. It was one of nine miniature chairs that come together to form a Chanukah menorah. Nine chairs created a complete Chanukah menorah. There was room for oil and a wick, and when lined up together, the tiny chairs formed a Chanukah menorah. Some say that the separate flames also served a practical purpose: if there was a hostile knock at the door, the candles could quickly be placed around the room and would appear to be a way to provide light to a room, not a way to celebrate Chanukah. I don't know if this is true.

Miniature chairs that form an oil menorah

I do know that my newfound friends, Jadwiga and Robert, were delighted to sell it to me. I paid them $25 for it. Jadwiga put the dreidels and the chair back into the pouch and handed it to me. As my collection grew over the years, I was able to acquire many such items. Some were only fragments, while others were in fairly pristine condition.

A side note worth explaining: Despite what the "Dreidel Song" says, dreidels were not made of clay. They were made of lead, and sometimes pewter – easy to make by melting the metal and pouring it into a mold. Apparently the word for lead did not rhyme properly with the next line of the song, so it was changed – for the sake of the rhyme – to "clay." Lead seals, about the size of a U.S. nickel, were melted down, attached to wire, and shaped in a way that it could be effectively used to seal a package securely, especially when it came to food. Packages that were kosher were labeled as such and were sealed to prevent opening the packages before delivery. I have many examples of these seals in my collection.

My collection of Jewish remnants has grown considerably since that first conversation with Jadwiga and Robert. I now have 5,000 pieces of metal artifacts in my collection: dreidels, miniature chairs that make up Chanukah menorahs, seals, pendants, jewelry, organizational pins, political pins, amulets of all shapes and sizes, and more.

The next item they showed me at our breakfast was an amulet. On the front of the amulet was the Hebrew letter *hey* representing the word *HaShem* (literally "the Name"), a synonym for the name of God. And on the back of the amulet was Hebrew text. The text reads:

Metal seals from the author's collection, including some that say "kosher"

Metal pendants (front) from the author's collection

*"May it be Your will, Hashem our God and the God of our ancestors,
that you rescue the infants of Your nation Israel, that diphtheria should
not afflict their mouths, and they should grow to a life of Torah, and may
You, in Your mercy, protect them. Amen."*

I looked at Jadwiga and Robert almost in disbelief. I held the amulet
and then, spontaneously, I kissed it. I had a strong suspicion that this
amulet, this good luck charm, may not have been effective. After all, it
was found in the ground, in an area that was once – but is no longer – a
Jewish neighborhood. In any case, this is what Robert explained. Often
people who do metal detecting will do their searching in a field that

Metal pendants (back) from the author's collection

used to be a road or a collection of houses. On what old road did the owner of this amulet drop or lose it? What was their ultimate fate?

This amulet would be the first of what would eventually become a large collection of dozens of Jewish amulets that I have acquired – all from metal detectors used by people in parts of Ukraine, Poland, Russia and Lithuania. I knew, of course, that each of the items in my collection of metal detector finds once belonged to Jewish people, and chances are likely that the owners were murdered. After all, most of the Jews in the western part of Ukraine and vicinity were murdered, either by a bullet or sledgehammer to the head or destruction in a death camp like Belzec. In my search for evidence of the Jewish world of Ukraine and Poland, I knew all too well that any evidence would be small – even tiny – remnants.

Metal seals, often used to secure kosher food packages

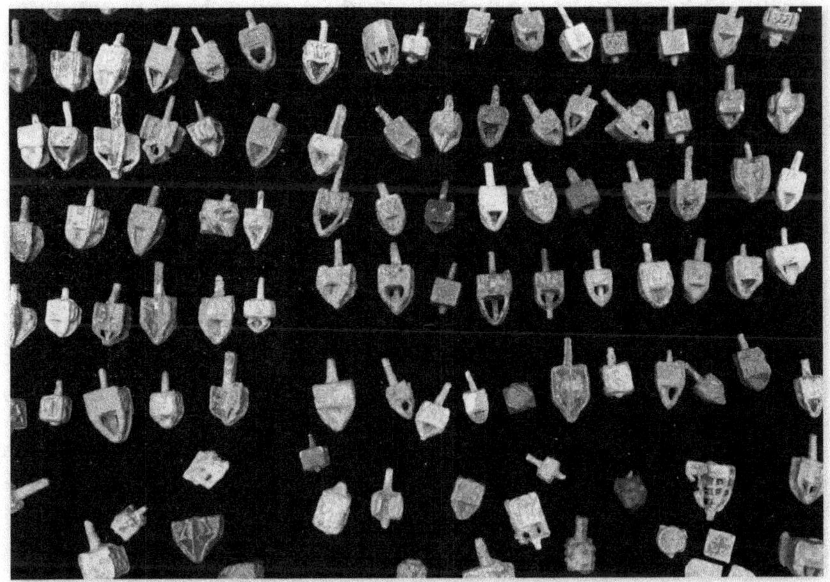

Dreidels from the author's collection

I looked at the amulet and mused over the situation I found myself in. There we were in a basement café of a small hotel in Ukraine. I was having breakfast with total strangers who were showing me Jewish objects discovered by metal detectors throughout Poland and Ukraine. The sellers don't know if the transaction is legal or not, although my research says it is legal because the value of the items is very low. For me, these items are priceless. In Poland or Ukraine, they are almost worthless.

Part of my search for signs of Jewish life was satisfied by these artifacts. After all, one of the purposes of my trips to Ukraine and Poland was to find evidence of my family. I had located the house where my father's family lived. These artifacts were not owned by my family, although sometimes I wonder if any of them were actually owned at one time by family members. But it wasn't enough for me. I was looking for something more; I just hadn't found it yet.

Toward the end of breakfast Robert said to me, "We have one more thing to show you." I waited patiently but eagerly as Jadwiga took a small envelope out of her shoulder bag. It was another amulet. This one was square and had the names of the Jewish patriarchs Abraham, Isaac and Jacob on it. Upon seeing and deciphering it, I got a little teary. Found underground in Ukraine was this handmade pendant of some sort, with the names of the biblical patriarchs on it. And in the middle of it was a Star of David with the letter *hey* engraved on it, signifying *HaShem*, another name for God.

Perhaps it was from a Jewish organization, or maybe it was simply a personal amulet. Whatever it was, I knew that I wanted it for my collection. As my collection of Jewish artifacts grew, I became aware of the power of them all being together rather than someone owning just one item.

"Would you like to buy it?" asked Robert.

"How much? I asked casually. I didn't want to seem too excited, figuring that the more excited I was, the higher the price.

"For the two amulets, $50."

I quickly said, "I accept."

Amulet with the names of Abraham, Isaac and Jacob (front and back)

Jadwiga put it back in the envelope and handed it to me. I handed her five U.S. $10 bills.

Robert then said it was time to go. We hugged goodbye and promised to be in touch. After that day I never saw Jadwiga or Robert again, but I have been in contact with Robert fairly regularly by email, as they find Jewish artifacts and offer them to me for sale. As for the dreidels, Robert often will send me a bunch of dreidels for free along with my purchase.

I had spent $75 and went home with five dreidels close to 100 years old, a chair-shaped piece that was part of a Chanukah menorah, and two amulets. This is not what I had in mind when I travelled to Ukraine to find evidence that my Jewish family lived in Dobromyl, but I had to have these items. They were all touched by Jews who perished, and I needed to save them.

Outrageous Love

visited Dobromyl, Ukraine, the birthplace of my father, eight times between September of 2016 and December of 2018. During that time, I never asked myself why. I thought I knew. But I truly didn't. And I still don't. Not really. Do I have to have a reason? Does there have to be some deep psychoanalytic motive?

I confess, as a believer in reincarnation, sometimes I wonder if I did something terribly wrong during a previous life in Dobromyl, and I needed to make amends. This is as plausible a reason as any I can come up with. I certainly did not do it for fame or glory. Until now, I have been perfectly satisfied with just a handful of people knowing about it. And even with this book, I know I am apt to get some bitter criticism from Jews who won't be able to understand why an American Jew, with over a hundred Holocaust victims on just one branch of my family, would want to embrace Ukrainians and Poles as friends.

What is it I could have believed that would motivate me to spend so much time and personal money to help this tiny town in western Ukraine where many people in my extended family and most of the other Jews were tortured and murdered?

But when I heard someone say, "The only response one can give to outrageous hatred is outrageous love," it resonated with me.

I went to visit the town where my father was born. After all, I heard him tell interesting stories about the town countless times as I was growing up. I could have planned a trip, visited the town for a few hours, looked around, and then left with a memory.

But when I arrived in Dobromyl for the very first time, I knew I had work to do there. If you encounter something broken you think you can fix, it is your job to do so. I saw Dobromyl as broken, physically and financially. It was not until I saw the faces of the children in town that I knew I had to try to help them, if only just a little, to grow up to live a full life. But why?

Was it my responsibility to sponsor the building of a playground and a park in the center of town? Was it my responsibility to create a GoFundMe campaign to collect thousands of dollars from my friends to get new computers, tablets, cameras, gymnasium equipment and other things for the school in Dobromyl? Did I have to personally fund the other projects in the town? I'm not a rich man by United States standards. But what I have I wanted to share with people in need.

Was there anything essential that I did? The town could have done without a playground and park, or a new awning for their soccer field, or indoor bathrooms for the young children. But I can't deny feeling I have really made a difference.

I certainly did not do any of this to make some kind of Jewish statement. I did not emphasize my Jewishness, though everyone in the town now knows me and knows I am a Jew. Do Jews owe Dobromyl anything anyway? Hardly. If there are reparations due, they should be coming from Dobromyl.

But I know one thing: in the depths of it all, I was looking for Abusch, my great-grandfather, after whom I was named. He was born

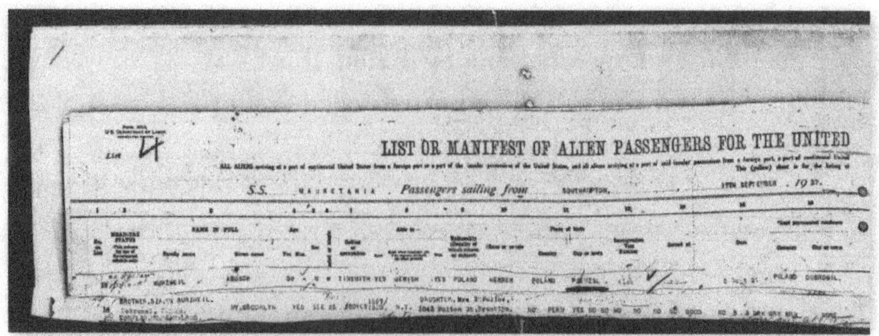

A fragment of the steamship passenger list with the author's great-grandfather recorded on the list

in what is now Ukraine and he died in New York, but for some reason I felt I would find him within me. I had this mystical sense that he and I would somehow finally merge into one person.

Kroscienko

Although my great-grandparents, my grandparents and my father all lived in Dobromyl (pronounced "Doh-**broh**-meal"), I learned, through my research, that the family originated in the nearby village of Kroscienko (pronounced "Crow-shee-**en**-koh"). A small village in southeastern Poland, I found a reference to it online. It was included in an old Polish business directory published in 1880.

In that directory, I found the name of my great-great-grandfather, Saul Kurzweil, who owned the tobacco shop in the center of the village. As is traditional in Jewish families, my father was named after his great-grandfather, Saul Kurzweil (1841–1897), just as I was named after Saul Kurzweil's son, my great-grandfather, Abusch Kurzweil (1867–1950).

It was suggested to me by a man I met in Dobromyl that there was a woman in Kroscienko who owned a coffee shop and was the unofficial village historian. She might be able to help me in my search. When I arrived in Kroscienko my driver, who knew Polish and Ukrainian and some English, asked someone on the street for directions, and he easily located the coffee shop. He waited in the car while I went in.

The proprietor of the shop was described to me as an exceptionally friendly person. She operated her coffee shop in a converted old barn, a rather charming, rustic place with an unfinished ceiling and exposed beams.

I introduced myself to the young woman and we greeted each other warmly. I suspected that not too many Jews ever come to Kroscienko.

The woman, with rosy cheeks and a pretty face, invited me to sit down. She brought me a cup of tea and some cookies, and told me, with a pained expression, that when the Nazis arrived in the village, they rounded up every Jewish family – about 200 people. All of them – men, women and children – were taken across the river that ran through the village and were shot. They are buried in a mass grave.

She also knew exactly where my great-great-grandfather's tobacco shop had been. Unfortunately, there is nothing to see today. Now it is just an empty plot of land, located at the intersection of two narrow main roads at the center of Kroscienko.

As I sipped my tea, I asked her if there were any remnants of Jewish life in Kroscienko, and with a sad face she said, in broken English, "There is a small memorial plaque at the spot where the massacre took place. I am afraid that is all there is."

I asked her where the plaque was and she said, "Go to the road, turn right and then walk across the river on the small bridge and then turn left into the forest. You will need to walk through the forest – it will take you about 15 minutes – and eventually you will see it. You will be walking close to the river."

It had rained that morning, but by the afternoon the sun was shining. I asked my driver to wait for me. I wanted to go in myself. The dark, silent forest was drying out. My sneakers got wet but otherwise it was dry. For me, it was a 20-minute walk on a rather narrow dirt path in between the lush, crowded trees. It was a little frightening, but I was too eager to see the memorial plaque to worry about it.

Suddenly, I walked into a clearing. I found the plaque. It was set in the ground. Engraved on it was a list of the surnames of Jewish families who were murdered and then buried in one mass grave.

I quickly glimpsed the list of names and I immediately saw my family name – Kurzweil. I began to cry. I cry easily, but this was different. I was sobbing.

I was standing on the very spot where my family from Kroscienko was destroyed.

Fucking Nazis!

Memorial plaque marking the site of the murder of 200
Jews from Kroscienko by Nazi forces in 1942

Kisielow

There was an underground organization in Poland after the Holocaust called the National Military Union. It was a Polish anti-Communist organization founded in November 1944. It is known that there were 16 units of this organization throughout Poland, and that several units were still active until the mid-1950s. It was also known to be one of the largest resistance organizations in post-war Soviet-controlled Poland. In the first half of 1945, it is documented that they perpetrated violence on surviving Jews in, among other places, Kisielow, Poland, where a branch of th Kurzweil family lived – and were murdered.

A highly regarded Polish scholar, Joanna Tokarska-Bakir, who completed her research on Kisielow in 2021, has documented a horrible incident there concerning my family. She based her research primarily on holdings in the Polish Institute of National Remembrance whose mission, since 1917, has been to research and disseminate the modern history of Poland and to investigate crimes committed from the date of its founding through the Holocaust, and up to the Communist period until July 31, 1990.

My family lived in several towns and villages near the borders of Poland and Ukraine. One of the villages where a branch of the Kurzweil family lived was Kisielow. My great-great-great grandparents, Eli and Machle Kurzweil, gave birth to three sons there: Harry, Saul and Yitzchok. I descend from Saul.

Harry Kurzweil and his wife Pessia lived in Kisielow. They had 10 children. Harry died there, at home, in 1892. Some of their children died before World War I. One of their daughters, Czelle Jutte, know as Gelita, was born in 1915 and died in 1935. Gelita Kurzweil had married Moshe Schlaf. They had seven children, one of whom was Saul Schlaf, who married Tauba Szyfman in 1929.

Saul and Tauba had three children. They were all murdered, in 1946, after the Second World War had already ended. During the Holocaust, they survived by hiding from the Nazis, but when the war ended, they returned to their home in Kisielow. One journalist, investigating the incident, quoted a local witness as saying, "They told them to prostrate into the shape of a Jewish star and then they shot them all." Murdered them – after the war was over!

The Schlaf/Kurzweil family were murdered by members of the National Military Union, who were known to cover up their murder of Jews by calling the Jews Communists collaborators. However, they murdered the Schlaf/Kurzweil children as well.

My cousin Josef Schlaf, who survived the Holocaust as a soldier in the Polish Army in exile, wrote a letter in 1961 to the Office for Complaints and Petitions at the Ministry of Internal Affairs and to the Head of the County Office of Public Security (*Powiatowy Urząd Bezpieczeństwa Publicznego*, PUBP) in Jarosław. The letter read:

"In 1945 in the village of Cieszacin Mały (Kisielów), Jarosław county, my family was murdered:

"Saul Schlaf [b. 1898, son of Gitla and Mosze], Tauba Schlaf [aka Tonka, née Szyfman, b. 1900 in Rożniatów], Józef Schlaf [aged 14], Fajga Schlaf [daughter of Tauba's relatives] and two other children [Chaim, aged 16, and Estera, aged 4 or 7, both of them the Schlafs' children]. For years I have been demanding information from the security authorities as to whether the perpetrators of this crime have been apprehended and punished."

While the crimes were officially acknowledged, there was never any evidence that the guilty individuals were found and brought to justice.

An investigation occurred in the 1960s. One witness said, "On March 1, 1945, around eight in the evening, I had accompanied the

Kisielow town border

Schlafs' daughter home, and a quarter of an hour later I heard a wagon approach from the direction of Cieszacin." The perpetrators "came on two wagons from Zarzecze in high spirits, and one of them was playing the accordion." The witness went on to say that the attackers surrounded the Schlafs' house, forced their way into an apartment, "ordered all those present to lie down with their faces to the floor," and then shot and killed seven Jews.

Another eyewitness said that one of the attackers demanded the victims hand over their money and jewelry. One of the victims replied, "We have no jewelry on us." They beat up the Jews, who were lying helplessly on the floor. The attackers began to kicked their faces and broke their fingers. The witness said one could hear the cries and begging of those who were alive to let them live.

One witness said that the attackers then demanded money, which the Schlafs gave them. The attackers murdered them all and stole their clothes and other belongings. They also killed two pigs and a cow and stole them as well. One witness said, "Other than the pig, there were such things on the wagon as clothes, fur coats, bedspreads, quilts, a feather-stuffed duvet, pillows, boots, and head scarves, all covered with a tarpaulin. The pillaged things were divided. I saw personally how [one man] carried a large fur coat over his arm, hemmed with black cloth, which he hid in the barn. Someone stole this coat from him; he even suspected his brother, and there was bad blood between them for some time. The following day I saw two green bedspreads that one of the murderer's wives was airing. From the things on the wagon, from the robbery, the wife received two green bedspreads, some sheets, a duvet, fur vests hemmed with black cloth, red fur jackets with sleeves, and head scarves."

Dr. Joanna Tokarska-Bakir wrote in her research:

> "The Kisielów perpetrators were religious people, as indicated by numerous records of personal searches revealing that they had rosaries and scapular medals on them and the fact that they went to confession The... partisans were in good relations with the parish priest... The priest harbored the bandits and was aware of their raids. We do not know if he approved of the latter but he probably gave the penitents absolution (we know that the perpetrators went to confession around Easter). They were also aided by the local organist, the monks of the Virgin Mary Monastery in Jarosław, and the Leżajsk monks."

Rabbi Elimelech

One day, on the way to Przemysl, in Poland, I asked my driver to go to the town of Lizhensk. I saw from a map that it was not too far out of the way, and I was eager to visit the grave of Rabbi Elimelech of Lizhensk.

Rabbi Elimelech was born in 1717 and he died in 1787. He was a *Chasidic* leader just two generations removed from the Baal Shem Tov, the founder of Chasidism. After the Baal Shem Tov, the Maggid of Mezerich took over the leadership of the *Chasidic* Movement, and his students included Rabbi Elimelech and his older brother, Reb Zusha. Many stories and legends exist about the two brothers, who were said to roam the countryside dressed as simple, poor Jews. The people they encountered never recognized the two saintly brothers.

One famous legend about Reb Zusha is this: When he was on his deathbed he said, "I am not afraid that the Almighty will ask me why I was not Moses. I am afraid He will ask me why I was not Zusha."

My favorite story, perhaps the most profound *Chasidic* story I ever heard, is about two students who were studying Talmud. The Talmud says that just as there are blessings to say upon experiencing each of the joys of life, there is a blessing to say on suffering. The students were confused and asked the rebbe, the Maggid of Mezrich, why there is a blessing on experiencing suffering. The Maggid suggested they go ask Reb Zusha; he would know. So, they went to Reb Zusha, who was poor and sickly, and asked him. Reb Zusha said, "I don't know why the Rebbe sent you to me. I never had an occasion to say that blessing!"

When I arrived in Lizhensk, it was easy to locate Rabbi Elimelech's grave. A local person walking on a dirt road knew exactly where it is located. After all, the Rebbe's grave is a popular pilgrimage spot. In fact, when we arrived there were a handful of Orthodox Jews davening (praying) at the grave. The grave of the rebbe was really an *ohel*, in this case a little house protecting the grave. On and around the grave marker was a pile of *kvitlach* – petitionary prayers from visitors to the grave.

I borrowed a prayer book from a small bookcase to the side of the grave and I began to daven. My prayers were mostly personal. I ad-libbed rather than read from the prayer book for most of my prayer session.

> There is a tradition among Torah scholars and pious individuals that Rabbi Elimelech of Lizhensk guaranteed he would help anyone who prayed at his grave, just as he had helped whoever came to him when he was alive. Furthermore, that person would not leave this world without having repented. The number of people praying at Rabbi Elimelech's grave each year on his yahrzeit continues to grow. Even Kohanim, who are unable to approach the grave themselves, send emissaries in their stead.... People asked Rabbi Elazar, the son of Rabbi Elimelech of Lizhensk, if his father left an ethical will after his passing. Rabbi Elazar replied: "If you want to read my father's will, look into his work Noam Elimelech. Although he delivered its teachings twenty-two years before his death, I know for a fact that he looked upon each day of his life as if it were his last.
>
> – Ohel Elimelech, Rabbi Avraham Chaim
> Simcha Michaelson, Premishlan, 1910.

I had been to a rebbe's grave before. When the Lubavitcher Rebbe died (and was buried in a Jewish cemetery in Queens, New York), Rabbi Steinsaltz asked me to take him to the grave for a visit. The grave is only about a 10- to 15-minute drive from JFK Airport.

I have been with Rabbi Steinsaltz a few dozen times. I didn't know how to behave at the grave of a *tzaddik*, so I just watched Rabbi Steinsaltz carefully and I imitated what he did. The first thing he did was to take a piece of paper and a pen, to sit down at one of several long table set up for just this purpose, and to write a letter to the deceased rebbe. I didn't know what to write, so I simply wrote a list of names of living people for whom I requested a blessing.

Peeking over at Rabbi Steinsaltz's *kvitl* as he wrote it, I saw that it looked much more like a letter. My paper was filled with a long list of people, including family members and close friends. I "asked" the Rebbe to join in my prayers for all good things for these people in my life.

Rabbi Steinsaltz finished his letter and walked over to a pile of rubber slippers. He took off his shoes and put on a rubber pair. I did the same. It is a custom not the wear leather shoes in a cemetery. This is because the grave of a *tzaddik* is considered to be holy and pure. Leather shoes are traditionally considered an earthly luxury and therefore inappropriate for a holy gravesite. This tradition goes back to the command to Moses when he approached the Burning Bush: "Remove your shoes from your feet, for the place on which you stand is holy ground" (*Exodus* 3:5).

Rabbi Steinsaltz and I then made our way outside on to a path leading to the Lubavitcher Rebbe's grave (as well as the grave of the previous rebbe, who was the Rebbe's father-in-law.)

It was only a 30-second walk to the grave, but it offered me enough time to say to Rabbi Steinsaltz, "Do you think this works?" referring to the writing of a *kvitl* addressed to the rebbe. Rabbi Steinsaltz said, "It can't hurt."

Once in front of the grave, the custom is to read the *kvitl* quietly and then rip it up and place it on the pile of *kvitlach* already there. Rabbi Steinsaltz told me that when he comes to the U.S. from Israel his pockets are filled with *kvitlach* from other people in Israel who would like Rabbi Steinsaltz to read them on their behalf in front of the Lubavitcher Rebbe's grave. Once a person finishes reading his or her *kvitlach* and reciting prayers that they have chosen, one leaves the inner chamber of the ohel and passes through the outer chamber where there are shelves with tealights. The custom is to light a candle

The author davens at the ohel of Rabbi Elimelech

on your way out (or on your way in). Outside there are spigots where a visitor to the grave can wash their hands ritually, as is the custom upon leaving a cemetery.

Rabbi Steinsaltz and I went back into the building which serves as an entrance to the cemetery, found our shoes, left our rubber shoes, and then we parted. But not before I took a few delicious home baked cookies that are always there for the taking.

Sometimes it's hard to know what is real and what is imagined. But I felt something unusual at the grave of Rabbi Elimelech. The vibes were palpable. Perhaps it was my imagination; perhaps it was my secret desire to feel something special there. It's not like me to manufacture any kind of mystical feelings, but not because I am not a believer in such things. Rather, it's the opposite. I *do* believe that a grave of a holy person that has been visited by countless people over the decades can feel special. It is because of this belief that I don't feel the need to make something up. The grave of the Lubavitcher Rebbe, for example, has an aura of sanctity that many people have reported feeling.

Dobromyl's Prison

once thought the Holocaust was simple: the Nazis murdered six million Jews. But...

Generalizations are always wrong.

I found this piece of wisdom among the pages of testimony I discovered regarding the massacre in Dobromyl in June 1941, in the book *Killing Sites – Research and Remembrance*, by the International Holocaust Remembrance Alliance (2015, Metropol Verlag + IHRA). I have been trying to make sense of that massacre. But what do I know about history?

The massacre in the prison in 1941 was not a Nazi action but a Soviet action ordered by Stalin. The *murderers* were also Ukrainians, Poles and Jews.

Of course, I don't want to believe this. Could Jews have murdered Jews, and others, during this massacre? But this is what the history says. It was a battle of Communists against those who wanted to maintain privatization.

Not everyone was in favor of the life that communism promised: *From each according to his abilities; to each according to his needs.* The goal of the Soviets was to get rid of those who wanted to hold on to privatization. In other words, they were to be murdered.

Order 270, issued by Stalin, declared that all Soviet military were to fight "to the end." Surrender was forbidden under any circumstances. Desertion, of course, was also unthinkable. Murder or be murdered. There was no other choice offered by Stalin.

I feel certain I would have been against the Communist revolution. I believe in capitalism and the freedom it defends and maintains. Milton Friedman's book, *Capitalism and Freedom*, had a big impact on me when I was studying for my Bachelor of Arts degree. In the book, Friedman argues that economic freedom is a precondition for political freedom.

*   *   *

The NKVD, translated as the People's Commissariat for Internal Affairs, was essentially the Soviet secret police. Among their activities were mass arrests, deportations, and executions. Between 1940 and 1941, they murdered political prisoners numbering in the tens of thousands.

It was June 1941 when a massacre, initiated by these secret police, happened at a prison located in Dobromyl. In this overcrowded prison, there were political prisoners from Dobromyl and from elsewhere in the vicinity. They were imprisoned because of their political beliefs.

The events in that prison were witnessed by many people who offered testimony. Some of these witnesses offer the following:

The prison was designed to hold between 60 and 70 inmates. In 1941, the terribly crowed prison held nearly 1,000 prisoners. The conditions were obviously horrendous.

Prisoners were stripped of their clothing and often shot in the prison hallways.

Some witnesses survived by faking their deaths after being shot.

Sometimes they were thrown into a pit filled with corpses but managed to pretend to be dead, escaping after nightfall.

If it wasn't horrible enough, sometimes prisoners were murdered not by bullets but by their heads being smashed by a heavy sledge-hammer. The prisoners' heads were often put on a chopping block and bashed in. When the governor of the prison protested this method, he was shot and killed by members of the secret police.

Even secretaries, with no political opinions, were murdered at the prison simply because they were Jewish.

Sometimes prisoners were murdered by being stabbed with bayonets.

There was also the almost inconceivable torture of breasts of women and genitals of men being severed.

Prisoners who were beaten to death had to wear gags to silence their screams.

Desperately, after the abject slaughter, family members tried to identify their murdered relatives.

As painful as it is to report, in Dobromyl there were Jews who collaborated with the Soviet secret police.

* * *

Lev, a new friend, lives in Great Britain with his wife, but he is originally from Dobromyl. He has family living in Dobromyl and visits them as often as possible. Lev was in Dobromyl during one of my trips, and he offered to walk with me through the town as he pointed out various sites.

He showed me where the main synagogue once stood (the Nazis burned it to the ground with 200 Jews inside).

He showed me the site of the large lumber mill where murders of Jews by Nazis took place.

We walked to the river, and I told Lev about my father and his recollection of the river.

And Lev showed me the location of the prison and took me inside the building. It is now used as offices. Lev introduced me to three women in one of the offices. They knew who I was, and they knew why I had come to their building. There is really nothing to see any longer, but I knew that the space itself reeks of the almost indescribable memories.

I knew that from the very hallways where I walked in that building bodies were taken out and buried in a large pit dug in the building's back yard.

I walked that staircase, and I climbed down to that yard.

I listened intensely to the silence in the yard, wondering if I could hear an echo of screams from the tortures, or the sounds of the bullets of the firing squads. But I heard nothing. I just stood in the middle of the yard in silence, wondering if any people in my family were among the victims.

There was a slight drizzle that day.

Salina

June 22 is a solemn day in Dobromyl. It is on that day when citizens from Dobromyl walk to nearby Salina, the scene of the most horrible massacre I have ever learned about. My mind cannot contain the horror.

I ask you, dear reader, to think twice about reading this chapter. What is the need to learn the details about atrocities?

Do the details serve any constructive purpose other than becoming the content for nightmares and day terrors?

It was in June 1941, after the Germans attacked the Soviet Union, that several hundred Poles, Ukrainians and Jews were murdered.

When the Nazis attacked the Soviet Union, the Soviets captured thousands of prisoners. This created a problem for the Soviets: what to do with the prisoners? They found a solution: the mass execution of their political enemies. Victims in and around Dobromyl included students, teachers, businessmen and even priests. The membership of patriotic clubs were also among the victims. All of them were taken to the nearby Salina salt mine.

What did the Soviets and their local supporters do? The Soviets smashed their prisoner's heads with sledgehammers (in order to avoid a shortage of bullets). Some victims were wrapped in barbed wire and thrown into the mineshaft. In cases where the sledgehammer blow did not kill its victim, they were thrown alive into the mineshaft and died of suffocation as the bodies piled up. Men, women, and children.

Most of the victims were intellectuals and activists (against Communism and the effort of Soviet domination of the region.) They refused to recognize the authority of the Soviet Union. Their bodies were thrown into the salt mine; a 100-meter pit was crammed with murdered bodies. Among the dead, residents identified 50 children.

Based on oral testimony, we know a lot of details about this location and its torturous deaths.

Prisoners from as far away (15 miles) as Przemysl were marched to Dobromyl to be murdered and thrown into the salt mine. If they passed someone on the way who protested, they were pulled into the line as well.

People were afraid to follow the marching prisoners. In time, a putrid stench filled the air. Engines were turned on by the perpetrators to drown out the sounds of the murders.

On June 27, 1941, people living in Dobromyl discovered this salt mine used as a burial site.

On occasion, bodies were pulled out of the mineshaft by local people to provide a normal enough burial, but often victims' faces had been eaten away by the salt brine. Sometimes body parts were taken from the mineshaft. Bodies were lined up and relatives tried to identify the bodies. When the terribly foul order was too much for the murderers to bear, the Nazis forced workers to close the shaft by cementing it shut.

Over the years, 3,600 bodies have been discovered. Each year on June 22, people from Dobromyl offer a religious service and march from the town to the location of the mineshaft.

Neighbors Kill Neighbors

In an almost desperate attempt to gain at least some understanding of why Jews were betrayed or murdered by their neighbors in Dobromyl, I buried myself in four books for several days:

The Towns of Death: Pogroms Against Jew By Their Neighbors by Miroslaw Tryczyk (Lexington Books, 2021)

Intimate Violence: Anti-Jewish Pogroms on the Eve of the Holocaust by Jeffrey S. Kopstein and Jason Wittenberg (Cornell University, 2018)

The Shoah in Ukraine: History, Testimony, Memorialization edited by Ray Brandon and Wendy Lower (Indiana University Press, 2008. Published in association with the United States Holocaust Memorial Museum)

The Great West Ukrainian Prison Massacre of 1941: A Sourcebook edited by Ksenya Kiebuzinski and Alexander Motyl (Amsterdam University Press, 2017)

Chapter 1 in the book *Intimate Violence: Anti-Jewish Pogroms on the Eve of the Holocaust* is titled "Why Neighbors Kill Neighbors." The authors list five possible reasons that might have compelled Ukrainians in many towns to murder their neighbors. The first is that Jews were seen as a political threat as indicated by growing Jewish nationalism. The second was also a political threat, reflected by Jews becoming one of several competing ethnically tolerant parties. The third was economic competition. The fourth was pure antisemitism (i.e., "Jews killed Jesus"). And the fifth was revenge against some Jews who were involved with Communism.

Not being satisfied, I read these four books carefully.

I went on to explore countless websites and chapters of other books.

I watched YouTubes on the subject of the Holocaust.

I listened to symposia on the subject.

I read books and articles on betrayal, forgiveness, neighbors.

I studied commentaries on the Biblical teaching, "Love thy neighbor."

I spent hours meditating on these things.

I prayed to God for insight and understanding.

I tried to put myself in the place of those who killed their neighbors or identified them as Jews to the Nazis.

I consulted professors.

I asked experts.

I studied the observations and theories of psychologists.

I inquired of historians.

I spoke to rabbis and theologians.

I discussed these matters with friends.

I searched for more books online.

I thought I would eventually reach some understanding.

One night I had a dream. The Nazis entered my town looking for Christians. They knocked on my door and insisted I identify the houses in the neighborhood where Christians lived. They said that if I didn't tell them, they would shoot my three children in front of me. I suddenly woke up. I was shaking and soaked with perspiration. And then I wept.

And I stopped my search for understanding.

The Cellar

Tatiana, who owned both the hotel and the convenience store Kopika (formerly my father's house), was excited one day when I returned from a walk around town. I walked with great confidence by then, my fourth or fifth visit to Dobromyl, knowing how everyone in town knew who I was by then. Tatiana's daughter Marika had just arrived from Lviv with her husband. They were waiting for me in the hotel hallway on the ground floor.

Marika was a journalist, the editor of an online publication with news and feature stories about Lviv and vicinity (including Dobromyl). Months earlier she had written the story about the sidewalk made from Jewish gravestones and the plans for building the Wall of Memory, and it was the information in this article which ultimately put me in touch with Mr. Rubinfeld, involving me in the project. Marika and I had become friends on Facebook and sent greetings to each other from time to time. In addition, I took her and her husband out to dinner one evening in Lviv, and after dinner I performed a magic show for them at the table as curious waiters looked on. Marika spoke a little English, which also helped a lot.

"My mother has something to show you," Marika said somewhat mischievously. Tatiana was holding a large old key. It actually looked somewhat ancient to me.

"Do you know what this is?" Marika asked, as though it was a riddle.

"It's a key," I said." A very old key."

"Yes," said Marika. "It is the original key to the Kopika building. My mother found it in the house a long time ago." Marika didn't go so far as to say that it was the key to my grandparent's home, but this was surely implied.

My eyes lit up, and I could see that both Tatiana and Marika thought that I wanted Tatiana to give it to me. Tatiana said something to Marika and Marika proceeded to say that it is an antique and Tatiana wanted to keep it. Somewhat disingenuously I said, "Of course. She should keep it. It is hers."

But Tatiana must have felt a little guilty, as though she had teased me by showing it to me, and she quickly said that she wanted to show me something that nobody but she is permitted to see. Tatiana went into the kitchen and brought out a key ring filled with keys, and found the one she was looking for. "My mother wants to show you the cellar of this building. Nobody ever goes down there except for my mother. She keeps old wine there."

Tatiana opened the door that was also off the same hallway we were all standing in. "Be careful of the stairs," Marika warned, again interpreting for her mother. "It is very dark down there."

It was the staircase to the original cellar before the hotel was built on top of it. My father had told me that one of his uncles and his uncle's family Eli and Dobroh Kurzweil and their three children) lived across the street in the basement. I had always naively imagined it to be like a finished basement, with a floor, walls, and a ceiling, but I was hardly ready for what I saw.

Tatiana and I walked down the steep, dark stairs and arrived at the bottom. She then found a hanging string connected to a lightbulb. She pulled on the string, and a dim bulb barely lit the room. There was no finished floor; it was pounded earth.

The ceiling was very low; a tall person would have to bend down to walk in it. The room was damp and cold; and there were no windows! The walls were unfinished cement. A small alcove existed off the main room. A large old wooden wine rack holding dusty bottles of wine stood against the wall.

After getting a sense of the place, in seconds I realized where I was:

the home of my great uncle (a brother of my grandfather) and aunt and their three children. I knew they lived in poverty but I was not prepared for the dingy, cold, cramped, damp, windowless basement room where Tatiana had led me. After being there for no more than 60 seconds, I said, "I go," to Tatiana, signaling that I had enough and was going back up the stairs.

The author's great-aunt, Dobroh, great-uncle Eli, and their children.

When I arrived on the main floor, I could tell on Tatiana's face that she was not sure bringing me down there was a smart thing to do. But I think she was trying to show me an authentic piece of my family history that nobody ever sees. I think she was trying to say that she well understood the conditions my family lived in.

I will never forget that little basement room, where five of my relatives barely lived before they were murdered by the Nazis.

Belzec II

During one of my trips to Dobromyl, when I was still in Poland, my driver asked me if I wanted to see Belzec.

"Is it far?" I asked. I didn't want to make any special effort, but had read that there is now a museum where there used to be nothing – as I had previously discovered.

"Not far," the driver answered.

So, we went to Belzec.

We arrived at Belzec and parked the car in front of what is now a museum. In 2004, Belzec was established as a branch of the Majdanek State Museum, founded in the Fall of 1944. It was the first museum in the world dedicated to the memory of atrocities.

I took a several steps towards the entrance of the museum, but I suddenly stopped. I ran back to my driver, who waited in the car, and I said, "I can't go in there."

Before he even had a chance to respond, I said, "No, I'll go in." I turned and I walked in the direction of the museum, and again I suddenly stopped. It was as though something was getting in my way, some invisible force field.

Once again, I ran back to the car and told the driver, "I cannot go in."

But then once again I said to the driver, "I need to go in – to pay my respects to the many relatives of mine who were gassed, burned and pulverized in Belzec."

So, I tried a third time, but as soon as I reached the point where I had stopped a few minutes before, I froze. I couldn't walk another step.

I actually felt as though hundreds of thousands of Jewish souls were occupying the large space leading to the doorway. It was packed with suffering souls, preventing me from going any further.

"I had enough," I said to my driver. "Let's please get away from here."

I sometimes still tremble at the thought of my attempted visit to that place.

The Dobromyl train station from where Jews were sent to Belzec

Atrocities in Dobromyl

"Tell me every detail
I've got to know it all,
And do you have a picture of the pain?"

Phil Ochs "The Crucifixion"

There are no people living in Dobromyl right now who have any direct connection to the Holocaust. It has been 80 years since the Nazis first entered the area in June of 1941. If anyone in the town is 90 years old today, they would have been 10 when the Nazis arrived.

Nobody in Dobromyl today is guilty as a collaborator. Even an adult who is 50 years old was born in 1961 (I was in the fourth grade).

There is nobody I could consider to be *them* or *they*. Poles and Ukrainians were also victims – of the Nazis and the Russian Communists. The local people today have their own suffering to endure. I would assume few people in Dobromyl are aware that before the war (wwii) half of the town population was Jewish.

Are there any people in Dobromyl today who descend from anti-Semites? Undoubtedly so. Do they hate me? I think not. Certainly, it is easy to imagine that adults today could think poorly of Jews. These kinds of prejudices tend to be sustained in families. There is the phenomenon of antisemitism without Jews.

Jews. Poles. Ukrainians. Russians. I can't keep track of them all. Eastern Ukraine. Western Ukraine. Southeastern Poland. Austrian Empire. Przemysl. Belzec. Nazis. The People's Commissariat for Internal Affairs (NKVD).

My head is spinning from the history of Dobromyl. Should I master the chronology? Will it teach me anything? Do I need to learn who killed whom? Who betrayed whom?

I read of many atrocities in Dobromyl. Caught between the Russian Communists, who were murdering intellectuals, and the Nazis, who were murdering everyone, how do I make sense of it all? Is there any sense to any of it? Can I keep track of whose side people were on? Can I understand the cruelty, the inhumanity?

The descriptions of the atrocities break my heart. They are unthinkable. Should I repeat them here so that you will also carry around mental images of horrible deaths? I think not. Learning the details is itself a kind of torture. I don't want to torture the reader. From time to time I recall some of the details I have uncovered through my research. Sometimes I can't get the images out of my head. To be honest, this chapter of this book was filled with many descriptions of atrocities in Dobromyl and during the Holocaust. When reviewing the manuscript, I reread the descriptions, highlighted them, and in one quick moment it was all deleted.

Letychiv and Medzhybizh

Bobby Kurzweil, the author's wife, at the road sign for
her maternal grandmother's town of Letychiv

My wife, Bobby, descends, in part, from Ukraine, so one day we travelled to the two towns where her maternal grandparents were born, Letychiv and Medzhybizh. Bobby's grandmother was from Letychiv and her grandfather was from Medzhybizh. Our driver and guide was familiar with both towns.

First, he took us to the Jewish cemetery in Letychiv. Like most Jewish cemeteries in Ukraine and Poland, the cemetery of Letychiv was filled with broken gravestones, missing gravestones, and overgrown shrubbery making it almost impossible to read any of the inscriptions on the stones.

A Jewish Cemetery in Letychiv

Within moments of our arrival in the cemetery, a woman appeared who identified herself as a local Jewish resident. She demanded to know why we had entered the land of the Jewish cemetery. She wasn't unfriendly but rather protective of the place. She explained that she knew the cemetery was in terrible disrepair but wanted to prevent any more destruction of the few gravestones remaining there. When we identified ourselves as Jews, and when we indicated that Bobby's maternal grandmother lived there before the Holocaust, the woman changed her tone and was quite friendly.

Bobby indicated to the woman (through the translations provided by our driver and guide) that she grew up on stories of Letychiv. Especially vivid were the stories Bobby was told about the puddles in the muddy roads and the source of fresh water in the town. Bobby's grandmother told her, "I bathed in the same water where the Baal Shem Tov bathed." Letychiv and Medzhybizh are close to each other, and the same source of water flowed through them. Remarkably, as we walked down the road, first passing the remains of the local synagogue and mikvah (also remembered by Bobby's maternal grandmother), we walked around puddles still there in the muddy street.

Bobby with a local Jewish woman in Letychiv

Bobby grabbed her phone and called her mother, who was in New York. What a magical moment it was as Bobby and her mother spoke on the phone as we made progress walking down the muddy street of their ancestors, the same steps Bobby's grandmother had taken so many times.

At the end of the road, we encountered the very body of water that Bobby's grandmother had spoken of. When we arrived there, we noticed that a few of the local residents were filling jugs with the fresh water flowing from a spring. It was the very same source of fresh water that Bobby's grandmother recalled from her childhood. Bobby was amazed: it was as if nothing had changed over the many decades since

The remains of the synagogue in Letychiv

her family lived there. Nothing except, of course, that the once Jewish town now had just a few Jews and a destroyed synagogue, destroyed mikvah, and Jewish cemetery.

After a short time, we bid farewell to the Jewish woman and Bobby handed her some American money as a gift. It was clear that the money Bobby offered made a difference for the woman. We then said our tearful goodbyes. And we were off to Medzhybizh.

Bobby Kurzweil at the road sign for Mezhbizh, home
of Bobby Kurzweil's material grandfather

Of the two towns, Medzhybizh was the more well-known of the two. In fact, Medzhybizh has been a pilgrimage destination for many thousands of Jews over the centuries. It is the town where the founder of the Chasidic movement, Rabbi Israel, known famously as the Baal Shem Tov is buried. He died on May 22, 1760. Pilgrims often travel to the grave of the Baal Shem Tov, offering their most heartfelt prayers

Synagogue of the Baal Shem Tov in Mezhbizh

with the hope that the soul of the Baal Shem Tov will bring the prayers to the Heavenly Throne itself.

As Bobby and I stood before the grave of the Baal Shem Tov, I confess I did not feel his presence. But what I did feel though was the presence of the thousands of people who stood, since 1760, at the same spot as us. The space felt like it was rich with the imprint of countless Jewish souls who took the same journey as we did, to the grave of a saintly individual.

Never Forget

A phrase among Jews regarding the Holocaust is "Never Forget." Each year on Passover, we read, *"And it is this that has stood for our ancestors and for us; since it is not only one person or nation that has stood against us to destroy us, but rather in each generation, they stand against us to destroy us, but the Holy One, blessed be He, rescues us from their hand.* (from the Passover *Haggadah*)

Even before I was old enough to understand, I have recited these words and have done so each year since. I grew up with the assumption that since time immemorial many people have wanted to destroy the Jewish people. And I believe that this is true. The mission of the Jewish people is to remind the world that there is a God, that God exists. But not everyone wants to hear this.

Jews have indeed been downtrodden in every generation, and without a certain kind of arrogance, the Jewish people might have disappeared long ago. Imagine if we came to believe that the world is right: there is no God. If we Jews did not have the extreme courage of our conviction, we would probably have abandoned our core belief and faith in God. And we would have disappeared.

The Torah describes Jews as a stiff-necked people, among other things. Our heels are often dug in. Where so many groups have perished over the millennia, we Jews have survived. What a strange paradox: the world is always out to get us, and we are the only ancient people who have survived. For the anti-Semite, this must be annoying and frustrating.

So, after the Holocaust, when a third of the Jewish people in the world were murdered, the slogans "Never Forget" and "Never Again" became popular. We Jews would insist that we will never forget the atrocities, the mass murders, the neighbors who betrayed us, the killing of innocent children. *Never Forget.*

And we have not forgotten.

But what is it that we should never forget? And to what aim? If it is a given that in every generation *they* are out to get us, what good will remembering do? It might prompt us to watch our backs, to minimize the destruction of lives.

Perhaps we can actually change the world so that a few generations are skipped in this relentless attack on the Jewish people? Would we have to edit this out of the Passover *Haggadah*? What if brilliant Israeli scientists were to find cures for all known physical and mental diseases, resulting in the world's gratitude? (Of course, down deep in my consciousness I have the feeling that *they* would always be able to come up with something to hate us for.)

Again, never forget. But what should I never forget?

Many Jews, prompted by Holocaust survivors, despise, for example, the Ukrainians. We've built up stereotypes about Ukrainians. They are all primitive, they are all Cossacks. But what is a Cossack?

Cossacks have been described as east Slavic self-governing Orthodox Christians. For some, the Cossacks have been romanticized as freedom and resistance fighters, while another perception of them is as a symbol of repression. They participated in countless anti-Jewish pogroms and were active in the Khmelnytsky Uprising of 1648–1657. An estimated 100,000 Jews were murdered by the Cossacks. They did not spare women and children, and their reputation included burying some of their victims alive, cutting them into pieces, and forcing their victims to kill one another.

How ironic: Ukrainians usually see Cossacks as a democratic, romantic group while the stereotype I have learned is that a Cossack is an anti-Jewish warrior responsible for pogroms and the murder of Jews.

I once asked a Polish acquaintance of mine who lives in Poland what she thinks of Cossacks. She said, "They murder Poles."

My question, of course, was absurd. In the same way that there is no typical Jew, there is no typical Ukrainian. Will we ever be able to get out of the *us* and *them* mentality?

So, I vow each year on Passover that I will always remember what *they* always want to do to us, and I vow every year on Yom HaShoah (Holocaust Memorial Day) that I will never forget. But what is it that I am never forgetting? If *they* – in every generation – want to annihilate us, then I will never forget.

In my conversations with Elie Wiesel, I once asked him, "What did you learn from the Holocaust?" He told me that he learned two things. One was not to let other people tell you what your questions should be. For example, if someone asks me why I am wearing a beard, I don't have to answer that question. It is not my question; I am under no obligation to answer questions that are not my questions. And the second thing Elie Wiesel said to me is that he learned not to be complacent with evil and think that things will get better. We must fight evil as soon as we see it. With evil, things usually do not get better; they get worse.

The classic symbolic figure of the anti-Jewish individual is Amalek (see Exodus 17:16). It is actually a mitzvah to "remember to forget" Amalek, to blot his name out. Similarly, on the Jewish holiday of Purim, we read aloud the Book of Esther from the Holy Scriptures. When we come to the name of Haman – the anti-Jewish villain in the story – we make noise to drown his name out. Again, we remember to blot his name out of history.

Perhaps this is the solution to my quandary. It doesn't surprise me that it is a paradox that might resolve the issue. We never forget how we don't want to remember our enemies. We should remember to forget our enemies, thereby remembering them.

We are told we must never forget the destruction of European Jewry during the Second World War, the Holocaust. But we betray ourselves if our remembering is merely how *they* murdered and betrayed *us*. Remembering how *we*, the good guys, were victims of *them*, the bad guys, can't be the point. If we stop short of any details, we are merely reinforcing stereotypes.

I remember once hearing a respected Jewish scholar at a lecture about the Middle East saying, "You have to understand the Arab mentality." The rather large audience didn't flinch. However, if an Arab were to speak and say, "You have to understand the Jewish mentality," I can just imagine the protests of such a "racist" comment. There is no one Jewish mentality. If anything, Jews are often disagreeing with one another. We joke and even embrace the joke of "Two Jews, three opinions." But we don't even realize when we do the same thing to others, with the same kind of generalizations we protest when we are on the receiving end of the stereotyping.

Perhaps what we need to never forget is not what *they* did to *us* but rather we must understand and keep in mind what it is that led up to the hostility and cruelty. It is the subtle and complicated history that we need never forget. We must be alert to the signs that something worse is coming. We need to try, through education, to cut physical destruction of each other off at the pass. What are the signs that it's bound to get worse? This may be what we need to learn and never forget.

We wish we could forget, but we can't. We must never forget.

Never Forget II

Sometimes I forget what I should never forget.

Sometimes I remember and wish I forgot.

Once I saw a terrible car accident. I couldn't get it out of my mind. But today, thirty years later, I don't remember anything about it.

Is memory a gift from God?

Or is it forgetting the real gift?

There are Holocaust photo images I can't get rid of; they haunt me every day.

There are descriptions of real torture I can't get rid of either. I wish I had never read about them.

After being introduced, it's usually impossible for me to remember someone's name; I'm too busy looking at a person's face to even listen.

What else don't I listen to? Does it matter?

I flunked high school Spanish. Too many words to remember. But I remember how to spell the names of the Polish and Ukrainian towns where my family lived and were murdered: Dobromyl. Przemysl. Kroscienko. Kisielow. Starjava. Jaroslaw. Rzeszow. Szczytna.

I remember how to spell the death camp where my family was destroyed: Belzec.

I remember that Lviv was once Lvov and Lvov was once Lemberg.

But sometimes I got lost just a few blocks from where I lived for 15 years. I have a hard time remembering a lot of things. But my friends tell me I have the best memory of anyone they know. I remember details of houses I haven't been in for over 50 years, but I don't remember what color my bedroom wall is.

Regarding the Holocaust, they say "Never Forget." What is it I should never forget? Six million Jews were murdered in the Holocaust. Nearly 1.5 million of them were children.

But sometimes I get stuck with the multiplication tables. 6 x 7 was always difficult for me. When I don't know how to spell a word, I look it up in my dictionary, but I often forget it by the time I get back to my keyboard. Sometimes I look up the word again, and again I forget it within seconds.

But I never forget the names of my grandparents, great-grandparents, great-great-grandparents, and great-great-great-grandparents.

When I was 12, my Hebrew school teacher made us memorize the names of the twelve tribes of Israel. 58 years later, I still remember them. I will always remember the names of the major death camps during the Holocaust. Auschwitz, Belzec, Chelmno, Majdanek, Sobibor, and Treblinka.

But what's the point?

Sometimes I want to forget the whole thing.

Abusch

The passage in the Bible where Abram was called by his new name, Abraham (Genesis 17:5), is both revealing and significant: Sarai, too, underwent a parallel name change and became Sarah (17:15). While we find in the Bible other name changes – as when Jacob became Israel… only one woman was granted this privilege, and that woman was Sarah. This change of name hints at a change in the whole essence of Abraham and Sarah's being, in their whole way of life. It is a profound transformation which involved them both equally, which had a double dimension, Abraham and Sarah together.

> – (from "Sarah: The Partner" in *Biblical Images*, Rabbi Adin Steinsaltz)

Is my search over? Have I completed my mission?

I had several goals since I first heard about Dobromyl sixty years ago:

1. To trace my family history. I have done so successfully. I have identified the names of my great-great-great-grandparents, Eli and Machla Kurzweil, and hundreds of their descendants. The current generation lives across the United States, in Poland, and in Israel.
2. To visit my father's *shtetl*, Dobromyl, and to connect with the people. Again, I have done so successfully. I am told that almost everybody in Dobromyl today knows of me.
3. To visit the places where members of my father's family were murdered during the Holocaust. I've been to Dobromyl, Belzec,

Kroscienko, and Przemysl. Kisielow. Starjava. Jaroslaw. Rzeszow. Szczytna. Stary Sambor. Chyrow. This goal was also a success.

Did I ever find Abusch?

Did I ever find the Dobromyl of my lifelong fantasies?

After it all, I still felt unsettled, somehow incomplete. I knew I could never return to Dobromyl when it was a *shtetl*. That world is gone, never to return.

But then, a remarkable thing occurred. It is one of those coincidences that feels more like it is part of some Plan.

Through a Dobromyl Facebook page I met a young man named Pavlo Bishko. One day, when Pavlo was visiting Krakow, he met a woman named Anna Baranowa who originally came from Dobromyl.

While Anna was showing Pavlo her old family photo album, he suddenly noticed a photo of interest. It is a picture taken of a Catholic Priest in 1935 in the town market square in Dobromyl.

And where was the priest standing?

In front of my great-grandfather Abusch's metal shop! The sign reads, "The metal workshop of Abusch Kurzweil."

It was an extraordinary genealogical find; surely the most exciting discovery in the 50 years I have been tracing my family history. Why? I don't know. Why have I spent five decades climbing my family tree? I don't know. Why did I spend so much time and money on Dobromyl? I don't know. Why did I want to learn the details of the Holocaust as it impacted my family? I don't know. Why do I want to remember? Why do I want to forget? I don't know. After all of my searching, after all of my research, after all of my tears, I am only sure of one thing.

My name is Abusch.

Abusch Kurzweil's metal workshop in Dobromyl, circa 1935

Appendices

Talmud Berachot 7a
with Commentary by
Rabbi Adin Steinsaltz

GEMARA: From where is this matter, that relatives are disqualified from bearing witness, derived?

The *Gemara* answers: It is as the Sages taught in a *baraita*: "The fathers shall not be put to death for the children, neither shall the children be put to death for the fathers; every man shall be put to death for his own sin" (Deuteronomy 24:16).

Why must the verse state this first clause?

If it is to teach that the fathers shall not be put to death for the sin of the children, nor shall the children be put to death for the sin of the fathers, this is unnecessary, as it is in any event stated: "Every man shall be put to death for his own sin."

Rather, the statement "The fathers shall not be put to death for the children" should be interpreted to mean that they shall not be put to death by the testimony of the children, and the statement "Neither shall the children be put to death for the fathers" should be interpreted to mean that they shall not be put to death by the testimony of the fathers.

The *Gemara* asks: And are children not put to death for the sin of the fathers?

But isn't it written: "Visiting the iniquity of the fathers upon the children, and upon the children's children, unto the third and unto the fourth generation" (Exodus 34:7)?

The *Gemara* answers: There, the verse is referring to a situation where the children adopt the actions of their ancestors as their own. If they do not behave like their ancestors they are not punished for their ancestors' sins.

Dobromyl Chronology

- Dobromyl was granted its town charter in 1566.
- Jews have lived in Dobromyl from 1570. They had equal rights as merchants.
- Jews were mostly involved with agriculture in the 16th century.
- In 1612, the Jews population received, from the town's owners, the right to live in town, to purchased plots for housing, and to build a synagogue. A small synagogue was built.
- In the 1720s, Rabbi Yitzhok Segal and his son Meir served as rabbis in Dobromyl.
- In the late 1700s and early 1800s, Jewish children attended a German-Jewish vocational school.
- In 1765, there were 1,253 Jews in Dobromyl.
- In 1870, there were 1,884 Jews in Dobromyl.
- In the 1800s, in Dobromyl, there were five synagogues including a big synagogue built in Gothic style. There was a tailors' synagogue and two *Chasidic* synagogues, one for Belzer *Chasidim* and one for *Chasidim* of Ruzhin.
- In 1890, the Jewish population had increased 2,035 (63% of the total population).
- At the beginning of the 20th century, a Talmud-Torah was founded. The sons of the wealthy Jews studied at the general schools and at the gymnasium of Przemysl.
- In 1900, the Jewish population was 1,845, 56% of the town's total population of 3,309.
- In 1910, there were 2,271 Jews in Dobromyl, 70% of the population.

- In 1914, the Russian army occupied Dobromyl on *Rosh Hashanah*.

- In 1918, after World War I, Dobromyl became part of Poland.

- In 1921, there were 2,120 Jews in the town, 61% of the total population of 3,431.

- Zionist activity in Dobromyl began in 1908. In 1909 the Theodor Herzl Society was founded.

- In 1912, the Agudat Ha-Haredim, an ultra-Orthodox organization, was founded.

- After World War I, the influence of the Belz Chasidim declined and the Zionists gained more recognition. There were branches of the General Zionists, Hitahdut, Hamizrachi, Revisionist Zionists, Poalei Zion and WIZO, the Women's International Zionist Organization. There were also active youth groups including Zionist Youth, Betar, Akiva, and Ha-Shomer Ha-Zair.

- In 1919, the gentile merchants organized their own trade association which competed with Jewish business. The Jewish community then organized an interest-free loan society that helped Jewish merchants and artisans.

- By 1922, Jews built an iron foundry as well as factories for manufacturing soap, matches, and textiles.

- In 1922, a supplementary Hebrew school of the Tarbut network was founded.

- In 1927, there were 19 Jewish councilors in the municipal council out of the total of 48.

- In 1934, a Jew was elected vice-chairman of the municipal council.

- There were 2,500 Jews in Dobromyl on the eve of World War II.

- On the 11th of September 1939, German forces entered Dobromyl.

- On September 17, 1939, Dobromyl came under Soviet rule in accordance with the German-Soviet pact. Jewish shops were nationalized and factories and homes confiscated. All Jewish institutions were closed down.

- In summer 1941, the Jews of Dobromyl were forced into a ghetto which also included Jews from Przemysl and neighboring towns.

- The German army occupied Dobromyl on June 28, 1941, a week after the German invasion of the Soviet Union.
- Jews were assembled in the market square where they were beaten and humiliated.
- Fifty young Jews were taken to an unknown destination. The peasants later reported that they had been murdered in an abandoned salt mine.
- The Ukrainians were given permission to harass the Jews. They attacked Jews and looted their property.
- June 30, 1941, ninety Jews were murdered in Dobromyl. German and Ukrainian police searched for Jewish men. Several Jews were burned alive.
- In June 1941, hundreds of innocent people were brutally murdered in the salt mine in Lacko (near Dobromyl) and in the prison in Dobromyl.
- Before the beginning of the Soviet-German war, the Soviet secret police began to empty out the prison. Prisoners were executed in cells, in corridors, cellars or in prison courtyards. Some witnesses survived.
- The Soviet secret police executed over 1,500 prisoners and dumped their bodies in salt mines near the edge of town. Local Jewish men exhumed the bodies.
- During June 1941, a Judenrat (Jewish council) was established by the Germans. Jews were forced to give large sums of money and other valuables to the German authorities. The German also established quotas to supply Jews for slave labor in and near Dobromyl.
- On June 27, 1941, a burial site containing 3,600 bodies of the victims of the Soviet Secret Police was found. The victims included Ukrainians, Poles and Jews considered to be intellectuals and activists. The victims included children from Przemysl and Dobromyl.
- A Jewish ghetto was established in Dobromyl in October 1941 and was enforced until July 29, 1942. Thousands of Jews from Dobromyl, Przemysl and other nearby locations were deported to death camp Belzec.

- Approximately 200 Dobromyl Jews were shot to death in the Jewish cemetery by the Germans, and about 60 Dobromyl Jews were shot to death by Germans on the streets of the town.
- On July 29, 1942, many Jews were assembled in the market square. Some were shot on the spot. The Grand Synagogue was set on fire with 200 Jews inside. The bricks and other materials from the synagogue were used to build a German army barracks nearby. Young men and skilled workers were sent to the labor camps in Przemysl. Some remained in Dobromyl and worked in the factories and lumber mills. Many were sent to death camp Belzec.
- On November 24, 1942, the remaining Jews in Dobromyl were taken to a lumber mill and ordered to dig a large pit. They were then shot and buried.
- On August 8, 1944 Dobromyl was liberated by the Red Army.
- Only 25 Jews of the community of Dobromyl survived the Holocaust.

About the Author

Arthur Kurzweil is a writer and teacher, and is the author of several books including *From Generation to Generation: How to Trace Your Jewish Genealogy and Family History, On the Road with Rabbi Steinsaltz, Pebbles of Wisdom from Rabbi Adin Steinsaltz, Kabbalah for Dummies, The Torah for Dummies,* and *My Generations: A Course in Jewish Family History.*

www.ingramcontent.com/pod-product-compliance
Lightning Source LLC
LaVergne TN
LVHW020025160726
843469LV00044B/1645